CARSMART

Save Hundreds on Car Repairs and Avoid Rip-Offs

Ron Coleman

Autowise Publishing
Athens, Alabama

Copyright © 1999 Ron Coleman
All rights reserved. This book may not be duplicated in any way without the express written consent of the publisher, except in the form of brief excerpts or quotations for the purposes of review. The information contained herein is for the personal use of the reader and may not be incorporated in any commercial programs or other books, databases, or any kind of software without written consent of the publisher or author. Making copies of this book, or any portion of it, for any purpose other than your own, is a violation of United States copyright laws.

Published by:
Autowise Publishing
807 Hwy 72 W
Athens, AL 35611
(205) 232-0307

Printed in the United States of America

Library of Congress Catalog Card Number: 98-70569

Coleman, Ron, 1966-
CarSmart : save hundreds on car repairs and avoid rip-offs / Ron Coleman. – 1st ed.
    p. cm.
    Includes index
    ISBN: 0-9663627-4-8

1. Automobiles—Maintenance and repair—United States. 2. Automobile industry and trade—United States. 3. Consumer education—United States. I. Title

TL 152.C65 1998   629.28'72'0296
                          QBI98-382

*To Bayleigh and Peyton, and to Melanie,
whose advice, input, and support were
more important than she thinks.*

TABLE OF CONTENTS

Introduction ix

SECTION 1

1) The Repair Industry Versus You 1
A Repair Shop on Every Corner • What You Don't Know *Will* Hurt You! • Unnecessary Repairs • Unlimited Profit • Why Are We Sitting Ducks? • Become Educated

2) Repairs for Less 7
Parts Are Parts? • One Price Fits All • A Fair Profit or a Scam? • Pre-Repair Price Check • Parts & Service Worksheets • Inside Information • Taking Charge • Hard Labor • Bring Your Own Parts • Determining Labor Costs • Smart Shopping • Old Faithful • A Competitive Edge • Was That Bob, or Rob? • Hook, Line, & Sinker! • Negotiating Price • Ask & You *May* Receive • Good Salesmanship • The New Kid on the Block • Tuesday's Special • Exercise Your Options • Two Heads Are Better Than One • Get It in Writing

3) A Shop You Can Trust 29
Trust Your Instincts • Mega-Shop or Mom-'N-Pop? • There's No Substitute for Experience...Or Is There? • Instant Status • Enough is Enough

4) Mechanics 35
The Good, the Bad, & the Parts Changers • A Rare Breed

5) Time for Repairs 39
Post-Repair Check-Up • Add-Ons • A Strong Signal

6) Becoming a Good Customer 43
Making New Friends • Spread the Word • Small Talk • The Superman Complex • Becoming a Bad Customer

7) Come-Backs 49
Keep Your Cool • And the Results Are... • The Number One Attitude • The Other Attitude • The Next Level • The Final Battle • Keep Those Receipts

TABLE OF CONTENTS

8) Far & Away **57**
The Best Trouble Is No Trouble • Be Prepared • Despite All Efforts… • The Traveler's Bluff

SECTION 2

9) Beyond the Basics **63**

10) Oil Change **67**
Every 3,000 Miles, Right? • Do It Yourself…Not! • If Not You, Who?

11) Tires **73**
Waste, Waste, Waste • Under Pressure • Cold Pressure • Flats • Patching Things Up • Rotations • Tire Cupping • Owner's Manual Error! • Rotating Styles • Keep Your Balance • Still Shaking! • See No Evil

12) New Tires: When, Where, What, and How 93
Time to Re-Tire! • How Thin Is Too Thin? • Tire Talk • Determining What You Need • Tire Lingo • Treadwear, Traction, & Temperature Ratings • Brand Names • Dial-a-Tire • Tire Warranties • Free Tires • Warranty Exclusions • Road Hazard! • Decision Time

13) Brakes **113**
The Basics • Disks, Drums, or Both? • Creating Friction, Destroying Pads • Pad & Shoe Replacement • An Early Warning • A Little Too Late • Shopping for Brakes • Rapid Pad Wear • Don't Over-Repair • Rotors • Thinning Rotors • The Problem with Thin • How Thin Is Too Thin? • Uncommon Knowledge • Brake Vibrations • Fluid Leaks • Where Does the Fluid Go? • The Falling Brake Pedal • Brake Pull • Many Solutions…Only One Fix • Tricks of the Trade • Low Brake Pedal • Tiny Bubbles • Bleeding Brakes • Anti-Lock Brakes • Brake System Glossary

continued next page

TABLE OF CONTENTS

14) Alignment **151**
Caster, Camber, & Toe • Asking For It! • Toe-In…Toe-Out • Standing Tall • Straight Ahead • Alignment Problem?…Or Not! • Pulling in Your Favor • Shaking Things Up • More Misconceptions • Finally! • Communication is the Key • Thrust Angle or Not?

15) Shocks and Struts.................................**173**
What are Shocks & Struts? • What's the Difference? • Out of Control • You Be the Judge • The Ups & Downs of Replacement • Shopping for Shocks & Struts

16) Front Suspension **183**
Rack-'n-Pinion • Racking Up • Tie Rods • The Ins & Outs • Boots, Joints, & Axles • Sounding Off • Axle Replacement Tips • A Mysterious Wobble • Front Suspension & Drivetrain Glossary

17) Driveability **201**
A Safe Bet • Seeking Professional Help • Are Tune-Ups Extinct? • The Burden of Repair • A Second Opinion • A Tune-Up on a Fighter Jet

18) Check Engine Soon! **209**
Artificial Intelligence • Sensing a Problem • Engine Alert Codes • Where to Go • What's That Smell?! • A Lack of Oxygen • Smelling Smoke

19) Air Conditioning **215**
Things to Know • A Cool Gas • More A/C Details • More is Less • Refrigerant Conversions • Losing Your Cool • Recharging • Blowing Hot Air • A/C Leaks • A Bad Connection • Leaky Hoses • More Serious Problems • After Repairs • Compressor Failure • Compressor Replacement • Cutting Compressor Costs • A New Clutch • A Compressor Bypass • Air Conditioning Glossary

Index..**240**

LIST OF ILLUSTRATIONS

T1	Tire Pressure	74
T2	Tires	77
T3	Irregular Tire Wear	83
T4	Rotation (Front to Rear)	85
T5	Rotation (Modified-X)	86
T6	Rotation (X Pattern)	87
T7	Tire Problems!	91
T8	Tire Sizes	97
T9	UTQG Ratings	103
B1	Brake System	115
B2	Brake Master Cylinder	116
B3	Disk Brake System	118
B4	Drum Brake System	119
B5	Brake Pad	121
B6	Brake Shoe	122
B7	Brake Rotor	131
B8	Brake Drum	132
B9	Wheel Cylinder	138
A1	Toe Angles	155
A2	Toe-In	157
A3	Toe-Out	158
A4	Negative Camber	160
A5	Positive Camber	161
A6	Uneven Tire Wear	167
A7	Thrust Angle	171
S1	Shocks	175
S2	Strut	176
S3	Shocks vs. Struts	179
F1	Rack-'n-Pinion	186
F2	Tie Rods	188
F3	CV Axle	191
F4	Front Suspension & Drivetrain (Front View)	196
F5	Front Suspension	197
AC1	The A/C System	218
AC2	A/C Electrical	227
AC3	Compressor and Clutch	228
AC4	Buying Time	237

INTRODUCTION

Almost everybody has heard someone proudly say that he or she doesn't have to worry about car repairs because their husband or brother or whoever is an auto mechanic. These blessed people can rest easy because *they* have someone on their side who knows auto repair. They probably don't realize how lucky they are.

Auto repair is one of the few remaining industries shrouded in lies, myths, and just plain ignorance. Many people go to an auto repair center with no idea about what they need, or how much they are going to be charged. They often leave wondering if they got their money's worth — or if they got what they paid for at all. Unfortunately, very few people actually get their money's worth from their repair dollars. Only people with close ties to the auto repair industry have the luxury of understanding how the industry works, and these few are the only ones who really get what they pay for, and more.

C A R S M A R T

But that was then, and this is now! Until now, practically no one has had access to the information you are about to read. There are thousands of books and other products out there that help the consumer get the best deal on everything under the sun — from cars to furniture to Barbie dolls — but I have yet to find one that gives consumers useful, easy-to-understand advice and guidance about car repairs. You are about to discover the next best thing to having a veteran mechanic in the family. I believe that this book is the first real attempt by someone within the industry, to help those without. For one reason or another, no automotive professional has ever shared his inside information with the public. Sure, there are a few TV shows and magazines that profess to help the auto repair consumer, but many seem to be primarily interested in selling a gadget or a product. Isn't it funny that they just "happen" to recommend the products made by the companies who buy advertising from them. Who are they really looking out for? Don't these people lose credibility when they get paid to endorse a product or a business within their own profession? But *CarSmart* isn't endorsing anything, *CarSmart* is 100 percent for you — the consumer!

I have always loved cars, and I've been working on them practically all my life. In fact, cars have been, and will probably always be, a significant part of my life, both as a hobby and as the means to support my family. At a very young age, I started "helping" my dad work on his own cars at home. Then in high school, I rebuilt and repaired cars for my family and friends. Naturally, back then, all the money I earned was spent on my own classic cars, but this kept me out of trouble...well...mostly. As one can imagine, my weekend tinkering became a way of life. At the age of 19, I was hired as the assistant manager of a tire and auto service center, and my professional career in the auto repair business began. This job was no picnic, but I was making more money than most people my age, and the title impressed my friends. After a few years, however, I decided I wanted to change careers, so I quit work and attended college full time. Although I maintained close to a 4.0 grade average in pre-engineering, I soon realized that my destiny was with cars. So, I returned to the same tire and service center and worked as the head technician for about three years. In 1992, I was offered the manager's position, and in

RON COLEMAN

1995, I became the owner of that store, where I continue to work every single day.

Each day, I learn more about people and more about cars. Over the past twelve years, I've worked on about 50,000 cars of all makes, and I have served thousands of customers. Over the years, I've worked with honest managers and technicians, and with dishonest ones, and I've read countless publications and articles about cars and the car industry. All of these experiences have taught me many things, good and bad, about automotive repair.

But the most important thing I've learned is that nearly all car owners feel that getting their car repaired is very intimidating and they fear they might not get honest, fair treatment. This is understandable. I have heard many stories about customers who were ripped off by repair centers. In fact, almost everyone has had at least one bad experience with a repair center — and my customers often discuss this with me or with other customers while they are visiting my shop. I have also witnessed a few of these scams. I once worked for a manager who added $100 to the retail price of a set of tires, just because the lady buying the tires made the mistake of trusting him. This single mom was struggling to make ends meet, but the greedy manager was more interested in making a bonus than in treating her like a human being. This is just one example at one store. Things like this happen to hundreds of people every day.

In contrast to this kind of behavior, I have always enjoyed helping people in every way possible, especially when it comes to repairing cars. When customers come to my store, I always try to explain the repairs and show customers everything that is going to be done to their car — and why! Instead of secluding my customers in a waiting area, I encourage them to come and see for themselves what is wrong and what should be done about it. Often they will say, "I won't know what I'm looking at," but just as often, they are surprised at what they learn when they see the worn part with their very own eyes. Even a novice will recognize a worn-out brake pad if he or she can compare it to a new one. A service manager can make any repair as mysterious as he chooses, and of course, mystery works in his favor. When my customers see and understand what is needed, they feel much better about the repair and they leave knowing they got what they paid for.

This is all well and good for those few thousand people who come to my store every year, but what about the millions of other people in the world? How do they know if they are getting their money's worth at a repair shop? The truth is, without an honest service center, or without enough automotive knowledge — they *don't!*

Until I decided to create *CarSmart*, I never imagined that I would write anything longer than a grocery list. However, a few years ago I realized that I knew things about automobiles and the auto service industry that could save the average consumer hundreds of dollars on car repairs, probably much more. I know the car repair industry inside and out. I know inside information that will change forever the way you deal with a repair center. I can also explain many techniques that will help you get the best price for service or tires or just about anything for your car. I know these techniques work — because they have been used on me!

Even though I try to treat everybody the same way, a few of my customers know how to get what they want for a little less than the next guy. Over time, I realized that I could share this information with consumers and they would reap huge benefits. *CarSmart* reveals these secrets and much more. *CarSmart* will show you how to become a knowledgeable, independent customer instead of one who must place his or her trust in the hands of a service manager or technician. With the information in this book, you will be confident and in control when you visit *any* repair center — not to mention that you will save some serious money.

CarSmart contains a wealth of information that will help everyone from the avid car nut to the person who thinks of a car as simply a mode of transportation. Although there are a number of people who can hold their own when it comes to car repairs, most people know little or nothing about their car. *CarSmart* was written with these people in mind. Therefore, most of you will be pleased to know that you will not find phrases such as "compression ratio" or "sequential fuel injection" herein. We leave these high-tech terms to car enthusiasts and to the mountain of publications devoted to these folks.

In *CarSmart*, easy-to-read, easy-to-understand language is used, and the only technical information explained is that which is necessary to ensure that you can take charge of your car repairs. This book does not assume that you have any technical background; thus, everything is carefully covered on a step-by-step basis. At the same time, this book explains only what you need to know and will not waste your valuable time with insignificant details.

Although *CarSmart* contains information that will help the do-it-yourself mechanic, it is not designed to teach you how to repair your own car. Most people don't have the time, the tools, or the desire to work on their own cars. Instead, *CarSmart* shows you how to hire someone else to do the work for you, without paying too much or otherwise getting ripped off.

CarSmart should not be considered a book for women only. Men can just as easily fall prey to auto repair rip-off, though it probably is not as common as with women. Why are women more vulnerable? Even though many men know little or nothing about cars, women get less respect because service personnel usually assume that every woman is totally lost when it comes to car repair. This assumption opens the door and encourages a dishonest technician or service manager to cheat when they deal with a woman. Therefore, women are much more susceptible to an auto repair scam *attempt*. (An attempt does not have to be successful!) In the back of his mind, a service manager often fears that a man *may* know enough about his car to catch a scam before it happens; the manager is therefore more reluctant to try a shady repair. But in truth, anyone can get ripped off and everyone can benefit from the information and techniques in *CarSmart* — whether they are a man or a woman, and whether they know nothing about cars or are somewhat "car smart" already.

CarSmart is divided into two sections. The first section discusses the repair industry, how to get the best price possible, and how to avoid auto repair fraud. It also covers things like how to find an honest repair center and a good mechanic, what to do when a repair goes bad or when you have trouble on the road, and much more. This section educates the reader about what the auto repair industry is really about, and it reveals little-known industry facts and secrets. The second section deals with specific repairs you are likely to need for your car, such as brakes, new tires, shocks, air conditioning, and others. Since *all* cars will eventually need most of these repairs, it is essential to prepare yourself for what will happen, *before* it happens!

The second section is just as important as the first, and it will be extremely valuable when it comes time to have your car repaired. After all, a basic understanding of what you are buying is essential to insure that you will not become a victim of fraud. Some of these repairs can cost more than one thousand dollars, so there is a significant amount of *your* money at stake. Carry *CarSmart* with you when you go in for repairs; it will be a valuable reference tool that can save you hundreds of dollars — *and* give you peace of mind. And don't forget to tell your friends about *CarSmart!*

SECTION I

THE REPAIR INDUSTRY VERSUS YOU

A Repair Shop on Every Corner

Automotive repair is one of the largest businesses in the United States. In fact, it is a multibillion-dollar industry. There are millions and millions of people out there, and there is an equally impressive number of automobiles. Each and every one of these cars will eventually need maintenance or repair, and most people will depend on a repair center to do some or all of this work. The average family spends several hundred dollars per year to keep their cars maintained. Some experts estimate that Americans spend more than 100 billion dollars every year on car repairs! This huge demand for auto repair produces the need for thousands of auto repair centers across the country, and all of them want a piece of the billion-dollar pie.

Although there *is* a big demand for repair centers, there seems to be more than enough shops to go around. It seems there is a repair center, tire store, national retailer, or small shop on every corner. Soon,

C A R S M A R T

> **Auto repair is not an exact science; it is filled with thousands of variables, and most consumers know little or nothing about what they are buying.**

there will probably be a restaurant chain that offers oil changes while you eat! Why do so many people fix cars for a living? One reason, other than the obvious financial opportunity, is that there is a large available workforce. Sadly, to *some degree*, almost anyone can become a mechanic. The most common repairs and maintenance can be learned easily by anyone with a reasonable amount of mechanical ability. Please note, this does not mean that anyone can be a good mechanic, rather, it means that with little or no experience, almost anyone can get a job at *some* shop. Therefore, the industry is overwhelmed with undertrained and inexperienced technicians.

Another reason for the huge number of repair centers is that an auto repair shop can be started with very little money. A technician with a little experience, a few hundred dollars worth of tools, and a place to work can start his own repair shop. If you compare this to almost any other type of business, it is easy to see why there are so many repair centers out there.

Most people assume that a highly competitive industry will equate to a better price for the consumer. This may be true for pencils or light bulbs where the consumer can compare product to product and from one store to the next, but it is not necessarily true for car repairs. Naturally, competition in the repair industry does ultimately give the consumer an advantage, but one still must be careful. Having your car repaired is much more complex than buying a light bulb. Auto repair is not an exact science; it is filled with thousands of variables, and most consumers know little or nothing about what they are buying. Of the thousands of repair centers out there, some are good and some are bad; some are honest, some are dishonest; some are competent, some are incompetent, but most are somewhere in between. The consumer must know how to find the right shop, which will be explained a little later.

What You Don't Know *Will* Hurt You

Unfortunately, the auto repair industry has a *somewhat* deserved reputation for taking advantage of people. Each year, it is likely that millions of dollars are wasted on unneeded repairs, overcharges on parts and services, and incompetent repairs. Almost everyone has been ripped off by a repair shop in some way, whether they know it or not. Many people in the industry know that auto repair fraud is very easy to get away with, and because of this, many otherwise honest people yield to the temptation to add an unneeded part here, or increase the price there, in order to increase their profits.

As with any wrongdoing, they may justify their deeds by believing, "What you don't know won't hurt you." Sadly, it is true: The consumer almost never knows that he or she has been taken advantage of — at least not until long after the repair has been completed and paid for. When this happens to you, you often get a very unpleasant feeling, as though you've been robbed, which is pretty close to what has happened. As a result, most people have learned to distrust *all* repair centers. It is a good idea to keep your guard up and use caution at any repair center, but there *are* shops out there that do good work and can be trusted.

Unnecessary Repairs

The most common type of auto repair fraud is when a dishonest shop sells a consumer repairs that simply aren't needed. It is just like getting a television repaired: Most people know nothing about electronics, so when they take their TV to the shop, they have no idea what is wrong with it. This lack of knowledge gives the repairman the opportunity to take advantage of them. The problem could be a 15¢ blown fuse, but a dishonest repairman can tell you that you need a $200 circuit board. Many of us would assume the repairman was honest and would say okay. Likewise, an automotive service manager who recognizes that his customer doesn't have a clue about what he needs can very easily sell services that are not necessary. People are often told they need a part or a repair, and they happily agree to whatever the service manager suggests. *If* the manager is honest, there is nothing wrong with this, but what if he's not? Unneeded repairs cause millions of hard-earned dollars to fall into the hands of dishonest people; fortunately, there are several ways to avoid this predicament.

UNLIMITED PROFIT

Not only do people buy parts or services they don't need, but they often pay too much for the services they do need. Overcharging for a part or repair is a common way that dishonest repair centers make *more* than a fair profit on their work. Consider the above example of a TV repair. If you do indeed need a circuit board, how do you know it should cost $200? Perhaps the retail price is only $50, and the repairman is making too much profit on the part. In the same way, most consumers don't know how much car parts should cost, so they have no idea if they are paying a fair price or not. Consumers often pay $150 for an ignition module that they could have bought at a parts store for $60, or perhaps they pay $300 for a new alternator, when a remanufactured one costs only $80! Some shops double or triple what they paid for a part when they sell it to you! These examples may seem extreme, but they happen every day. Time after time, consumers pay much more for parts or services than they should, and never know it.

WHY ARE WE SITTING DUCKS?

Why are so many people so vulnerable to auto repair fraud, and why is it so easy to pull off? The answer is the same as for any other product or service you buy: **A lack of knowledge about something being repaired or purchased puts you at risk.** Although almost everyone drives a car, most know practically nothing about how cars work. When you know nothing about what you are buying, whether it is car repair or anything else, you are at the mercy of the person you are buying from. Consider this example: A lady sends her husband to a department store to buy facial makeup. If this man knows little or nothing about makeup, he is totally at the mercy of the salesperson. If the salesperson is dishonest, she can tell him anything, and he will have no choice but to believe it. She could sell him too much of one item, or sell him things his wife didn't need. She could even double the price and he wouldn't have a clue that he had been ripped off — until he returned home and his wife hit the roof! However, if the wife had taken a few minutes to explain what she needed and how much to expect to pay, the husband could have immediately recognized that something was wrong.

This is exactly what happens to thousands of men and women when they have their cars repaired. If they understood just a little about the systems being repaired, they would greatly reduce their chances of getting ripped off. Although few of us know someone who could educate us about electronics, most women could tell a man enough about makeup to prevent a scam. **Knowledge makes you less vulnerable to repair fraud.**

Become Educated

You are probably thinking that you have no chance of understanding enough about cars to prevent yourself from becoming a victim of fraud. Although it is true that some systems *are* too complex and specialized for the average consumer to understand, most common auto repairs are reasonably simple. Every car owner can, and should, learn enough about these systems to know what is a typical repair, and what is not. By simply learning the names for these repairs and parts, and the terms commonly used in the industry, you can greatly improve your communication with the people at the service center.

Consider how you would feel if you went to a foreign country and didn't know the language. Then, imagine that you had to trust a person whose language you didn't understand to exchange your currency! It is much the same if you go into a repair center for brake service, and you don't know a brake rotor from a master cylinder. **If you can speak the automotive language well enough to let the service manager know that you are knowledgeable about your car, you will change the way he thinks of you as a customer.** Every manager knows that he cannot easily trick a person who understands what is going on. On the other hand, a person who knows nothing about cars can feel totally helpless when dealing with a repair center and is much more vulnerable to fraud. A general knowledge of repairs and terms will greatly increase your confidence. You will also be able to make educated decisions about your car's repairs instead of depending entirely on someone else. When you read the sections that cover individual systems and repairs, you can gain the basic knowledge that you will need in order to get respect at a service center, and perhaps you will recognize a repair fraud before it happens.

C A R S M A R T

> **If you can speak the automotive language well enough to let the service manager know that you are knowledgeable about your car, you will change the way he thinks of you as a customer.**

Another way to prevent repair fraud is to learn some of the methods used to take advantage of you. Several common repairs are especially susceptible to fraud. There are many ploys, which offer no real benefit, that are used get more money out of your bank account and into the shop's. In addition, there are myths perpetrated by the repair industry and the general public that can cost you time and money. One common myth is that you must replace the front and rear brakes at the same time. This is simply not true, but some service managers assume you don't know this and sell you brakes you don't need. Knowing the methods and myths can help you look for and recognize fraud before it happens. This type of inside information can be invaluable for obtaining the best service for your money. These methods and myths will be dealt with on an individual basis, as they apply, in the following sections.

REPAIRS FOR LESS

Today, consumers are smarter than ever before. They seem to know what everything on this earth should cost. *Except auto repairs*. But there is absolutely no reason to go to a shop for car repairs with no idea what it's going to cost. In fact, this should never, ever, be done!

First, we will cover some things you can do to make sure you get the very best service for the very least amount of money. There are no big secrets here (although there are a few small ones). Mostly you will learn common sense rules that you probably never thought of. These rules apply to buying tires, service, or parts. In later sections, which cover individual systems, you will learn more specific ways to save money.

CARSMART

PARTS ARE PARTS?

When a car needs maintenance or repair, it will usually require parts. Brake pads, rotors, water pumps, fan belts, and thousands of other parts constantly wear out or break. When these parts fail, you must purchase new parts and pay a repair center to install them. This sounds simple, but buying parts from a repair center can be risky. Many people pay much more than they should for parts and service, and this is how many consumers are ripped off. However, you can prevent this from happening by knowing what the parts for your car should cost — before going to a repair center.

ONE PRICE FITS ALL

Because parts can vary *greatly* from car to car, there is no single price for a certain type of part. Consider a brake rotor for example. A new brake rotor for a 1990 Ford Taurus costs under $30 from a parts store. On the other hand, a new rotor for a 1997 Ford Explorer with anti-lock brakes, which at the time of this writing is available only at the dealer, costs over $150! Why the huge difference?

Some of the difference comes from the size and type of the rotors. The rotor for the Explorer is much larger and has more components than the rotor for the Taurus, and therefore will always cost a little more. However, most of the difference is a result of, first, the total number of rotors made, and second, which companies produce the rotors. The huge price difference between our two rotors is the result of Taurus rotors being produced by the millions and by many different companies. The greater the volume and the more companies that compete to produce a specific part, the lower the price will be.

Explorer rotors are much more expensive because the dealer has a monopoly until "aftermarket" companies begin to produce them. (Aftermarket companies produce parts to replace the ones produced by the car companies.) As more companies produce more and more rotors for the Explorer, the price will begin to fall. After a few years, the price will probably go below $60. It follows that when a body style or brake system is changed, the price for the rotors will be much higher for a year or two until aftermarket parts start to surface. The longer a car maker uses the same rotor on a car or group of cars, the less it will cost.

Now, apply this reasoning to a car that is relatively rare — a Saab 900 Turbo for example. This car is sold in very small quantities in the

US compared to the Ford Taurus or the Chevy Cavalier. Therefore, rotors for such a car will probably be much more expensive and may be available only at the dealer. An aftermarket company may not want to spend thousands of dollars to set up their machines to produce only a few thousand rotors. Think of this as buying power. All Chevy Cavalier owners constitute a huge buying group; in fact, Chevy Cavaliers use the same rotors as the Pontiac Sunbird and Grand Am, the Olds Calais, and the Buick Skylark. This means that a company can produce one rotor that will fit millions of cars. As a result these car owners can expect to pay less. Not just for rotors, but for every part manufactured in quantity.

A Fair Profit or a Scam?

So, how do repair centers determine how much the consumer will pay for a part? First you must understand one thing — **many auto repair centers do not have a fixed price for parts or services**. Since there are thousands of different parts required to repair all the different types of cars, most shops only stock a few parts. They simply buy the parts they need, only when they need them, from a local parts store. Then they add a percentage to their cost, for profit. There is nothing wrong with this — *if* the profit is reasonable. Marking up the price of parts is one way a service center must make money in order to stay in business. But how much they add to their cost is what makes the difference between a fair profit and a scam. Unfortunately, this markup can depend on who they are selling the part to.

A shop may add 25 percent to their cost for one customer, but a whopping 200 percent

> **A shop may add 25 percent to their cost for one customer, but a whopping 200 percent for another — on the same part.**

for another — on the same part. But why? Well, if the shop suspects that you have no idea about what a part should cost, they know they can often get away with making the price much higher than they would for someone who once worked in an auto parts store and knows what parts should cost. For instance, let's say you are having new brakes installed on the front of your car, and the service manager informs you that you also need a new brake rotor. If the service manager knows you have no idea what the rotor should cost, he could double or triple the price, and you may never suspect you were being ripped off. On the other hand, if you know *approximately* what the rotor should cost, you can spot an excessive charge in an instant. Then, you could refuse the repairs or negotiate a fair price. Variable profit margins are usually more of a problem at locally owned stores, which often don't have strict rules about markup percentages, but overcharges can happen at any store where unethical individuals are responsible for the retail price.

Pre-Repair Price Check

How do you know how much a specific part or service should cost for your car? One way is to check the sections in this book that describe the automotive systems; you will find prices for many parts and services listed there. These prices are somewhat conservative and are only a general guideline, but they should get you in the ballpark. The price you will pay may be a little less or significantly more than these because price can vary depending on not only the make and model of your car, but also on where you live. If you live in a large city or anyplace where property, rent, utilities, and wages are relatively high, the labor and the markup on parts will be higher. Service centers in these areas must charge more to pay for their higher operating expenses. In addition, remember that service centers with million-dollar buildings, lavish waiting rooms, and modern equipment must pay for these amenities somehow. Ultimately, the consumer must always pay for these things. In contrast, if you live in a rural area where expenses are lower, you may be able to buy parts or services for less.

But the best way to find out *exactly* what price is typical for a part or service in your area is to pick up the phone and do some shopping. On the facing page, you will find a pricing worksheet. On this sheet you will find a list of some of the most common parts and a few services any car will eventually need. Fill in the parts section by calling at least two

R O N   C O L E M A N

PARTS WORKSHEET

Make: _____ Model: _____
Year: _____ Engine size: _____

BRAKE PARTS	PRICE	SOURCE	PHONE	NOTES
Front brake pads				
Front brake rotors				
Front brake calipers				
Rear brake shoes or pads				
Rear brake drums or rotors				
Rear wheel cylinders or calipers				
Brake master cylinder				

SHOCKS/STRUTS

Front struts or shocks				
Rear struts or shocks				

SUSPENSION/DRIVETRAIN

Outer tie rod ends				
Inner tie rod ends				
Rack-n-pinion				
Idler arm (found mostly on trucks)				
Outer CV boot				
Inner CV boot				
Left CV axle				
Right CV axle				

BELTS AND HOSES

Serpentine (one-for-all)*				
Alternator belt*				
Power steering belt*				
Air conditioner belt*				
Timing Belt (some models)				
Upper radiator hose				
Lower radiator hose				

*Most 1985 and newer cars use only one belt, older cars may use three or more individual belts.

ENGINE PARTS

Spark Plugs				
Spark plug wires				
Air Filter				
Alternator				
Ignition Module				
Water pump				

AIR CONDITIONING

A/C compressor				
Dryer or accumulator				
Expansion valve or orifice tube				
A/C relay				

C A R S M A R T

SERVICE WORKSHEET

Make: _____ **Model:** _____
Year: _____ **Engine size:** _____

BRAKE SERVICE	PARTS	LABOR	TOTAL	SOURCE	PHONE
Basic front brakes					
Basic rear brakes					
Front brakes (incl. turning rotors)					
Rear brakes (incl. turning drums)					
Turn brake rotors					
Adjust rear brakes (some models)					
Bleed brakes					

ALIGNMENT SERVICE					
Front wheels only					
Thrust angle					
Four Wheel (some models)					

TIRE SERVICE					
Tire rotation					
Tire balance					
Rotate and balance					
Flat repair					

TUNE UP SERVICE					
Maintenance tune up (plugs only)					
Complete tune up (plugs, wires…)					
Timing belt replacement					
Diagnostic check					
Transmission service					

NOTES: _____

_____

_____

_____

_____

_____

_____

_____

_____

_____

parts stores (not service centers) and asking for the prices of all the parts on the list for your car. Before calling, make sure you know the make, model, year, and engine size of your car, for example: 1990 Buick LeSabre with a 3.8L (3.8 liter) engine. You can find the engine size on a sticker under the hood. You may want to drop off a list of the parts you need at a parts store and pick it up later. If the parts store clerk tells you one of these parts is not required or is not available for your car, make a note of this.

Also, on some parts there are different prices for different warranty levels. For example, a store may offer one alternator with a lifetime warranty and one with a one-year warranty, so the clerk may give you more than one price for the same part. Exact figures are not as important as getting a general idea about part costs for *your* car. The worksheet should be placed in the glove compartment of the car it applies to and left there for reference.

INSIDE INFORMATION

Why get prices from a parts store, when you will be buying them from a service center? The answer is — the prices you collect on your worksheet will be very close to the price a service center pays for the parts. When you are told you need a part on the worksheet, simply take a quick glance at the sheet and you will know approximately how much profit the service center is making — thereby revealing whether or not you are dealing with a fair, honest shop. It doesn't take long for the worksheet to pay you back for the time you spent chasing down the prices.

Ten years ago, this wasn't as effective as it is today. Back then, a service center could buy parts for much less than a person off the street could. But because of fierce competition in the auto parts business, you can now buy parts at or near the wholesale price. True, a service center may be able to buy parts for slightly less if they buy in quantity, but the cost difference is usually insignificant.

Keep in mind that you will almost never buy a part at a service center as cheaply as you could at a parts store. Most service centers add from 50 to 80 percent to their cost, so you can figure that you should pay no more than twice the price on your worksheet. This worksheet is a valuable tool that will save you hundreds of dollars. Not only will it help you get a fair price every time you need car repairs, but it will also show you whether the repair center you're dealing with is honest. For your own sake, please take the time to fill out a separate worksheet for each car you own as soon as you can.

Taking Charge

If your repair center is charging more than twice the price on the worksheet, you can simply refuse the service or politely ask for a better price. Let them know you called a parts store before coming in and that although you understand that they must make a profit, you also know how much the parts cost. In addition, ask if they have other options for the part you need, such as a rebuilt part instead of a new one, or a part with a one-year warranty instead of a lifetime warranty. You may even want to ask them if you could purchase the part at a parts store and pay them to install it (see "BYOP," facing page). Remember — you are the boss! But also remember to always use a polite and professional tone when discussing prices. There may be a legitimate reason for the difference in price. It is easy to offend someone if you come across as though you are accusing them of over-charging you. Give them the benefit of the doubt until you know otherwise.

Hard Labor

The labor rate, in dollars per hour, also affects the price you pay for a service. Labor rates can vary a great deal depending on many factors. Independent shops usually charge about $40 per hour. Dealers, on the other hand, may charge over $80. Why the big difference? Dealers charge a higher rate because they can. Most people prefer to take their car to a factory dealer even though they know it is more

Ask the repair shop if you can purchase parts at a parts store and pay for installation.

Remember — you are the boss!

BYOP
[BRING YOUR OWN PARTS]

Most repair centers will only install parts that you buy from them — not only for the purpose of making money, but for liability reasons as well. However, some service centers may be willing to let you buy the parts from a parts store, then pay them to install them. In other words, you supply the parts, they supply the labor. This can save you a considerable amount of money. It not only eliminates the service center's profit on the parts, but it allows you to shop around as much as you want to find the lowest price on the parts you need. A service center may only use two or three parts suppliers, but you could call dozens and find the absolute best price.

There are a few things you should know about bringing your own parts. First of all, the service center's liability may be reduced when you don't buy parts from them. If a part fails, for instance, the service center may blame the problem on the part, and the parts store may blame the service center. This can get pretty complicated if there is a serious problem. In contrast, when you purchase the entire job from a service center, there is no question about who is at fault. Another thing to consider is that the warranty on the part is from the parts store, not the service center. Therefore, if you have a warranty claim, you will probably have to pay labor charges a second time to have the parts re-installed. All of a sudden, bringing your own parts is more expensive than buying them from a service center. Some technicians may even pay less attention to details when installing a customer's parts because they will not be warranting the job, and because they probably aren't making as much. Finally, a service center that allows you to bring your own parts may charge more labor to install them compared to the labor for installing their own parts. Many service centers add 20 percent or more to the labor cost, and this is another case where you may not save money by bringing your own parts. Moreover, consider what will happen if the parts store gives you the wrong part. This happens often, and you may be stuck at a service center with no transportation. As with any money-saving technique, you should carefully investigate the situation before you decide to bring your own parts, to insure that it's right for you.

CARSMART

expensive. A dealer can charge more than everyone else and still expect to stay busy.

Operating expense also affects the labor rate. A service center that employs top-notch technicians must pay relatively high wages to hire and keep them. These technicians deserve more pay because they have spent time and money on school and training; they also attend seminars and buy expensive tools and service manuals. Therefore, a service center who employs the best technicians and invests in high-dollar equipment must charge more per hour. On the other hand, a shop that hires inexperienced technicians just out of school, with less expensive facilities and equipment, can charge less for their labor. The question is — which do you prefer? Do you want only the best technicians, or is it more important to save a little money?

Sometimes the answer depends on what kind of repairs are being done. A simple oil change, lube, or tire rotation can be done equally well by a $5-per-hour trainee or a $30-per-hour master technician. If you have a serious brake problem or tricky engine trouble however, the extra money spent at a shop with an experienced technician and the best equipment may be a good investment in your safety. Often, a technician with years of experience under his belt may even save you money by fixing your car right the first time, instead of guessing at the problem. Of course there are always exceptions. You may be lucky enough to find an independent shop that has an excellent technician who charges only $40 per hour, or you may pay $85 per hour at a dealership that has an inexperienced person working on your car. Don't think that just because you carry your car to the dealer or a high-dollar repair center that you will automatically get the best technicians available.

DETERMINING LABOR COSTS

Have you ever wondered how a shop determines how much labor to charge for a repair? Most service centers use a book, or computer software, called a labor guide. This book lists practically every repair, for almost every car. This guide lists how long a specific repair should take for any make and model car, which allows a shop to estimate the labor charge before a job is started. The guide gives the labor in time (hours), not in dollars. The service center must multiply their hourly rate by the number of hours listed in the guide. For example, if a labor guide shows 2.5 hours to install a water pump, the service center would multiply its rate, let's say $40 per hour, by the number of hours, to get the price for their labor ($100). Of course, some shops also consider their own experience when estimating the time for a specific repair. Look for a shop that specializes in a particular car make or a specific type of repair; it is likely that they can do a job in their specialty in half the time it would take a shop that does general repairs. Note also that for some common jobs like a brake job or an alignment, there will be a universal price that covers most cars. Example: Front brakes — $79.95 — most cars.

If you are in a shop for a repair and you suspect that you are being overcharged for the labor, try calling another service center and asking them to look up the time in their labor guide. Most service centers will be glad to help you — because they have a chance of getting a new customer. Ask them for the amount of time for the repair you need and the name of the labor guide they are using. (There are about three different brands.) If the labor price you are being charged does not agree with the labor guide, stop the repair before it starts and ask the service manager how he determined the labor price. If he cannot offer a good explanation, get out of there! **Remember, you are the boss, and it is your right to decide what repairs you want and where they are done.**

The pricing worksheet mentioned earlier also has a service section. This lists a few of the most common services your car will likely need. Many of these repairs pop up unexpectedly, so it can be a big help to have a quick price reference at your fingertips. If, for instance, you are in a shop for an oil change and you find that you need front brakes, you can compare the price at that service center to the quote on the

Don't think that just because you take your car to the dealer or a high-dollar repair center that you will automatically get the best technicians available.

> ...a service manager who knows (or thinks) that you always bring your car to his shop may assume you are not checking around and may be tempted to add a little to the price.

worksheet. This not only insures that you are not being overcharged, but can also save you the time and hassle of calling other repair centers for a price comparison. If the shop gives you a price that seems much higher than the price on your list, you can wait before doing the repair, or you can use the information on the worksheet to negotiate a better price.

You may notice that the service worksheet is smaller than the parts worksheet. This is because many variables affect the final price for many of these services, so these prices are not as exact as the prices for parts. Also, if you can plan ahead for a repair, you should call before you go to confirm the price and to set up an appointment. Fill in the service worksheet by calling two or three service centers and getting basic quotes for the services listed. Again, there are countless variables that can affect the ultimate price for a service, so you will probably be quoted the "best case" price on the phone. Use the worksheet as a guide only.

SMART SHOPPING

Whenever you need a repair other than routine maintenance, you should call around before going to any shop. This does two things. First and foremost, it lets you know what to expect to pay for the service and who has the best price. Second, it lets the shop know that you are shopping around for the best price. This is very, very important. When a repair center knows you are shopping around, they will want to give you their best price in an attempt to secure your business. Your best chance for getting the lowest price is always on the phone. If you just pop in, there may be an entirely different pricing structure!

Old Faithful

Even if you have a favorite shop, you should call ahead to let them know you are shopping around. Many times, a service manager who knows (or thinks) that you *always* bring your car to his shop may assume you are not checking around and may be tempted to add a little to the price. (Hint: If you call your favorite shop for a price, don't tell them who you are *until after* they give you the price.) It is always a good idea to let the service manager know that he is competing with other shops for your business.

If your favorite shop quotes a higher price than some of the competitors, and the difference is enough to bother you, ask them why their price is more. It may be because they are using more expensive parts or are doing more service than the others. A shop that knows you and your buying habits may take the liberty of giving you a price for a more complete job than someone hoping to lure you into their shop. Always use tact and professionalism when discussing prices with anyone, especially your favorite shop. Let them know that you like their service and plan to continue doing business with them, but you also expect to get the same service and price you could get elsewhere. Never have a smirk on your face when you tell them you found a better price somewhere else, they may just tell you to go there! If your favorite shop is reasonably close to the other shops in price, and you like their work and trust them, you probably shouldn't mention it at all. **A trustworthy shop is worth the extra money.**

Frequently, many people regret going to a shop for a lower price, only to get poor quality work or inferior parts, when they could have paid a little more at their favorite shop for a much better job. Besides, if your favorite shop finds out that you don't totally trust them, they may develop a less positive attitude towards you, which is never a good thing.

A Competitive Edge

When shopping for service or tires, don't forget to ask each service center if they will match a competitor's price. You may be pleasantly surprised. Since the automotive repair industry is one of the largest in the world, it is *highly* competitive. Because of this fierce competition, profit margins are at an all-time low for tires, parts, and service. This, of course, is good for the consumer in most cases. This may allow you to do business with a shop closer to you, or one that is highly recommended, for the same money you would spend at a store in another city that started with a lower price. Almost everyone knows that they should wheel and deal when buying a new car or a refrigerator, but most people don't realize that auto repair is usually open for negotiations. Like new car dealers, many repair centers know that if you don't get a fair price at their store, you can go down the road. Few service centers can afford to be totally independent. Always be sure that the person on the phone is aware that you are price shopping.

WAS THAT BOB, OR ROB?

When phone shopping, always remember to write down the price you were given and the name of the person you spoke with. This is very important when you arrive at a service center for repairs. If you failed to write this information down, you may spend several minutes going over what you need, what the price was, and whom you spoke with. Sometimes, you can't even get the price you were given on the phone when you arrive at the shop. Many people have been quoted a price on the phone; then when they go in for repairs, "no one at the store knows anything about it." By providing the person's name and the price you were given, you will eliminate the chance of this happening to you.

HOOK, LINE, & SINKER!

When phone shopping, be wary of receiving a low price that is a "bait-and-switch" ruse. This old trick didn't originate within the automotive industry, but it is frequently used with tires, brakes, or just about any repair. The old bait-and-switch works like this: A service

If a price sounds too good to be true — it probably is.

center quotes you a very attractive price on the phone; then when you go in for service, you are told that they're out of that particular tire, or that you need additional brake repair that was not included in the price you were given. This tactic gets you into the store for a low price, but then switches the offer to a product that has a price that is not so low. Throughout the industry it is a well-known fact that once a customer is in the door, there is a good chance that he or she will fall for the bait-and-switch and purchase more expensive products or repairs. This sounds sneaky, and it is.

Even so, this technique is used everywhere and all the time. Some advertisements use this same principle. A tire store would be glad to sell you those $9.99 tires you saw in the ad, *but* they just happen to be fresh out. By a remarkable coincidence, they *do* have some $59.95 tires in stock, ready to put on your car! If you find a shop that has a much lower price than most others, this *could* be the reason. If a price sounds too good to be true, it probably is! If you suspect you have been targeted for a bait-and-switch, simply refuse the service or products until you take the time to think it over or call around.

One of the best ways to avoid the bait-and-switch routine is to get as much information as you can on the phone — *before* going to the repair center. Ask all the questions you can think of about the products or services you need. Make sure you are quoted the total price, including labor, tax, shop supplies, waste disposal fees, and so on. Ask for the total "drive-out" price — the price you will pay when all is said and done and you drive your car away. When you work hard to compare apples to apples, you often find there is a much lower price difference from shop to shop.

NEGOTIATING PRICE

As mentioned earlier, many repair centers and tire dealers are often willing to sell their service or products for less in order to get your business. Many times the first price you hear can be reduced with a little friendly "dealing." This is especially true when trading with an independent or locally owned repair center. These small businesses often have a higher markup on their products and therefore have more room for price discounts. An independent manager or owner may also have more *authority* to reduce the price if they so desire. Small business owners know that making a few dollars less on a product or repair is much better than not doing the repair at all — something is always better than nothing!

In contrast, a salesperson at a company-owned chain store may not be able to cut one dollar from his price even when he wants to. Of course, many of the larger chain stores will meet a competitor's price if you bring them a written estimate, so it never hurts to ask.

Let me give you a few suggestions that will help you negotiate the best price for repairs or a set of tires. Some of these may not be right for you, but most are very easy to use and could save you serious money.

Ask & You *May* Receive

When shopping for tires or service, either on the phone or at the store, it is always a good idea to come right out and ask the manager for his best price. After the price is quoted, ask if he can do more, or if he will match a competitor's price. You will be surprised to discover how many dollars these few words can save you! If you are phone shopping, emphasize the fact that you are shopping around to find the best price, and that you want the absolute lowest price they can give you. This puts fear into the mind of a manager because he knows that his price will be under the spotlight with his competitors'. He may even offer extra services or throw in a free oil change to make his price sound more attractive. It never hurts to *ask* for a free oil change or a tire rotation and balance when negotiating a price for a relatively expensive purchase. These services cost a service center only a few dollars, so why shouldn't they go the extra mile to get a new customer or keep an old one? If you are a regular customer, call and check the price before you go; if the service manager thinks he is talking to a potential new customer, he may discount the price more than he would for someone who is already his client.

Good Salesmanship

Rule number one: When negotiating a price with a service manager, always do it with a friendly, professional attitude. Use your best salesmanship. After all, you are selling your money to someone who wants it, and the shop is paying you with its services. Remind the manager that there are other shops out there that want your business. This is not rude; it's just a simple fact — there are many places where you *could* take your car. So, what can this repair center offer in the way of better service or better price to secure your business?

This is a good time to let the manager know that you are not ignorant about the service you need. Use terms and mention parts that prove you are knowledgeable about the service you need, and that show that you can tell the difference between better price and better value. If you will be paying in cash, make sure the manager knows this. Credit cards cost the store about 1 to 3 percent, so when you give them cash or a check, they make a little more profit. Cash also gives them quick money to pay their own bills, and it can help you communicate that you are interested in saving as much money as possible. If you wish, explain that you are on a tight budget and only have a limited amount of money to spend at this time. (Of course you should never tell how much money this is!) Most service managers will respect your need to save money and will try to match their price or the amount of service to your budget. After all, if a product costs more than you can afford, you can't buy the service even if you wanted to, which means you both lose. If you state that a price is simply more than you have to spend, a manager may find a way to cut the price a little more.

THE NEW KID ON THE BLOCK

A new business, or one that is still growing, may be more receptive to bargaining than a business that already has all the work it can handle. A new and growing service center will often bend over backward to get your business. They may be willing to make less on a given repair, with the intention of making you a regular customer. On the other hand, a well-established business with a strong customer base may be much more independent when it comes to price breaks. If they have all the work they

Tips for Negotiation:

1) Maintain a professional, friendly attitude.

2) Convey your knowledge of terms and parts.

3) Tell them if you're paying in cash.

4) Buy when the store is not busy.

need, why should they do a job for less? If you walk, someone else is waiting to get in. Remember however, it never hurts to ask for the lowest price no matter who you are dealing with, because few businesses have all the work they need.

TUESDAY'S SPECIAL

Another way to get the lowest price possible is to buy when a store is not busy. A repair center may need more work on a Tuesday, but may have more than they can handle on a Monday or Saturday. If you can schedule your repair at a time when a shop needs work, your bargaining power is increased. In addition to having slow days, most repair centers slow down a great deal in the winter months. Again, your bargaining power goes up as their business slows down. Therefore, for repairs that aren't needed immediately, such as tires or struts and shocks, you might wait and get a great deal during the slow months. You not only have a chance at a better price, you will also find that a center does better quality work when they are not rushed. They will probably give you and your car more attention. Of course, they may also look harder to find something wrong with your car on a slow day, so keep your guard up!

EXERCISE YOUR OPTIONS

Service centers like to offer a "good–better–best" plan for repairs. Although some of these options are legitimate, many times the "best" plan is essentially the same as the less expensive plan, or it may add some very high profit items to the ticket that offer no real benefit. Often, the only difference between plans is a higher markup (profit) or extra services that you don't really need. One example is the minor tune-up versus the major tune-up. The major tune-up *does* include a few more parts, but they may only cost the service center a few dollars. The price you pay, however, may be two or three times the price of the minor tune-up, and there is a good chance that the less expensive tune-up is all you need.

Because a center makes more profit on higher-priced options, the person selling the service usually makes a bonus or extra commission if he sells luxury services. This is why there is pressure to buy the "best" service.

Salespeople are trained to make more expensive repairs sound as though they are a better value, even if they aren't. If you are offered such a choice, don't be afraid to ask questions. Have the salesperson explain exactly what the difference is, and get all the details. Use your own judgment and make your own decisions. Also beware: Sometimes you may have to ask about a less expensive service; some service managers offer only the highest profit repairs at first. Whenever you are given a price for a repair that seems high, ask if there is a less expensive (economy) service, or perhaps less expensive parts.

Many service managers will attempt to find everything on your car that needs repair and then try to convince you that all of these repairs must be done right away. If you have an older car, this could get expensive! It would probably cost over $2,000 to replace every worn or less than perfect part on a 10-year-old car. Don't do everything at once. Express your desire to do only what is necessary to keep your car dependable and safe. Have the service manager list everything your car needs in order of importance. In his opinion, what is the most important repair to do right now, and what can wait? Things like brakes should be at the top of the list, but things like shocks and struts or a tune-up probably won't jeopardize your safety or the safety of others. Do only a few repairs at a time. Remember, you are the boss! You may find that your car works just fine for thousands of miles, *without* some of those additional repairs.

Two Heads Are Better Than One

If you don't know exactly what your car needs, have at least two shops inspect your car before you authorize any repairs. This gives you a chance to compare prices and get two opinions on what your car needs. Start by calling a few repair centers and describing your problem to the service manager. If the manager

> **Never go into a service center and ask them to repair whatever is needed without first getting at least one more opinion, unless you have total confidence in your shop.**

seems interested in doing the repairs, ask when he would like to inspect your car and give you a written estimate. Letting the service manager know that you will be comparing his opinion and price with his competitors' will almost always keep him 100 percent honest! Never go into a service center and ask them to repair whatever is needed without first getting at least one more opinion, unless you have total confidence in your shop.

Depending on what type of problem you have, a shop may inspect your car free of charge. Some problems, however, require a good deal of time to diagnose, which will necessitate a charge. If a shop charges you for an estimate, ask the manager if he will refund some or all of the price you paid for the inspection if you decide to let his shop repair your car. Some centers will offer this and some will not. You should ask this *only after* the estimate is written, to prevent the inspection fee from being hidden in the estimate.

GET IT IN WRITING

When getting an estimate, have the service manager explain exactly what repairs are needed and give you an itemized list of all the parts and labor. This is also the time to discuss warranty information. This will make the job of comparing estimates much easier and will help you decide who really has the best service for your money. Make sure the estimate is signed and dated, and find out how long the price is valid — and by all means, hang on to the estimate!

In some cases, two shops may disagree on the proper method of repair. Because of the many variables in repairing cars, there can be legitimate disagreements about what repairs are needed. But sometimes the difference in "opinion" is really just one shop trying to sell you more than you need. When getting an estimate, tell each shop that you want to know your options. You need to know what is necessary to make your car safe, as opposed to what they may be "recommending." Ask each shop if they will be responsible for their diagnosis. In other words, will they charge you the full price if the repairs do not correct the problem? If more repairs are needed, will you have to pay for repetitive services? Will you be charged again for more diagnostics? Make the manager understand that you want your car fixed right the first time. If necessary, have the shops write on the estimate what will happen if the repairs are not successful. Most likely, a shop that stands behind its opinion in some way is certain that they are recommending the right repairs. If you are not convinced by any of the repair centers you visited, getting another opinion may be in order.

A SHOP YOU CAN TRUST

     Once you've collected some information on the phone or perhaps from visiting a couple of shops for an estimate, you must decide where to go for the repairs. This is a very important decision. Ask anyone who depends on others to keep their car running, and they will probably state that their biggest concern is finding a car repair shop they can trust. A dependable shop can actually make your visit to the repair center enjoyable. Enjoyable? This may sound strange, but all cars need repair, so if you find a trustworthy service manager who does only what is necessary, and who will charge you a reasonable price, consider yourself lucky and enjoy your good fortune. There are good service centers out there; the question is, how do you find them? There are no magic tricks for doing this, but there are some things you can do to help.

C A R S M A R T

TRUST YOUR INSTINCTS

One of the biggest mistakes you can make when choosing a shop is jumping to the center with the lowest price. Location, appearance, reputation, and even your instincts should also play a role in your choice. Perhaps a shop that is close to home, or one that is willing to pick up your car at work, is worth a few dollars more. A shop with clean facilities and neat workers will probably show more respect for your car than a shop that looks like a junkyard. It's not a bad idea to drive by a shop and notice what kind, and how many, cars are being serviced there. A shop with a good reputation will likely earn clients with newer cars and have a strong business, even if their prices are slightly higher than some of their competitors'. In addition to these tangible things, you should trust your instincts. Perhaps you communicate better with one of the service managers you spoke with, or maybe he or she seemed more tuned into your needs as a customer. Some people are genuinely concerned about helping their customers, and some are only interested in making money. Most of the time you can tell the difference by talking to them for a few minutes. Keep all this in mind when you are looking for the shop that is right for you.

MEGA-SHOP...OR MOM 'N POP?

First of all, is there one type of auto repair business that has a better reputation for being honest than another? Can you trust a shop just because it is a big retailer with a self-made image for being honest and has a nationally recognized name? Are small independent shops more trustworthy? Do you always get a better price at the national chain stores and tire dealers? The truth is that any business is only as good as the people in it. All of the above stores can be on either side of the coin. There are good and bad service centers of all shapes, types, and sizes.

One thing to consider is that big chain stores may be able to offer better prices on some products because of their buying power. If a chain of stores collectively buys a million dollars in products every month, you can bet they will be paying less than an independent store who buys only a few thousand dollars worth of the same products. However, in hot competition with other stores, chain stores may advertise unbelievably low prices, sometimes below their cost, to lure you into their store. As we all know, a business *must* make a profit to stay open, so these stores must try (very hard) to make up for the money they lose on an advertised item by selling high-profit products or services as well. So be careful!

These larger stores are usually operated by employees, not owners. Therefore, you may find that they have less concern for your business and for their store's reputation than a person who owns his own service center. Small business owners or managers often will give you the best service you can get. They not only depend on their store for a living, both now and in years to come, but are also placing their personal reputations at stake. Another thing to consider is that the personnel at the large chains may not have the authority or motivation to negotiate prices, while a small business owner would much rather make a few dollars less than nothing at all!

Of course all this is only a generalization and may be totally wrong in some cases. There are locally owned stores that are less than honest. There are some chain stores that offer long-term benefits to their employees and pay them by the hour instead of a commission on their sales, which tends to give them pride in their work and helps reduce the temptation to add unneeded services.

THERE'S NO SUBSTITUTE FOR EXPERIENCE...OR IS THERE?

The only way to know for sure if a shop is trustworthy is by experience. It usually takes many visits over several years to determine if a service center is honest or not. This may sound like bad news, and it is for many people. But the good news is — *you* don't have to be the one "testing" the repair center. Let the experience of others work for you. Everyone has access to hundreds of people who can help them find a good repair shop. You can ask your family,

Ask family, friends, co-workers and acquaintances to recommend a service center.

Let the experiences of others work for you.

friends, workmates, or even strangers to recommend a service center. Practically everyone has had good and bad experiences at various repair shops, and most people are more than happy to share them! You may even get tired of hearing all of these stories.

If you get a good report on a shop from several people, the chances are excellent that the repair center can be trusted. Likewise, several bad reports is a sign that you should avoid a shop. But be careful not to base an assessment, good or bad, on a report from just one person. No matter how honest and competent a shop is, there will always be a time when someone thought they were ripped off or had an incompetent repair, whether it is true or not. Auto repair has thousands of variables, and every shop will eventually make a mistake or simply have some bad luck. There's not a repair shop in the world that has pleased every customer every time. Auto repair professionals are human! Keep in mind that the more people you ask, the better your chance of finding a good shop. You will get a more accurate picture of what a service center is really like. It is also a good idea to write down the names of the good and bad repair centers. It takes time to gather all of this information, so if possible, check around before you need repairs.

INSTANT STATUS

When going to a shop that has been recommended, be sure to tell them so, and mention the name of the person who told you. This is very important; it tells the repair people that their good work is paying off and puts pressure on them to continue doing high quality work. When a service manager finds out you were recommended to his business, he will immediately think of you as a good customer. The service center gets instant credibility from the recommendation, and you get instant good customer status. It's like climbing a ladder without having to start on the first step. Likewise, when you find a trustworthy shop, tell others about the good service and ask them to mention your name when going in for repairs. This will definitely help establish you as a great customer and you *will* reap the benefits!

Of course, your own interaction with a shop is the best way to develop trust. **There is no substitute for a long-term relationship with a service center.** Like everything else, practice makes perfect. There is nothing that compares to going into a shop thinking that you need major repairs, and the service manager tells you that he found a loose

ENOUGH IS ENOUGH

Early last summer an elderly lady brought her car to my shop because her air conditioner was not working. The summer before, she was told by another shop that her car would need a new air conditioning system, which would cost about $600. We had done some work for her before and had earned her trust and respect. She told me that she was ready to spend the money to have the new system installed and was prepared to leave her car with us for the day. My wife was about to take her to work, but I told her to wait a few minutes so I could give the air conditioning system a quick check.

I raised the hood and noticed that the a/c belt was missing. This usually means that the compressor is locked up, and I knew the $600 repair was probably needed. But to my surprise, when I tried to turn the compressor with my hand, it moved. This meant the belt had simply worn out and broke, and the compressor was probably good after all. Ten minutes later, I had a new belt on the car and the a/c was working fine! Her car was fixed in a few minutes for about $30! Needless to say, she left with a smile. The rest of the day I thought about how easy it would have been to install the new system and make about $300 profit. I could have justified the expensive repairs in my mind by telling myself that the compressor was probably worn out anyway. I wondered how many shops would have done the expensive repairs.

plug wire, and he is not charging you for putting it back on. Or, perhaps you were told that you needed a new air conditioner compressor, and your shop finds that you only needed a new belt. Simple things like this will save you hundreds of dollars. Auto repair shops can easily do costly repairs and take advantage of you without a hitch. So when a shop chooses to be honest and make much less money by doing the right thing, they deserve a pat on the back — *and* your future business!

MECHANICS

THE GOOD, THE BAD, & THE PARTS CHANGERS

There are many mechanics in this world, and mechanics are no different from any other professionals. Some are good, some bad, with plenty in between. So how do you define good and bad for mechanics?

A good mechanic is a person who can quickly solve difficult automotive problems. He actually understands what makes a car work and *why* things happen the way they do, instead of simply knowing how to replace old parts with new ones. A good mechanic can repair a car on the first attempt without guessing. A bad mechanic bluffs his way through every repair. Even if he figures out how to do a repair, he doesn't really understand what happened. A bad mechanic can actually do more damage than good to a car. There are plenty of bad mechanics out there, and they have given the industry a bad reputation.

CARSMART

Somewhere between the good and the bad are the parts changers. The parts changers have a decent amount of experience and can do specific repairs with confidence and skill. A parts changer may not have the training or be intelligent enough to be a top-notch technician, but he is good at what he does. When a new or unusual problem is introduced however, the parts changer may have no idea what to do. Parts changers however are a valuable part of the auto repair industry.

A RARE BREED

It takes three things to make a good mechanic: knowledge, experience, and intelligence. Intelligence was listed last, because it can sometimes be replaced with hard work. A person who may not be among the most intelligent can study and work hard to develop a high level of skill.

There is, however, no substitute for knowledge and experience, which must go hand in hand. No matter how much technical schooling is completed or how many technical books are studied, a technician will not be top notch until he has actually worked in the field for several years. Experience teaches things that cannot be learned in the classroom. A veteran mechanic learns something new every day. Without experience, knowledge is little more than useless. On the other hand, experience can only go so far without a basic knowledge of automotive systems. A person who has worked on cars for years can be easily stumped if he does not really understand why things happen the way they do. Experience without knowledge usually equates to a good parts changer, which is not a bad thing.

Within his field, a good parts changer is just as good as a master technician.

Where and how do you find good mechanics? The best mechanics *usually* work at the shops that have the best reputations and the highest prices. This is because a good mechanic will rightfully earn more money than a bad one. Therefore, he will usually end up at a shop that charges enough to pay for his higher wages. Usually, you can't find the best mechanic in town working at the shop with the lowest prices. You should have no problem guessing where you will find the worst mechanics. Just like anything else, you get what you pay for when it comes to a technician. Of course there are exceptions. In the end, the only way to know for sure that you have a good mechanic is by your own experiences or the experiences of other customers. For instance, does your shop usually find and repair your problem quickly and on the first attempt, or does it take a little guessing to get it fixed? When you leave the shop, do you have to go back and have the problem fixed again? What about a mechanic who fixes a problem that several others worked on and failed to fix? These situations should give you a good idea as to the competence of your mechanic.

The fact that good mechanics cost more may sound like bad news, but you don't always need the best mechanic in town. If you have a simple repair such as an oil change or a basic brake job, a parts changer may be just what you need. Within his field, a good parts changer is just as good as a master technician. A person who works on brakes, day in and day out, will know brakes, and it makes no difference whether he knows how to tune a car. Imagine you go to an eye doctor instead of to an eye surgeon for an eye exam. Sure, the far more knowledgeable eye surgeon *could* give you a prescription for new glasses, but you'll get the same glasses either way, and how much more will the surgeon cost? Just as the eye surgeon should be called for serious eye problems, an ace mechanic is needed for a tricky engine problem or an anti-lock brake repair. Don't forget — a good, experienced mechanic may cost less in the long run by fixing your car quickly and fixing it right the first time! More on this later.

TIME FOR REPAIRS

Now that you know how to get the best price and how to find a shop that is right for you, it is time to discuss what to do when you walk into the service center. First, be sure to let the service manager know that you called ahead, or that you have a written estimate. Mention the person's name you spoke with and repeat the price you were given. This tells the manager that you already know how much the repair should cost and should eliminate any chance for price adjustments without your knowledge. Immediately, let the service manager know that you are knowledgeable about the repairs you need. Discuss information or terms you have learned about the repairs if you feel comfortable doing so. Avoid saying anything that gives the impression that you know nothing about your car. Never admit to your lack of knowledge! Be sure to give all the details about what your car is doing wrong. You may want to write down these symptoms before going in, because they can be easy to forget.

The more information you place in the hands of the service manager, the more likely he will be able to solve your problem. It is also a good idea to supply the manager with a written list of all of this information and state exactly what repairs are authorized. If you want to be really cautious, make two copies and keep a copy signed by the manager.

Before repairs are started, be sure to tell the manager that you want to be notified *before* any additional repairs are done. If your schedule permits, it is best to stay at the shop during repairs. If you choose to leave the shop, give the center a number to get in touch with you if the need arises. Never tell them to do whatever is needed unless you have already determined that they can be trusted with such power. Another good idea is to ask them to save any old parts that come off of the car, when possible. All of the above hints are very powerful ways to give the service center the message that you are looking out for yourself.

POST-REPAIR CHECK-UP

If you suspect that a service center has replaced a part that was not worn or damaged, you may want to take the old part to another technician to get his or her opinion on the condition of the part. If you do this, don't reveal the name of the shop you are checking on, even if they ask. Depending on their integrity, competitors may give you false information in order to cover or damage the reputation of a another shop.

If you find that a part was replaced that was not defective, you may want to carry the part back to the original shop and peacefully discuss your concerns with the manager. The service manager may not be aware that a technician is unnecessarily replacing parts, and you may help prevent this from happening to the next person. Note: Parts stores require that *some* old parts be returned to them for future remanufacturing. If you want to keep these parts, you may have to pay a "core charge."

ADD-ONS

Consumers often go into a shop for a specific repair, and the service manager tells them that additional repairs or parts are needed. Although there are many legitimate reasons for additional repairs, or "add-ons," many service centers make extra money by selling add-on parts or services that are not needed. Throughout the car industry, it is a well-known fact that if a shop has your car on the rack, you are more likely to purchase additional repairs than to ask them to put your car back together and let you go. This philosophy is used not only in the automotive industry, but in other types of retail business. Many centers quote a price on the phone or in an advertisement that is so low that they will lose money if they don't add something to the ticket. A service manager in this position will push his technicians to find something wrong with your car, even if they have to fudge a little. Likewise, service centers who give lifetime warranties on a service, such as brake pads for example, must find additional repairs if they expect to make money on a warranted brake job. Remember, all stores must make a profit to stay open, so you are not likely to get one free brake job after another. This may sound a little hard to believe, but in fact it happens every day.

In contrast, a service center that quotes a price that allows them to make a fair profit on the service you actually need will not be so motivated to sell you things you don't. When shopping around for a service, a store that gives you a slightly higher quote that includes more extras may actually cost you less. For example, let's say you called two service centers for a price on a front brake job. Shop A gives you a price of $89.95 that includes the best pads, labor, and machining the rotors; shop B gives you a price of $69.95, but does not mention machining the rotors or the quality of the pads. You would probably find that if you took your car to shop B, they would wait until your car is on the lift, and *then* mention that your rotors need machining and that they would recommend the

> A service manager in this position will push his technicians to find something wrong with your car, even if they have to fudge a little.

best pads for your car. These additional repairs could add $50 to the repair! This is a common technique used to get your car on the lift before you are told the *actual* price. This is another example why it is very important to get all the details while you are shopping for a service.

A Strong Signal

If a service center advises you that you need additional parts or repairs, ask them for an exact description and price for the extra work and a total for all the work you need. You can also ask them to escort you to your car and show you what they have found. **These small details may not seem like much, but they definitely give the service manager the message that you are not a pushover and that you are not a good candidate for a scam.** (You may be told by the manager that his insurance carrier will not allow customers in the shop area. Although insurance companies vary on this policy, most will allow you into the shop if you are escorted by an employee. If you are told otherwise, this may be a reason for suspicion.)

If you suspect that a shop is trying to sell you something you don't need, it is your right to tell them to put your car back together and let you get a second opinion. Don't believe anyone who says that you must buy from them. Some service managers try to pressure their customers to buy add-ons by telling them that it would be unsafe to keep driving the car or that it would be against the law to drive the car without the repair. If someone tries to scare you into buying something, look out! If your car was *that* bad off, you probably would have known it way before now! It is your car, and you have the right to get another opinion. Also remember, if the part or service you need is on the price worksheet, you can tell at a glance if the prices are in line. If the repair is not on the list, and you have reason to think you are being overcharged, don't be afraid to use the shop's phone or a nearby pay phone to call another service center or a parts store for a price.

BECOMING A GOOD CUSTOMER

Becoming a good customer is one of the best ways to get good service, good prices, and honesty from a repair center. One definition of a "good customer" is one that the service manager likes to see walking in the door. This should not be confused with a "sucker." Some service managers also like to see these walk in! A sucker lets the shop do anything they want to his or her car and charge anything for it. A good customer is someone the service manager enjoys dealing with, to whom he can offer the best service and price and go the extra mile. Dealing with a good customer is one of the service manager's biggest joys. **Knowing how to become a good customer can save you a lot of money and will make your visits to a repair center much more pleasant and enjoyable.**

> Developing a real friendship with the people at the shop can make a big difference in how they perceive you as a customer.

There are several ways to become a good customer. If you have plenty of money to throw around, you can simply tell the manager you want whatever your car needs and only the best parts, leave your car with them a few days and don't ask how much it will cost until you pick the car up, then pay them cash. You can bet your last dollar that such a person will be considered a good customer by any service manager.

Of course few people can afford to do this, but anyone can become a customer the manager enjoys seeing in his store. One of the best and easiest ways to be such a customer is with a smile. When you walk into a shop with a smile and a friendly attitude, the person who greets you will probably appreciate this and return the gesture. This sounds simple, but it works! If you've ever worked with the public, you already know this makes a big difference. On the other hand, if you go into a business with a bad attitude and express negative feelings about having your car repaired, the service manager may develop a negative attitude towards you, and a negative attitude between a manager and a customer is never good.

MAKING NEW FRIENDS

To go a step beyond a smile and a good attitude, you should learn the owner's or manager's name as soon as possible. It is a proven fact — people respond in a more positive way when you call them by name. It shows that you think of them as a person, or even a friend, instead of just an employee. Ask how they are doing or how their family is doing; this adds even more to the relationship. Developing a *real* friendship with the people at the shop can make a big difference in how they perceive you as a customer. This should include not only the owner or manager, but everyone at the service center. If you know the names and talk with everyone who will be working on your car, the entire shop will begin to think of you as a good customer. This really works!

This is especially true with the technicians. If you develop a friendship with the technician, he will be much less likely to suggest repairs that you may not need. A technician may even estimate in your favor when the service manager asks him for the time or labor he put into your car. In many cases, service managers know much less about repairing cars than you think. They often depend on the technicians to tell them what your car needs, and sometimes, how much the repair should cost. If the technician likes you and is looking out for you, your chances of being taken advantage of are much less.

When a technician can put a face with the car he is working on, he is much more likely to be conservative with his repairs. Also, if you are pleased with the repairs and service you received, you may want to call the shop or visit them to tell them that you are satisfied. Thank them for the work they did. Let them know that their good work and honesty was not taken for granted. This is like music to their ears, and they will surely have a smile on their face the next time you see them!

Spread the Word

Another way to be a good customer is to recommend your service center to others. When you've established that you have found a competent and trustworthy shop, tell the service manager and the technicians that you appreciate their work and that you will tell your

---

A Good Customer:

1) Knows the manager's name

2) Develops friendships with shop employees

3) Introduces himself to the technician

4) Thanks the technician for the good work

5) Tells others about the shop

6) Can ask for advice

friends about them. This is also music to their ears! The best advertising in the world is by word of mouth and they know it. A person who is referred to a shop is usually a good customer because they have a certain level of trust that would not be there if they had simply walked in cold. When you refer someone to a center, be sure to have them say who sent them. When your shop hears your name, it demonstrates that you have kept your word and that you could provide even more new customers. This benefits everyone, and makes you a *very* desirable customer.

Once you've developed a good relationship with a service center, you may get help from them in many ways. You can call them for advice on repairs they don't do, or they may be able to recommend a good shop for certain repairs that they don't specialize in. They may also give you advice or help with a do-it-yourself repair at home, or even let you borrow a tool you need. There is nothing like having a friend in the auto repair business.

Small Talk

You may think that you are not outgoing enough to successfully befriend a shop. The truth is, you don't have to be very aggressive with this strategy. Just think of the people at the shop as regular folks, which is what they are. They get up in good and bad moods and have good and bad days. They all have families and feelings. This is true for the lowest man on the totem pole to the highest. If you place them on the same level as yourself, you will probably find that they are easy to talk to and will show an equal amount of concern for you. If you don't feel confident talking about your car, talk about the weather, sports, or anything you may have in common. Just be yourself and they will learn to like you as you are, whether you have an outgoing personality, or are a little bashful. If you find that you simply don't click with one person at a shop, try dealing with another. Don't continue doing business with a center that has a service manager you detest. Having your car repaired should be a positive, enjoyable experience, not a clash of personalities.

The Superman Complex

When developing yourself as a good customer, be careful you don't allow the service center to feel invincible. Trust them, but not to the extent that you will do anything they say. Always let them know that you are the boss. Make them aware that you are knowledgeable and that you know what a repair should cost. To do this without seeming too obvious, ask them to take you into the shop to see the parts that need replacing, or tell them that a friend insisted that you call their favorite shop for a price. You could even mention an ad you saw in the newspaper for a specific repair. Simply letting them know that you are thoughtful about handling your car's repairs should be enough to keep them on the straight and narrow. It's a good idea to mention that you appreciate their honesty. This puts pressure on them to continue being honest with you.

Becoming a Bad Customer

In case you were wondering, there are a few things you must avoid if you want to establish yourself as a good customer. First, don't bicker too much over the price. A customer who constantly begs and argues over a price can get on a manager's bad side in a hurry. Try to get the price settled quickly without bickering. You should know what the job will cost before you authorize it, so don't complain or argue about the price after the work is finished. If you've done your homework and know you're getting a fair price, there's nothing wrong with acting as if you don't mind paying the price.

It's also good business not to talk too much. Managers and mechanics are busy people. They may *seem* interested in hearing your family history or your medical problems, but they probably don't have the time. A few kind words and a little small talk is all you need. This is especially true with phone calls. You should state your business and get off the phone! Phone time takes a manager or technician away from his work or another customer and can cost them money, which of course rubs them the wrong way. And if you see someone from your shop at the grocery store, don't ask them about repairing your car. Most people try to forget about their jobs when they clock out. Never call a manager or technician at home to talk about your car problems!

You can stay off a technician's most unwanted customer list by never hanging over his shoulder and watching him work. This makes most mechanics nervous and may give them the impression that you don't trust them. Wait in the customer lounge unless you are invited into the shop. And finally, if you take your car to several different shops, don't constantly remind the centers of this fact. If a manager thinks his is your only shop, it's to your advantage.

COME-BACKS

In the automotive repair industry, a "come-back" is a repair that must be checked or fixed. Come-backs are inevitable. All repairs centers eventually make a mistake or have some bad luck. Most of the time, this will result in a come-back. Almost everyone has had to return at least once to have a repair checked or done again. All shops have come-backs, and all shops handle them differently. Some repair centers receive a come-back with a smiling face and open arms, some can get downright nasty and try to lay the blame on you or something else. Learning how to handle a come-back can help you get the results you want, quickly, without having to argue with the service manager. Every situation will be different, and there is no secret way to handle all the possibilities, but there are a few basic guidelines.

If something goes wrong after a repair, call or return to the shop as soon as possible, even if the problem seems minor and may not need immediate attention. A call should be made *especially* if you can't go back to the shop right away. This call informs the service center about the problem and lets them know the time frame in which the problem occurred. This is also a good time to set up an appointment to bring your car in. When discussing your problem with the service manager, give only the facts. Refrain from giving your opinion about the problem or the shop's work, you may have to eat those words later. Above all, remain calm and control your temper, even if the problem seems severe. A customer who can handle a come-back with a good attitude is more likely to get his or her problem fixed without a hitch.

> It is much easier to get the problem fixed under good terms, and almost all managers are much more likely to help you if you go to them with a friendly, professional attitude.

Keep Your Cool

When you go into the shop with a come-back, greet the service manager with a smile. Remember, the problem could be unrelated to the recent repair or could be just a simple mistake; it is never intentional. Make sure you bring the receipt for the work with you and ask the manager to take a test drive *with* you, so he can hear or feel the problem for himself. Tell him exactly what seems to be wrong and be sure he acknowledges that there is indeed a problem. The worst thing you can do is go into a business angry and tell the service manager what a sorry job the shop has done. This will make the manager defensive, and it will be much harder to get your car repaired to your satisfaction. Many people think that a business *must* do whatever it is told. The truth is, a business can tell you to get lost if they choose. Sure, you can get a lawyer or go to small claims court, but the time and expense can be significant — not to mention the fact that you could lose. It is much easier to get the problem fixed under good terms, and almost all managers are much more likely to help you if you go to them with a friendly, professional attitude.

And the Results are...

When the car is checked out again, there are several different results you may get. The two most common are as follows:

#1. The technician found the problem, and it *is* directly related to the recent repair. The shop is willing to make all the repairs at no charge.

#2. The technician found the problem, but it *was not* related to the repairs the shop had done. They may offer to repair the new problem for a price.

Although these examples are general ones, most situations can be roughly placed into one of these two categories. How you should react to these situations will be dealt with next.

The Number One Attitude

If a shop tells you that they were responsible for the problem and they will take care of everything at no cost to you, hats off to them! It takes a good person, or repair center, to admit to a mistake, especially if it is going to cost them money to fix. It is often easy for a shop to lay the blame on a new problem and charge you for *their* mistake. If your shop admits they made a mistake, you should tell them that you appreciate their honesty and will continue doing business with them. Be careful not to judge a shop harshly after only one or two come-backs. Any shop can make a mistake, but a shop with a #1 attitude deserves a second chance. Naturally, if you have come-backs on a regular basis, this is an important sign that the technicians are less than competent.

The Other Attitude

If you are given the #2 excuse, ask the manager to escort you to your car and show you the problem. If the shop has previously proved themselves honest, and they can give you a reasonable explanation of the problem, they are probably telling the truth. If you are not sure about the honesty of the people involved, you may want to go to

> ...before entering into a friendly battle with anyone, be sure you are talking to the most powerful person available at the time.

another shop for a second opinion. Getting an unbiased opinion can make a big difference in how you proceed from that point on. It can shed new light on the subject and may even convince you that the original shop was not at fault. When you get a second opinion however, don't tell them who recently repaired the car, even if they ask. Some repair centers may feel that certain other centers are their enemies. A repair center that is not on good terms with another may claim the other is at fault, even if they are not. Likewise, two shops on good terms with one another may try to cover for each other.

If the new shop believes that the first is at fault, you should have them write down what they think the problem is. They don't have to write whose fault the problem is, just the problem. This gives some responsibility to the second repair center. Next, call or go back to the original shop, tell them what you have found, and ask them if they wish to reconsider. Tell them that they are at risk of losing you as a customer if they do not repair the problem to your satisfaction. They could have made an honest mistake and may be willing to repair the problem at no cost, or they may value you enough as a customer to do the repairs, instead of losing your business. If they refuse to check the car again and tell you to get lost, they probably know they were at fault.

THE NEXT LEVEL

What if a shop has caused a new problem, and they claim that they are not responsible; what should you do? First of all, don't lose your temper! A heated argument almost never solves your problem. Also, before entering into a *friendly* battle with anyone, be sure you are talking to the most powerful person available at the time. The manager or owner is usually the person most concerned with the future effects of how he or she handles your problem. They are aware of the possible damage you could do to their business if you are not satisfied. If a manager or owner is not available, you may want to wait and discuss your problem with them later.

Before discussing *what* you think a shop should do to correct a problem, be sure to tell them exactly *why* you feel the way you do. Start at the beginning — describe the original repair and what happened afterwards. Give as much information and detail as possible. Do your best to make them understand why you believe they are responsible. Try to make them see the problem through *your* eyes. You can even come right out and ask them, "Do you see why I feel the way I do?" or "Place yourself in my shoes." Don't forget to keep an open mind and listen to their side of the argument with respect. A disagreement can't be resolved if either party has a closed mind. If the service manger begins talking over your head with technical terms, ask him to slow down and explain in plain English what these terms mean. If the manager presents a good argument in his defense and you feel that he may be making a legitimate point, you may still feel that they should do something about your problem. At this point, it is often wise to offer to pay half of the regular price or pay enough to cover what the repairs will cost the shop. A manager who truly believes that his shop is not responsible may be willing to do this to keep your business and to keep you happy. At least your offer prevents them from losing money on the repair.

THE FINAL BATTLE

After you have presented your best argument and the manager still does not offer to repair your car, what does this mean? It could mean that the manager whole-heartedly believes that his shop was not the cause of your problem, or it could be that he simply does not care. In either case, another visit to an unbiased shop may be helpful. If after all of this, all fingers are still pointing to the original shop, it's time for the heavy artillery. You should call or visit the manager and tell him how you feel. Tell him that you whole-heartedly believe that they *are* responsible and that you will stop doing business with them in the future. Tell him that you will tell your friends about what happened. The threat of a small claims suit can be mentioned, but should not be thrown around casually. Make this person believe that you mean what you say.

If the manager is suddenly willing to do the repair, he is probably only trying to save his reputation, or perhaps he knows that he would lose a small claims battle. If it would cost a significant amount of money to have the work done elsewhere, you may want to go ahead and let the original shop do the repairs. If repairs can be done inexpensively at another shop, it would probably feel better to say, "You had your chance," and go elsewhere. If you decide to tell others about your experience, refrain from stating strongly opinionated information, just give them the facts and let them be the judge. If there is a significant amount of money involved, you may want to consider a small claims suit. This may be the only way to get what you deserve. A small claims suit can be handled without legal council and is fairly inexpensive compared to hiring a lawyer.

KEEP THOSE RECEIPTS

Time after time, customers come into my business wanting a brake job or some other repair that they feel should still be under warranty. When asked if they have their receipt, they usually say, "I have it somewhere at home," or "Don't you guys keep a record?" Sure, we keep records in the computer as well as hard copies, but it could take hours to find one record out of thousands. A service center writes thousands of tickets, while a customer needs to keep up with only a few. Most businesses who keep records of warranty information do so only for their own convenience and protection; they don't have to keep any records at all. Many shops will not consider a warranty without seeing a receipt. Therefore — keep up with your receipts — burden the shop only with working on your car. When you walk into a shop with your warranty in hand, you present yourself as a customer who knows what they are doing and takes their warranty seriously.

Another common mistake is assuming a shop can remember you and your repair. I think I can speak for most managers out there when I say that it is impossible to remember every car and every repair my shop has done over the years. You may have had only one or two repairs done over the last six months, but a busy repair center has done thousands!

Also, don't underestimate the time or mileage since the repair was done. I have often had customers tell me that a repair was made a few months ago, when it was over a year ago. Recently a customer complained that his tires were worn out with only about 30,000 miles on them. When the invoice was found, it revealed that the tires were seven years old and had over 60,000 miles on them! This kind gentleman was not being dishonest, time had just slipped by faster than he thought. So, when you go into a shop without a receipt, be careful about estimating how old a repair is; you could be embarrassed. Of course, if you have your invoice, there will be no need to guess.

Some people insist on keeping their automotive receipts in a file at home, but the best place for receipts is in the car to which they belong. You will always know where the receipts are. If you have a problem while driving, you will have the invoices with you when you need them. If you keep records at home, make copies and keep the originals in your car.

FAR & AWAY

One of our biggest car-related fears is having car trouble away from home. An on-the-road repair can take the fun out of almost any trip. Having your car repaired miles from home can be frightening and intimidating. Almost everyone has heard at least one horror story about a car that had to be repaired on the road. It seems the chance that you will be ripped off is multiplied many times over if you are in another city or state. And it is more likely — because a dishonest shop manager knows you will probably never see him again, and you are not in a position to shop around or damage his business if you are not satisfied. Many roadside shops were built with the helpless motorist in mind. Some of these service center owners don't even care if you *know* they are ripping you off!

CARSMART

To avoid repairs away from home:

1) Practice prevention.

2) Have a safety inspection before leaving home.

The biggest problem with having repairs out of town is paying ridiculously high prices for parts, tires, or service. A dishonest manager or owner knows that if he charges triple the price, the traveler really has no choice but to pay it. Sometimes, the victims don't know they are being ripped off; other times they simply pay astronomical prices because they think there is no alternative. Convenience can also play a role. A business person or someone in a hurry to start their vacation may be willing to pay too much to keep the show on the road. Even though your chance or willingness to be a victim of repair fraud does go up when you leave home, there are some things you can do to help reduce these chances. You do have a choice!

THE BEST TROUBLE IS NO TROUBLE

The best way to avoid repair fraud when traveling is to not have car trouble. Of course, there is no way to guaranty this, but keeping your car well maintained helps a lot. Most automotive problems can be prevented if a car is properly inspected and maintained on a regular basis. Before going out of town, you should take your car to a repair center and ask them to do a thorough safety inspection (or preventive maintenance check). They will check your battery, brakes, belts, hoses, and all other systems to make sure there are no obvious signs that a problem may soon occur. Also have them check the tires and inflate them to the proper pressure, which can save you some gas money.

If your (trusted) repair center advises you that repairs are needed, don't try to wait until after the trip, do them now! It is much better to do the repairs now, even if it's sooner than

BE PREPARED

The Boy Scout motto is "Be Prepared." This is always good advice, but it is especially true when traveling in your car. Being prepared can save you from being stranded on the side of the road, or from getting ripped off by a towing service or auto service center. Before leaving on a trip, have your car inspected by a professional mechanic. Also check the spare tire, the jack, and all its components. If you have never changed a tire, and you won't have someone with you who can, get someone to help you practice changing a tire at home. This could make a huge difference if the need arises.

There are also a few things you should carry with you. Make sure you have a flashlight, and a pair of jumper cables is also a good thing to have in your trunk. Many people may be glad to help you jump your car, but if there are no cables, you may have to call a wrecker anyway. A jug of clean water (at least a gallon) is also a good idea. This water could be used to fill the radiator if your car overheats, which can save an engine. Water is a better choice than antifreeze, because clean water, in a clean container, can also be used for other purposes such as for drinking or cleaning. A spare pair of wiper blades can also come in handy. Of course an extra quart of oil, transmission fluid, and some brake fluid should be included. Transmission fluid can also be safely used as power steering fluid. You may want to purchase a can of tire inflator–sealer to keep in the trunk. This may inflate or fix a flat tire enough to keep you on the road without having to change a tire. (See the section about flat tires in the tire section).

Another suggestion is to keep your old drive belts when you have new ones installed. Since parts stores close at night, that old belt may keep you on the road if a belt brakes at night or in the middle of nowhere. It can be quite unpleasant to stay at a service station all night waiting for a parts store to open! These few items can give you peace of mind and can make a big difference if you do have trouble. If you don't think you have room for these things, check in the spare tire compartment. These compartments often have extra room under or around the spare. And by all means, remember to bring *CarSmart* and your parts and service worksheets!

necessary, than to risk paying three times the price on the road. Your service center may charge for this inspection (under $20), but the money you spend could save you hundreds of dollars later. Many service centers offer a free safety inspection with an oil change or with a tire rotation and balance. A few phone calls will probably get you an inspection for free.

DESPITE ALL EFFORTS...

If worse comes to worse and you need repairs in another city, ask a few local folks whom they would recommend. They should be able to steer you away from shops that are known for taking advantage of travelers. (Almost every town has at least one rip-off service center.) Tell them that you're from out of town and that you are looking for an honest repair shop. Most people will be glad to help you, if you just ask. Another good idea is to call the local chamber of commerce or police for suggestions for an honest shop. (Don't call 911, except for emergencies.) If you are going to be towed, try to find a shop via phone *before* your car is on the tow truck. Towing services charge by the mile and by their time, so you don't want to have your car towed to several different shops before deciding on one. The tow truck driver may give you the name of a shop, but be cautious about this. **Wrecker services are often tied to repair centers who may or may not be honest.** A recommendation from a local citizen is probably more trustworthy.

There are no rules for finding a shop that will treat you fairly, but **many times a dealer or a national chain store is the best choice for out-of-town repairs, especially one that has a store in your home town.** These businesses are less likely to have a price structure that fluctuates depending on where you are from. Also, if you find that you were overcharged, or if you are not satisfied in any way, you can call the franchise store in your town and explain what happened. They may handle the problem or give you the number of the corporate office, where you should be able to get satisfaction. Whenever possible avoid service stations near the interstate, or even near a remote highway. These businesses are prone to preying on innocent travelers. This does not mean that all stations of this type are dishonest, but the reputation *is* there. If you can get your car to a busy part of town, you will have a better chance of finding an honest shop.

If your troubles occur at night or on a weekend, what you do depends on your traveling situation. If you are in a hurry or in a small town, you may be forced to have repairs done at a roadside service station. If, however, you are in town for a few days, you may be able to wait until the chain stores open. More and more, chain stores and department store shops are open late and on weekends.

The Traveler's Bluff

If you decide to go with an unknown service station, muster all your confidence — it never hurts to start off with a good attitude and give them the benefit of a doubt. You may be lucky and find a shop that is genuinely concerned with helping you fix your car for a fair price. If this doesn't seem to be the case, and you get the feeling that you may be the next sitting duck, put on your war face. Tell them you have other options, even if you have to bluff a little. If you don't like the price, say that you might go to another service center or stay in town and wait for other shops to open. You may even want to tell them you have family or friends who live in town. This may give you one more advantage, and you'll need every advantage you can get. If possible, use a pay phone to check prices at another shop before authorizing repairs. If worse comes to worse, and the shop calls your hand by refusing to give you a fair price, you still have other options. It may cost a little more initially, but having your car towed to a larger town or waiting until another repair center opens could save you hundreds of dollars in the long run, not to mention making you feel better by avoiding a repair fraud.

SECTION II
BEYOND THE BASICS

Knowledge Is Power

Now that you know some of the basics for becoming a smart auto repair consumer, it's time to get into more detailed information about specific repairs. The sections that follow will be very useful when the time comes for these repairs. From these sections, you can gain the knowledge you need to become a confident, informed consumer who will command respect from service managers. When you have the respect of a service manager, you will feel more comfortable when you walk into a service center, and you will be much less likely to get ripped off.

In the following sections, each of the most common repairs are discussed one at a time, including brakes, tires, alignment, front suspension, oil changes, shocks and struts, air conditioning, and driveability. Naturally, every possible repair for every car couldn't be covered in a book even one hundred times the size of this one, but the ones you are most likely to need are. Because cars vary greatly from model to model, repairs are explained in a general way. In reality, when repairs are stripped down to the bare basics, they are surprisingly similar from car to car. The repairs and principles covered will apply to the vast majority of cars on the road today. Since you need to learn only the most basic principles and terms to communicate effectively with your service manager, useless details and technical explanations are avoided. Instead, you will learn the buzz words that will be recognized immediately by people in the repair industry.

Every effort has been made to keep the following sections simple, and easy to read and understand. In many cases, technical terms and principles have been replaced by everyday language and simple explanations. Illustrations are provided to help you learn what some parts look like and to better explain their functions. Despite these efforts, some technical terms must be used, and some people may find this a little difficult. However if you feel at all lost, simply study the illustrations and read the paragraph over again; then the explanation will probably become clear. Remember, this information is vital if you want to prevent auto repair fraud from happening to you. Before you call or visit a repair shop, it would be a good idea to review the section that covers any problems you are having and refresh your memory with the pertinent terms. You may get helpful insight into the nature of your car's problem at the same time.

When you find a word in **bold** print, this is a term that is used by service professionals. Industry people use these terms to describe the parts they use and the services they perform. This is their language, so to speak. Therefore, these terms are important to understand, especially when it is time for repairs. If you can understand these terms and use them when discussing problems with the service manager, you will establish yourself as an educated customer. You may feel a little awkward using these unfamiliar terms around service professionals, but these terms won't sound a bit strange to them! When you speak the automotive language, you will communicate much more effectively with auto repair personnel. As you know by now, a knowledgeable customer who can communicate this knowledge to a service manager will earn his or her respect and is *less* likely to fall prey to repair fraud.

When you find a word in **BOLD SMALL CAPS,** this is an industry word that is also defined in the glossary that appears at the end of the section where it is found. Glossaries are found at the end of several sections where there are many terms you may not be familiar with. Reading the glossary may also reinforce your understanding of the system being covered. Or you can use it as a quick reference if you find that you need additional parts or service while at a shop for other repairs. In the glossary, you will find the definition of the part, its average price, and its size and location. Actual prices and descriptions may vary from car to car, but this will give you a good idea about what to expect. If you do not know what system includes a term in question, a general index in the back of the book will point you in the right direction. Now down to business!

OIL CHANGE

When automobile maintenance is mentioned, most people think of oil changes. Oil changes are the most common routine maintenance cars require. In a car, the engine oil gets dirty from the residue left behind by the burning gasoline, and the oil filter keeps the oil as clean as possible between oil changes. Because every engine needs clean oil to keep it lubricated and to make it last as long as possible, it is very important to change the oil and oil filter regularly. This simple procedure only takes a few minutes and costs less than $20 in most cases. It involves draining the old oil from the engine and removing the old oil filter, then replacing them with new products. This simple, inexpensive routine can add thousands of miles to the life of your car and can save you hundreds of dollars in engine repairs. You may already know this, so what else should you know about oil changes?

CARSMART

EVERY 3,000 MILES, RIGHT?

How often should you change the oil and filter? Most people would quickly say every 3,000 miles. This is what most people have been taught to think. But this is not how most manufacturers see it, as reflected in the owner's manual. If you read your manual carefully, you will probably discover that it recommends changing the oil and filter every 7,500 miles — unless you drive in extremely dusty conditions or under extreme driving conditions. Keep in mind, the manufacturers designed, built, and tested your vehicle, not to mention that they are warranting most cars for about 36,000 miles. If they don't know when you should change your oil, who does? This means that more than 90 percent of all the people who change their oil every 3,000 miles are wasting their hard-earned money! Most modern oils will last much longer. Tests on cars used as taxis have shown no advantage to changing the oil every 3,000 miles, even under those heavy-duty conditions. So why does everyone think their oil should be changed every 3,000 miles?

The notion that automobile oil should be changed every 3,000 miles is mostly supported (and promoted) by those who profit from changing oil. Have you noticed who sponsors advertisements or articles that make you feel guilty if you don't change your oil every 3,000 miles? Oil companies and oil change shops! If these businesses can convince you to change your oil every 3,000 miles instead of every 6,000 miles, their profit doubles! If someone is told to change their oil every 3,000 miles over and over again, they soon begin to feel as though they are risking their engine if they go longer. But this is simply not true. Today's oil is of good quality

Suggested maintenance:

Have the oil and oil filter changed and the tires rotated at the same time — every 5,000 to 6,000 miles.

and will protect your engine even if you choose to leave it in there for as long as 7,500 miles. Please allow a word of forewarning as well: New car dealers are starting to realize the potential for profit in performing routine maintenance such as oil changes and brake service; as a result, you may soon see a shift in the manufacturers' recommendations for oil change intervals to the magic 3,000-mile mark.

So what *is* the correct interval for oil changes? In truth, there are as many opinions about the proper mileage for changing the oil as there are people interested in the debate. Some swear by changing their oil every 3,000 miles, and others say they have great luck changing it every 10,000 miles or more. When someone believes in what he has done for years, there will be no changing him. If you don't have an opinion, consider yourself lucky; you will not have to be de-programmed. Of course, no set mileage interval will be right for every car and driver.

However, when all factors are considered, the smartest interval for changing the oil and oil filter may be from 5,000 to 6,000 miles, which also happens to be the best time to have the tires rotated. Having the tires rotated and oil changed at the same time not only saves you time, but also helps you remember the interval. Instead of having to keep up with two mileage figures, you need only remember one. This also gives the shop a chance to do a thorough inspection of the car, since they will have the tires off the car for the rotation. This interval is still more frequent than the 7,500 miles that most manufacturers recommend for the average driver, so don't feel that you are pushing the limit. If you have a relative or friend who thinks the eleventh commandment is, "Thou must change thine oil every 3,000 miles," don't tell him you are going 5,000! "What he don't know, won't hurt him." If you are one of those 11th commandment people, it certainly won't hurt to change the oil every 3,000 miles, except in your wallet. Over a 100,000 mile period, changing your oil every 6,000 miles instead of every 3,000 miles saves you about $300 and about 20 hours of your time!

One thing to remember, especially if you are changing your oil every 5,000 miles or more, is to check the oil level every 1,000 miles or so. All engines are designed to use a small amount of the oil to lubricate the cylinders, so your car's engine *must* have enough oil in it to prevent permanent damage. As an engine gets older, it will use more and more oil. Therefore, all engines will need oil added, *unless* the oil is changed before this happens. Naturally, the longer you go between changes, the more likely that you will need to add oil between changes. The only way to know if an engine needs oil is to check the oil level. If you don't know how to check your oil, have someone at a shop show you how. You need not add oil until the engine is one full quart low, with the possible exception of some sub-compact cars that hold only three quarts. These cars should not get lower than about one-half quart.

Do It Yourself...Not!

Many magazine articles and TV shows will tell you to save money and experience the joy of changing your own oil. But you only save about ten dollars or less per oil change. Lying on the cold ground with your nose pressed against a red-hot muffler and oil dripping in your hair may not prove to be such a good time either. You will also have to deal with hazardous waste oil and filters. Burned motor oil has been proven to cause cancer if it remains on the skin too long, and it is very hazardous to animals, plants, and groundwater. Then, you still need to have your tires rotated, which can be dangerous when done without the proper tools. All these factors add up to one thing. **Paying someone to change your oil is probably the best ten dollars you ever spent.** Don't forget, you get about $10 worth of oil and filter when you get an oil change. In addition, a trained professional will be doing the work, and he will be inspecting the rest of the car for possible problems such as worn belts or hoses and brake problems.

This inspection may save you money or prevent a more serious problem in the future. However, if you can change your own oil and do indeed enjoy it, good for you! It's money in your pocket! Just remember to rotate those tires!

If Not You, Who?

Where is the best place to have your oil changed? Of course, there is no clear answer to this question. The ideal shop would be one that has experienced technicians, a good price, tire and brake service, a convenient location, and is fast and dependable. Wow! This is a fantasy for most people, but a shop that meets most of these criteria can usually be found with only a little investigation and some common sense. As always, you will find that preparation and investigation are two of the most important things for insuring that you get your money's worth from any repair.

If your tire dealer offers oil changes, this could be an excellent choice. This way you combine two or more stops into one. Another good choice is a quick oil change center *if* they also offer tire rotation services. Since these shops are set up especially for changing oil, they will probably have well-trained people and can change oil faster than most. Again, this combines two services into one convenient stop. Big chain stores that offer oil changes usually have the best price, but these shops sometimes have inexperienced technicians. If a service center charges several dollars less than the other shops, they may have to hire technicians with little or no experience just to make a profit. Many aspiring technicians use this type of job as on-the-job training, to gain experience for a better paying job elsewhere. A person with limited experience is more likely to make a simple mistake such as leaving the drain plug loose or installing the wrong oil filter, which can cause major problems including ruining the engine, which leaves you without your car for about two weeks. These examples are only general ones; there are some exceptions. For instance, a chain store may require a training period for their oil change technicians, and of course, even a veteran technician can make a mistake.

When searching for a shop to do your oil changes, you may want to visit a few and ask the manager some questions. First, ask how long the oil change technician has been working for them and how much prior experience he or she has. Every technician must start somewhere, but you may not want them to practice on your car! Ask the manager if his shop uses brand name oil and filters, or if you must accept whatever *they* choose. Many bargain oil changes include low-quality oil and oil filters, which may not protect your engine as well as needed. Also, ask the manager if they offer services such as tire rotation and brake repair. Even if you do not choose them to do these repairs, they will at least be able to give you their opinion about what is needed, which can be very helpful later. This could be a way of getting a free inspection and repair estimate.

When visiting a shop, also look at the shop area and the employees. Make sure the shop is reasonably clean and the people are neat and professional. It is also a good idea to ask your friends and co-workers where they get their oil changed and whether they are satisfied with the service. They may be able to steer you away from a less than upstanding shop. A little work before you choose may save you a lot of headaches in the future.

TIRES

Most people know that tires are one of the most important items on an automobile. Every car or truck needs good tires to operate safely. Tires not only hold your car up off of the road, they also grip the road on wet and dry pavement to keep you in control of your car. They make cars drive smoothly and quietly, and help today's cars drive better than ever before. Most people know these basics, but understand very little else about tires. Like any other product, a good understanding of tires can save you a lot of money. The good news is, this stuff is easy!

T1 - TIRE PRESSURE

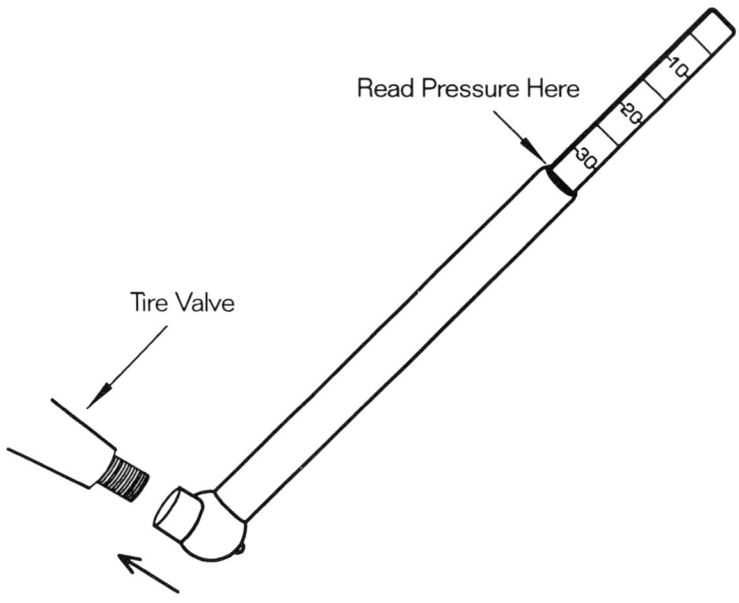

To check the tire pressure, the tire gauge is carefully aligned with the valve stem and pressed in firmly. A scale will extend to show the exact pressure reading. The pressure at each tire should be checked at least two times to insure accuracy. After each reading is taken, the scale should be pushed back into the gauge. There is a small pin on the end of most gauges that can be used to depress a small pin inside the valve stem to release excess air. The gauge shown is called a pencil-style gauge. This is the most accurate and dependable tire gauge you can buy, and at $3, it's also the least expensive.

Waste, Waste, Waste

Millions of dollars are wasted every year by consumers who buy new tires too often. It takes several gallons of crude oil, a lot of energy, plus other valuable resources to produce just one tire. Added up for millions of people around the world, this becomes a significant amount of energy and money. Why is all of this money wasted? Poor maintenance of the tires is the number one cause. The failure to keep tires properly maintained can decrease the life of a set of tires by 50 percent or more! Since the average price for a set of tires is close to four hundred dollars, poor tire care can cost you dearly. But why do so many people throw money down the drain? Because most never learned how to get the most from their tires. The next few paragraphs can literally save you hundreds of dollars.

Under Pressure

Tire pressure is the simplest and most cost-effective type of tire maintenance. Low tire pressure not only causes tires to wear prematurely (*also see the section on alignment*), but it can also cause a car or truck to handle poorly and can significantly reduce the fuel mileage. Fuel mileage suffers because underinflated tires are harder to roll. A car that is harder to push down the road uses much more gas per mile. Underinflation also causes heat to build up in the tires. Tires can be permanently damaged by the increased heat caused by driving with low pressure. In fact, low pressure is probably the biggest reason that otherwise good tires suddenly blow out, which is also very dangerous. Since most people don't realize how important tire inflation can be, they simply do not take the time to check the tire pressure regularly (*see illustration T1*).

Even if you can't change a light bulb, you can probably check your tire pressure. All you need is a three-dollar tire gauge. Pencil-style gauges are best. Each wheel has a small, black valve called a valve stem. This device is on every tire so you can check the pressure and add or remove air. These valve stems usually have a small cap that protects the valve from dirt. This cap should be removed before checking the pressure. If the valve does not reach out far enough past the wheel cover, you can buy valve extensions that will solve this problem. After removing the cap, place the tire gauge over the end of the stem and press in firmly. The gauge will move out to show you the exact pressure of the tire (*see illustration T1*).

> **Never try to guess the pressure, you will almost always overinflate the tires, which can be very dangerous.**

It is normal to lose a small but insignificant amount of air each time you do this. If you are losing a lot of air when you check the pressure, change the angle of the gauge slightly. The gauge must be properly aligned with the valve to prevent too much air from escaping and to get an accurate reading. It may take some practice to get the technique right. If you still have trouble, take your car to a tire dealer or repair center and ask them to check it for you. Ask them to teach you how to use your gauge. Most will be happy to show you, because this means you won't be coming in every month to ask them to check your tires! Check the pressure two or three times at each wheel to insure you get an accurate reading. Please be aware that it is impossible to judge whether a tire is low or overinflated by looking at it. Today's radial tires are constructed in such a way that the sides of the tires will bulge out slightly even when properly inflated (*see illustration T2*). Never try to guess the pressure, you will almost always overinflate the tires, which can be *very* dangerous. **Use a gauge!**

How much pressure is enough? Believe it or not, almost every car has the recommended tire pressures printed on a label located in the jamb of the driver's door. The manufacturer determines the best pressure to give each model the best ride and handling and prints it on this label and in the owner's manual. This pressure can be different for the front and rear tires. If you cannot find the recommended pressure, call a tire dealer. Most tire dealers have a book that gives the manufacturer's recommended pressures for all car makes and models. If you still can't find the pressure, 35 PSI should work just fine at all four wheels. This is generally very close to most recommended pressures.

T2 - TIRES

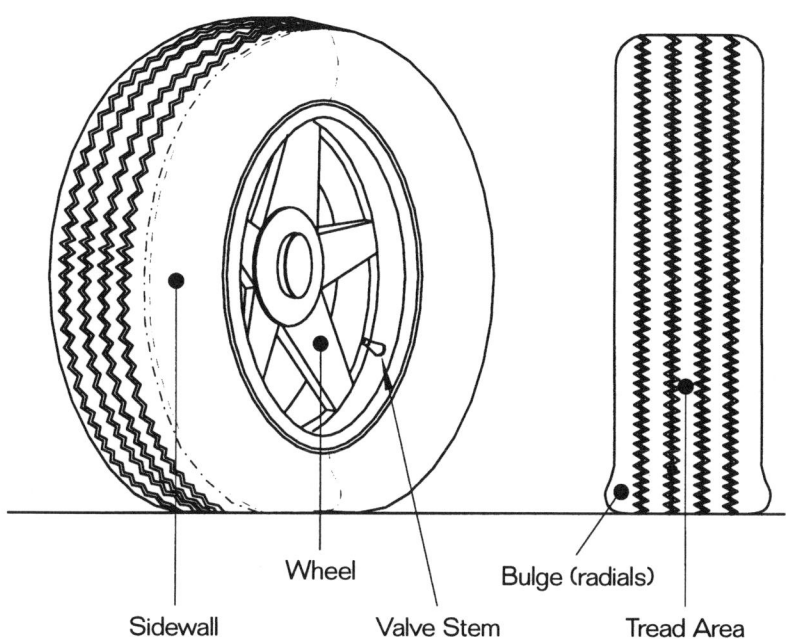

Sidewall   Wheel   Valve Stem   Bulge (radials)   Tread Area

All of the important information about the tire such as the size, speed rating, and tire quality ratings can be found on the sidewall.

Here you can see the components of the tire and wheel unit. The wheel is made of metal, and the tire is constructed of rubber with polyester and steel reinforcing material. The valve stem is a small rubber device used to check the tire and add air. The grooves in the tread area shed water and grip the road. The sidewalls are much thinner and softer than the tread to help the car ride smoothly over bumps. The tire above is a radial tire, which bulges under a load. This makes a radial tire look as though it has low air pressure even when it doesn't. For this reason, the air pressure must be checked with a gauge, not by guessing.

This is also the maximum cold pressure for most tires made today. Before inflating the tires to 35 PSI, read the fine print on the side of the tire. Each tire will have the maximum cold pressure printed on the sidewall. This cold pressure will be the same for all tires in a matched set and should never be exceeded.

Cold Pressure

No, this does not mean that the weather must be cold; it means the tires should be cold when they are checked. In other words, before you drive on them. Tires heat up significantly when you drive, and this increased temperature causes the pressure to increase. It is a law of nature that if a gas (such as air) is confined to a given space (such as the inside of a tire), when the temperature rises, the pressure will also rise. Likewise, if the temperature decreases, so will the pressure. Therefore, if you have to check the tires after you have driven more than about five or ten miles, the pressure will be about two or three pounds more than the normal cold pressure. In other words, if the tires are warm, it would be normal for them to have as much as 38 PSI. This is also the reason why tires need air added when the weather turns colder; in some cases, air may need to be released in the summer.

Because tires tend to lose a small amount of air over a period of time, the pressure should be checked once every month. If your tires only lose a pound or two between checks, this is probably normal. Air can sometimes escape through the tiny pores in the rubber, much in the same way that a rubber balloon loses air after a few days. An older tire may be more prone to this type of leak because the rubber gets dry and can develop small cracks, allowing air to escape. If after checking the tires two or three consecutive months and no air is needed, you can begin checking them every other month or even longer. However, if you are adding more than a few pounds between checks, the tire may have more than the normal leakage and should be checked for a puncture or another source of a leak, such as the valve stem or even the metal wheel.

Air is added in much the same manner as it is checked. A **tire chuck,** which is connected to an air hose, is pushed onto the valve stem to add air and increase the pressure. Many gas stations have compressed air, or you can go to a tire dealer and ask for help. After adding air, the pressure should be checked a few times. Most tire gauges have a small nipple that is used to push in the valve to let excess air escape if you get too much pressure. If you purchased new tires from a tire dealer, they should be happy to add air for you at no charge. This will help assure them that you will get the most from the tires you purchased from them, which benefits both parties.

FLATS

If you find you have a tire that deflates every few days, you should take your car to a tire dealer and ask them to check the tire for leaks. They may find an obvious leak such as a nail stuck in the tire, or they may need to remove the tire and wheel and submerge it in water to look for air bubbles, which indicate a leak. The most common cause of a tire leak is a puncture. A puncture simply means the tire has a hole in it. Often times a nail, screw, or other sharp object will find its way into a tire. If this object penetrates several layers of thick rubber and steel belts, and then through the thin inner liner of the tire, it will cause a leak. Even a tiny hole in this inner liner can cause a slow leak. Many times, a nail goes into a tire and stays there. The nail sometimes plugs the hole effectively and can almost completely seal the leak. This type of puncture can cause a leak that occurs over several weeks instead of several days.

A patch is the safest and most permanent method of tire repair.

PATCHING THINGS UP

Most experts and tire manufacturers recommend that a puncture be repaired with a patch. In this process, a tire is removed from the wheel and a small rubber patch is glued to the inside of the tire, sealing off the hole. This is the safest and most permanent method of tire repair. If a tire is patched properly, it will never leak at that location again and will be as good as before the puncture. When patching a tire, the tire technician should mark the exact location of the valve and the wheel weights and assemble the tire back in the same location. This prevents the need for rebalancing. In most cases, only a tire shop will have the equipment required to remove the tire from the wheel and patch the inside of the tire.

The next best method for repairing a puncture is with a tire plug. This is a small rubber plug that is pushed into the tire from the outside. This rubber plug is coated with a glue that seals the hole and stops the leak. Plugs are not generally as permanent as a patch, but are relatively safe and effective. The advantage of a plug is that it costs less and is much faster to install. Another advantage of the tire plug is that it requires little skill and no special equipment. For this reason, many shops that don't have tire equipment can plug a tire. The drawback with some plugs is that they begin to leak after some time, although this is not very common. If you have a plug that begins to leak, patch the tire to fix it.

A third method of repairing a tire is by using a can of tire sealer. It is recommended that these liquid tire inflator–sealers be used only in emergencies, and only temporarily. These sealers contain several ounces of a liquid that can cause the tire to become out of balance, which can make your car vibrate. These chemicals can also be flammable and can sometimes damage the inside of a tire. They can however be very helpful in a situation where you cannot change a flat tire. They not only temporarily stop most small leaks, but also inflate the tire. If you use such a product, be sure to read the instructions on the can; then have the tire properly repaired as soon as possible. Be sure to tell the shop that you have used a liquid tire sealer before they begin repairs.

ROTATIONS

A bad habit that causes just as much damage to a tire as low pressure is the failure to properly rotate them. **It is a fact: If you do not rotate your tires when you should, they will not last nearly as long as they were designed to last.** Lack of rotation causes several problems, premature wear being the biggest among them. This is especially true since front-wheel-drive cars have become the norm. Most cars made in the last fifteen years are front-wheel-drive, which means that the front wheels not only steer the car, but also pull it down the road. The rear tires on the other hand are simply used to keep the rear of the car off the ground and are just along for the ride. As a result, the front tires wear much faster than the rear tires. In fact, they can wear up to three times as fast! Therefore, if you never rotate the tires from front to rear, the front tires will be worn out in a short time, and the rear tires will still look almost new. Even rear drive vehicles like trucks and sport-utility vehicles need frequent tire rotations.

TIRE CUPPING

Another problem that stems from insufficient rotation is *irregular* tire wear. Irregular wear can occur on the front tires of some vehicles, but is especially a problem for the back tires on a front-wheel-drive car. If two tires remain on the rear of a car too long, they can develop humps and valleys in the tread pattern. This type of wear is sometimes called CUPPING or "heel-and-toe" or "high–low" wear (*see illustration T3*). This wear pattern can cause a rough ride and a noise that sounds like the roar from the huge mud tires on a four-wheel-drive truck. You can rub your hand along the tire's tread and feel these bumps if the problem is severe. What causes this wear? The truth is, there is no concrete explanation. When this type of wear first started to appear in the eighties, experts blamed everything from shocks to car design to the tires. No one has a definite answer *why* it happens, but we do know *when* it happens. Cupping occurs when the tires are run too long without being rotated. How long is too long? This figure varies from car to car, but this wear will usually begin to show up at around 10,000 miles. The important thing to know is that proper tire rotation will almost always prevent this wear.

If you find that your have the dreaded cupping on your tires, you should have them rotated immediately. If you were hearing a

> **Be sure the front and rear tires always trade places.**

roaring sound from the rear, you may find that it is louder after the tires are moved to the front. In fact, you may not realize your tires are cupped until you rotate them and begin to notice this roaring noise. You may also feel the roughness of the tread more than before, and it may feel like you are driving over small bumps at slow speeds. If you can live with these symptoms for a few thousand miles, they will probably improve. If, however, these symptoms are too severe to put up with, you can either move the cupped tires back to the rear where they will get worse, or you can replace the tires. Just be sure to keep the new tires rotated as needed. Although this type of wear is usually not considered a defect in the tire, some tire makers will warranty such a problem, especially if you can prove that you rotated the tires properly. It never hurts to check with the appropriate tire dealer before you buy new tires. Many rear-wheel-drive vehicles, such as trucks, are prone to cup the front tires. These same procedures should be followed on such vehicles.

OWNER'S MANUAL ERROR!

How often should tires be rotated? If you read the owner's manual for your car or truck, it may recommend somewhere around every 10,000 to 15,000 miles. **This is wrong!** This is far too many miles for most tires and vehicles. We can trust automakers regarding the frequency of oil changes, because they designed the engines; by the same token, let's believe the tire makers when it comes to rotation intervals. Almost all major tire manufacturers and tire specialists recommend tire rotations every 5,000 miles. This is the best interval to use to insure that your tires do not develop irregular wear, especially if you have expensive tires with a long mileage warranty. In fact, most tire makers *require* 5,000 mile rotations to keep the tire warranty in effect. If you own tires with a mileage warranty, you should keep a record of every rotation. If the tires wear out or wear irregularly before the warranty expires, you may be asked to show evidence of tire rotations every 5,000 miles. If you get free tire rotations from your tire dealer, ask for a tire maintenance schedule and have them fill it out each time you are in for a rotation. This record can mean the difference between getting some money back on a tire warranty and getting nothing. If you change your oil every 3,000 miles (see *"Every 3000 miles . . . Right?"* section), you should have no problems if you do a tire rotation every 6,000 miles (every other oil change). This would be much more convenient, but check your tire warranty first.

T3 - IRREGULAR TIRE WEAR (CUPPING)

This tire has a wear pattern called "cupping," also known as heel-and-toe wear, or high–low wear. Cupping can be described as a bumpy tread pattern. The bumps in the tread can be felt by rubbing your hand along the tread. A tire with severe cupping will make a roaring or humming noise as the car is driven. Cupping is not caused by an alignment problem, nor is it a defect in the tire. This wear usually occurs if the tires are not rotated properly, but bad shocks or front-end components can speed the process along. A front-wheel-drive car will cup the rear tires, while a rear-drive vehicle, such as a truck, will cup the front. A tire rotation every 5,000 miles should prevent this type of wear.

Rotating Styles

There are about four different ways to rotate tires, but which method is best? The front-to-rear rotation is the most common method. This method always keeps the left and right tires on the same side and swaps the tires only front to back (*see illustration T4*). The front-to-rear method is easier to keep up with and works just fine in most situations. However, if you find the front-to-rear method allows some irregular wear, try the modified-X pattern (*see illustration T5*). This takes the tires from the rear straight to the same side on the front, and crosses the front tires as they go to the back. This pattern will eventually work each tire into every position. You can mix and match these patterns from one rotation to the next if need be, just be sure the front and rear tires always trade places. The owner's manual for your car may also have some suggestions on rotation patterns. (*If you find that your car begins to pull to one side after a tire rotation, please read the section on alignment.*)

A common myth about rotating tires is that you cannot take a tire from the left side and place it on the right side. Switching tires from left to right causes them to rotate in the opposite direction, which is believed by many to damage the tire. This is simply not true. This *was* however a major problem with radial tires built before about 1980. What happened to many of these tires was that after the tire was run in one direction for a few thousand miles, the steel and fiberglass belts inside the tire would flex in that direction. Then if the direction was changed (swapped from left to right), the belts in the tires would unwind and separate. This separation would render the tires useless *and* dangerous. Millions of tires were ruined by changing their direction, therefore many people were told that they could not rotate tires from left to right. However, the industry changed the way radial tires were built after 1980, and they can now be rotated in any direction. **Although many people are still to this day afraid of rotating tires from side to side, all major tire manufacturers strongly disagree.**

Keep Your Balance

Tire balance plays a role in getting the most from your tires. A tire that is properly balanced will ride smoother, wear more evenly, and last longer than a tire that is not balanced. When a tire is out of balance, one side of the tire is heavier than the other. This is similar to what happens to a washing machine when too many clothes gather on one

T4 - ROTATION (FRONT TO REAR)

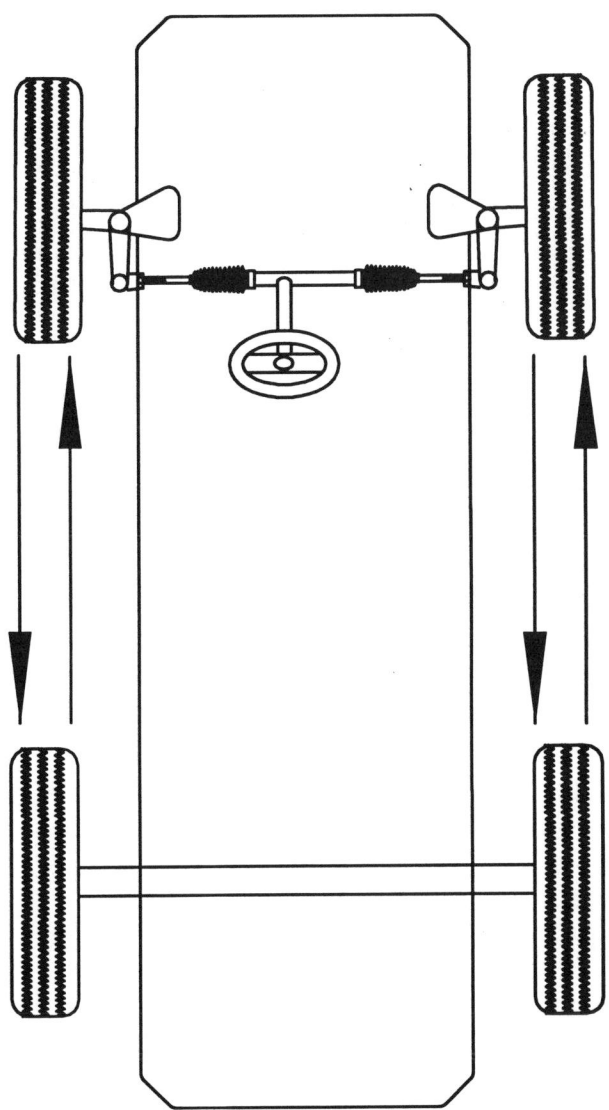

The front-to-rear rotation is the most common tire rotation used today. This simply involves switching the front and rear tires without changing the tires from left to right. Although this method is effective on most cars, the modified-X pattern may keep the tires from wearing unevenly on cars prone to cupping the tires. A tire rotation should be done every 5,000 miles.

T5 - ROTATION (MODIFIED X)

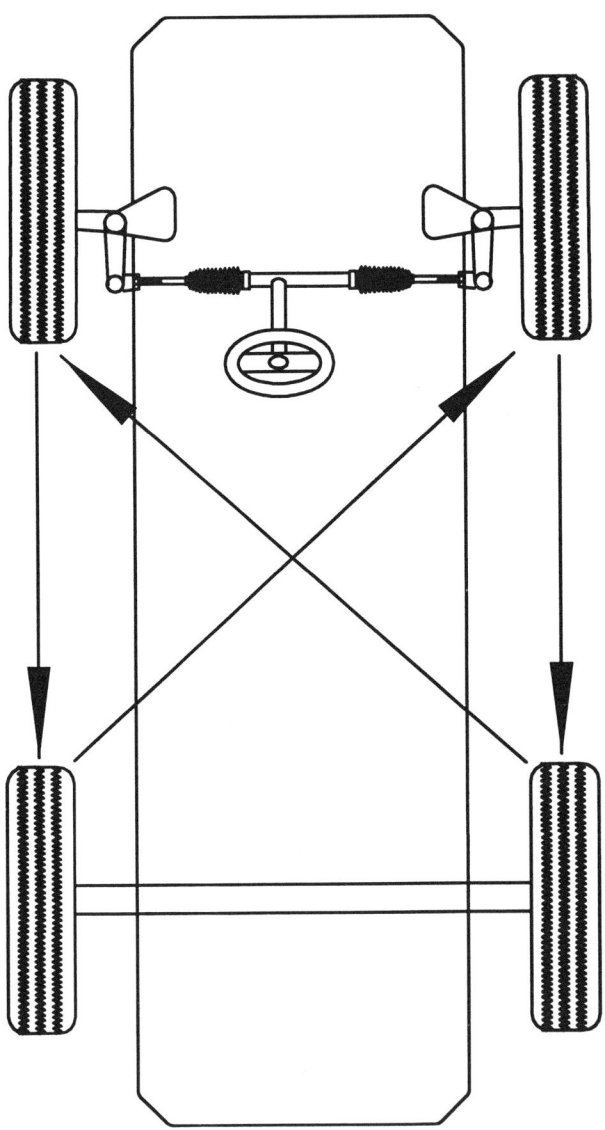

The modified-X rotation moves the front tires straight to the rear, but crosses the rear tires as they are moved to the front. After three of these rotations, each tire will have spent time at every position. This helps to reduce the chance of uneven wear because tire position and direction is constantly switched. Contrary to popular belief, it does not harm radial tires to switch them from side to side. Regardless of the method, rotations should be done every 5,000 miles.

T6 - ROTATION [X PATTERN]

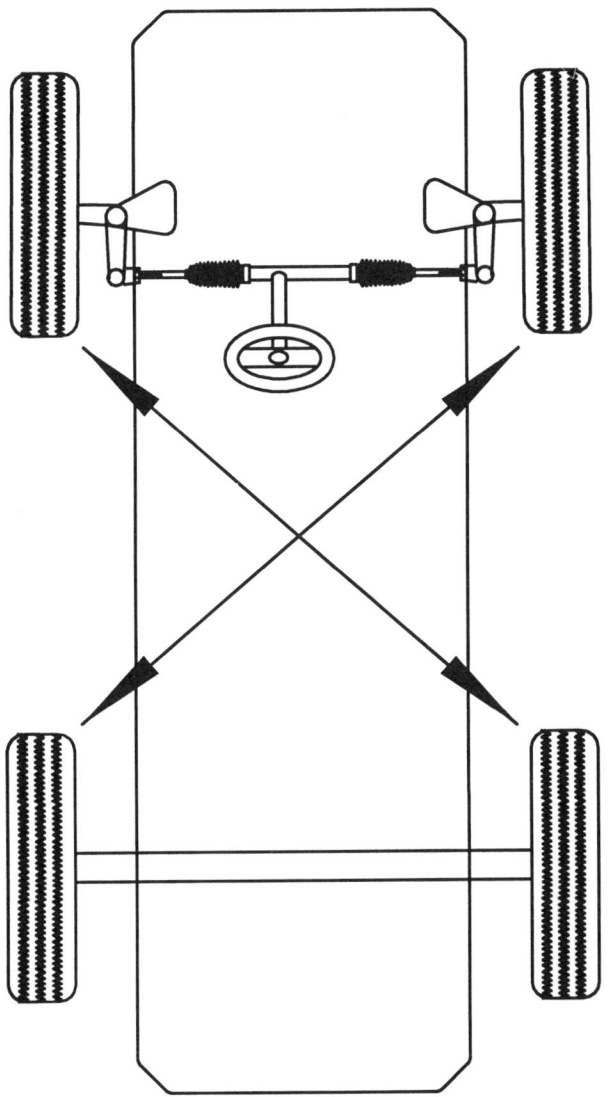

As the name implies, the X rotation switches the tires from corner to corner. Although this method does change the direction of the tires, the tires will only occupy two positions. The modified-X pattern is therefore better than the X method in most cases.

side of the tub. When the washer starts the spin cycle, it will be out of balance and will begin to shake. The greater the difference in weight, the harder it will shake. Likewise a tire can have more rubber in one spot, which will cause it to be out of balance. All new tires should be balanced when they are installed. A tire is balanced by removing the wheel and tire from the car and spinning both on a balancing machine. This machine detects where the heavy spot is and tells the technician where wheel weights should be added to make the tire and wheel perfectly balanced. Most tires require about two ounces of weight to correct normal irregularities in the tire and wheel. A tire that requires a relatively small amount of weight is usually of better quality than one that requires several ounces.

Still Shaking!

Out-of-balance tires make a car vibrate or shake. Usually the vibration starts around 40 MPH and gets worse as the speed increases. The more the tires are out of balance, the more severe the vibration will be. Since this vibration is something you can feel when you drive, you don't have to depend on someone else to tell you that your tires need balancing, you can be the judge. If you car rides smoothly at all speeds, you probably don't need the tires balanced. If, however, you have a noticeable vibration at any speed, your tires may be out of balance. You may need to have them balanced every time they are rotated, or they may never need to be rebalanced after the initial new tire balance. Just balance them as they need it. Generally, expensive tires will hold their balance better than economy tires, but this is not written in stone.

> ...If you are paying a shop to balance all four tires, they should not charge you for a rotation.

The best place to have your tires rotated or balanced is at a tire center. A store that specializes in tires will have the best equipment and the most knowledgeable staff for tire-related work. People who work on tires everyday can recognize and correct tire problems better than someone who does not. Ideally, the tire dealer who sold you the tires is the best choice. In fact, many tire dealers will rotate (and sometimes balance) your tires *free* if you purchased the tires there. In some cases, you can purchase a free rotate-and-balance policy with your new tires. This policy usually costs about $10 per tire and is usually well worth the money, especially if you buy middle- to upper-priced tires and you plan on keeping the car for a year or two. You may even be able to buy this policy for the original equipment tires, so it never hurts to ask. If you don't have such a policy you can expect to pay between $2 to $4 per tire for a rotation and about $5 to $10 for a balance. **If you are paying a shop to balance all four tires, they should not charge you for a rotation.** All of the tires will be off anyway, so they will simply put them back in a different location. No extra work is required! You should be charged only the fee for balancing four tires.

What if you have your tires balanced and the car still vibrates? Tire balance is only one of many conditions that can cause a vibration. A vibration can be caused by other tire problems, or it can result from mechanical problems.

A common tire-related vibration is caused by a tire that is "out of round" or "separated." These conditions can cause a vibration even if the tire is perfectly balanced. If a tire is out of round, the outside of the tire is not a perfect circle. Instead, the tire is slightly oval or egg-shaped. A tire in this condition can make a car bounce and vibrate at highway speeds and can make it wobble at low speeds. Unfortunately, an out-of-round tire will probably always be that way. The one hope of correcting such a tire is to let the air out, dismount the tire from the metal wheel, and reposition the tire on the wheel in a different place. Sometimes this changes the way the tire seats to the wheel and corrects the problem. If you are told that you have an out-of-round tire, you may want to ask the manager to try this technique before you buy a new one. A tire store manager hoping to sell you new tires may be reluctant to mention this trick! Of course, if you bought the tires from a tire dealer, this should be done at their expense. This trick will probably never fix a tire that is severely out of round, and it will need to be replaced. If the tire is reasonably new, the tire warranty should cover this type of problem.

CARSMART

...a tire separation starts out as a barely noticeable wave in the tire and later develops into a huge bulge that can cause the tire to blow out.

A separated tire can cause the same symptoms as an out-of-round tire. When a tire separates, the cords and fibers inside the tire unwind, unravel, and separate (*see illustration T7*). This usually causes a bump or high spot to form in the tread of the tire. Every time this high spot rolls over the road, the car has to bounce over it. This can cause a severe wobble at low speeds and a bad vibration at highway speeds. If a separated tire is on the front, it may cause the car to pull to one side. Usually, a tire separation starts out as a barely noticeable wave in the tire and later develops into a huge bulge that can cause the tire to blow out. A separated tire will not last many miles, so it should be replaced as soon as you find out about it. There is no way to repair a separated tire. A tire separation is a severe defect, so it should be covered under warranty by the tire manufacturer whether you bought the tires new or they came with the car. Check with any tire dealer that sells the brand you have.

Mechanical problems can also cause a vibration that a tire balance will not correct. The most common vibration, which is not related to the tires, comes from the brake rotors. When a brake rotor is warped, the car may ride smoothly under most conditions, but will vibrate or pulsate when the brakes are used (*for more information on brake rotors, see the section on brakes*). Drive axles can be another source of vibration. A worn axle usually causes vibration that is noticed when you speed up, but goes away when the gas pedal is released. This vibration can feel very much like a separated tire, but a tire vibration will not be affected by the gas pedal (*see the section on front suspension for more on axles*). A warped wheel can also cause vibration. A tire may be perfectly round,

T7 - TIRE PROBLEMS!

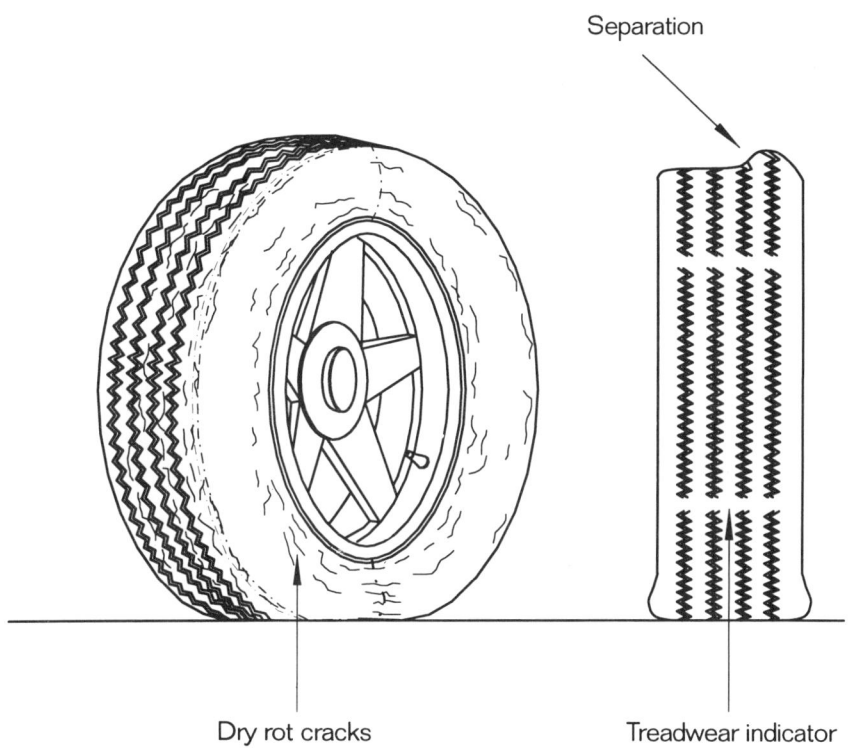

Separation

Dry rot cracks

Treadwear indicator

Above are a few examples of serious tire problems. The tire on the left has many cracks from dry rot. This can occur after the tire is about four years old and is caused by the natural aging of the rubber. The tire on the right has two problems. On the top of the tire you can see a bulge in the tread caused by the steel belts unwinding inside the tire, weakening the tire where this occurs. This will cause a bad vibration and will usually cause the car to pull to one side. It will also cause the tire to blow out very soon! This tire is also showing its treadwear indicators. This is the solid line across the tire, which appears when the tire is worn down to $2/32$ inch of tread. Any or all of the above problems should be corrected by replacing the tire as soon as possible.

but if the wheel it is mounted on is not, the entire assembly will be out of round. This will cause the same symptoms as an out-of-round tire. A warped wheel should be replaced with a new one, or perhaps with a used wheel from a salvage yard. Of course, there are several other mechanical problems that can cause vibrations, but these relatively easy-to-find and easy-to-repair problems should be checked first.

SEE NO EVIL

A vibration that cannot be explained by the dealer from whom you purchased your tires is often easily diagnosed by another dealer. How can this be? Unfortunately, since a tire dealer can lose money when he replaces a tire under warranty, he may be reluctant to do so. He may turn the proverbial deaf ear to an out-of-round or separated tire. In fact, this is fairly common. **If you have a persistent vibration that your tire dealer can't correct, visit another *tire dealer* for an unbiased opinion.** They may agree that the tires are *not* the cause, indicating a mechanical vibration, or they may indeed find a tire-related problem.

If another tire specialist finds a problem with your tires, have him write down exactly which tire is causing your vibration and why. This should help get the problem solved at your dealer. If you still cannot get satisfaction from your tire dealer on a vibration, or any tire warranty problem, kindly ask the manager for the customer service number for the manufacturer of your tires. Most tire makers, especially the big ones, have a toll-free number you can call to get help with a tire warranty problem. These customer service centers usually have liberal policies. They may direct you to another tire dealer who sells this brand, and they will work with that dealer to get your problem solved. They may even reimburse you for the money you spent on the second opinion, if you ask! If your dealer refuses to give you the number, try calling another dealer who carries the same brand.

NEW TIRES: WHEN, WHERE, WHAT, AND HOW

TIME TO RE-TIRE!

Most often, new tires are needed because the tread has worn down and is too thin. So how thin is too thin? The old method of using a penny is an effective way to make a judgement about your remaining tread depth. This is done by placing a penny head first into the tread of a tire to see if the tread is deep enough to touch Abe's head. If it is deep enough, you have at least $1/16$ inch of tread ("$2/32$ inch" in the language of the tire trade). This is the minimum amount of tread that is considered safe. In many states, it is also the minimum *legal* amount of tread.

You can also look for the treadwear indicators that are built into every tire. A tread indicator is a small hump, down in the tread, that shows as a solid rubber line running across the tire tread when the tread is less than $1/16$ inch deep. If you can see these lines, it's time for new tires (*see illustration T7*)! Of course, if you see metal wire sticking through the edge of the tire, it should be replaced immediately. The metal cords in the tire can become exposed if the outside rubber is worn off. Also look for bulges in the tread or on the sides of the tire, or for a large number of cracks in the tire (called dry rot), which mean you must have your tires checked as soon as possible. Any and all of these conditions indicate that you will need tires very soon! Note: If you feel around the sidewalls of a radial tire, you will feel three or more small dips in the sides. These indentations are normal; they are a result of the way tires are constructed in sections. However, if you feel a bulge that protrudes *out*, this is *not* normal and could be a sign of an upcoming problem.

Although $1/16$ inch of tread is considered safe by many, it is not nearly as safe as a new tire, especially on wet roads. The grooves (or tread) of a tire are put there to give water a place to go during wet driving. If the grooves are not deep, they will not hold very much water. If the grooves cannot handle enough water, the tires will ride on top of the water instead of through it. This is called hydroplaning. It is a lot like waterskiing. If the speed of the skier is fast enough, he just skids over the top of the water. Hydroplaning in a car is not nearly as fun as waterskiing and can be very dangerous if it causes a car to slip and slide over the road. **The thinner the tire tread and the faster the speed, the more likely hydroplaning will occur.** In other words, thin tread is more dangerous than deep tread. Tires with thin tread are also more susceptible to punctures or flats, simply because a shorter object can make it through a thinner tire.

How Thin Is Too Thin?

So what is the minimum safe tread depth? It is a matter of opinion. Although $1/16$ inch is the minimum that is considered safe to insure you are not taking any chances, most experts recommend not going under about $4/32$ inch ($1/8$ inch). This is about 35 to 40 percent of the original tread depth on most passenger tires. This may seem like a lot of waste, but there are ways to turn this waste into profit. How? If you purchase new tires before the old ones are completely worn out, you may be reimbursed for trading in your old tires. There is a huge demand for good used tires. Many tire dealers, especially smaller independent stores, sell good used tires to the public or sell them to a recycler for resale or re-treading. Such a store may give you five to ten or more dollars for each good used tire. When shopping for new tires, even on the phone, ask if this is a possibility. You may be surprised! Another way to profit from your old tires is to bring them home and sell them to a friend or at a garage sale for $10 to $20 each! There is always someone on a tight budget looking for used tires. Of course if you are on a tight budget, you may have to run your tires down to the minimum tread depth. If this is the case, be sure to slow down in wet weather.

Although it is common to replace all four tires at the same time, this is not always necessary. If you have only two tires that need replacing, there is nothing wrong with replacing just two. Be sure to buy the same size and the same basic type of tires already on your car, and you will never know the difference. The brand name does not have to be the same. If you have fairly new tires and need only one new tire, try to find the exact same tire and replace just the one. If you cannot find an exact match, you can try one of another brand or type. If the mismatched tires are on the front, this may cause your car to pull to one side, though this is unlikely. When your tires are somewhat worn, it is better to get at least two at a time. When you buy only two tires, it is common practice to put the new tires on the front. This is usually a good idea, but if your rear tires are still good and they are ready to be rotated to the front, put them on the front for at least 5,000 miles. Then, later, you can rotate your tires as necessary. If the two tires you are *not* replacing are nearly worn out, however, it is

Buy at least two tires at a time — and put them on the front.

best to keep them on the rear where they will not be subjected to the harsher conditions of the front.

TIRE TALK

When you are ready to purchase new tires, the first thing to do is to get some information from the sidewalls of your old tires. On the sidewall you will find the size, the speed rating, and the treadwear, traction, and temperature ratings for your tires. You will need this information when talking to a tire salesperson. The size will consist of seven numbers and two letters, such as **P195/70R14**. What do these numbers and letters mean? The "P" means you have a passenger tire and "R" means a radial tire. The last two numbers are your car's rim (wheel) size. Here the "14" stands for 14 inches. The "195" represents the width of the tire in millimeters, and the "70" is the aspect ratio, which is the relative height of the tire, in this case the sidewall is 70 percent of the width (see *illustration T8*). Some tires may also have their speed rating included in this sequence, such as 245/50VR16 where "V" is the speed rating. Most new tires, however, put the speed rating, if they have one, after the size, such as 205/70R14 98S. The "98" represents the load rating of the tire and "S" is the speed rating.

Next are the UTQG ratings (uniform tire quality grade ratings) These three figures represent treadwear, traction, and temperature (example: TREADWEAR 420 TRACTION A TEMPERATURE B). These figures show how the tire performed in a standardized government test that measures how long the tire lasts, how well it grips a wet road under braking, and how well it withstands high temperatures (see *chart T9*). Every passenger tire sold in the US is required to undergo these tests, and the manufacturer must print the results on the side of the tire. There is, however, a catch to these ratings. Although the government sets the standards, the tire manufacturers are responsible for their own tests and ratings. This is similar to giving high school students a test, and then letting each student grade his own test privately! For this reason, these ratings should not be taken for absolute facts. Consider this: Ten years ago, a tire that would last around 60,000 miles would have had a treadwear rating of about 180. Today a tire with the same mileage expectancy may have a rating as high as 420 or more! In competition with one another, manufacturers have pushed these figures higher and higher, but the test standard is still the same. These figures can be helpful when comparing tires, but be careful not to put too much

T8 - TIRE SIZES

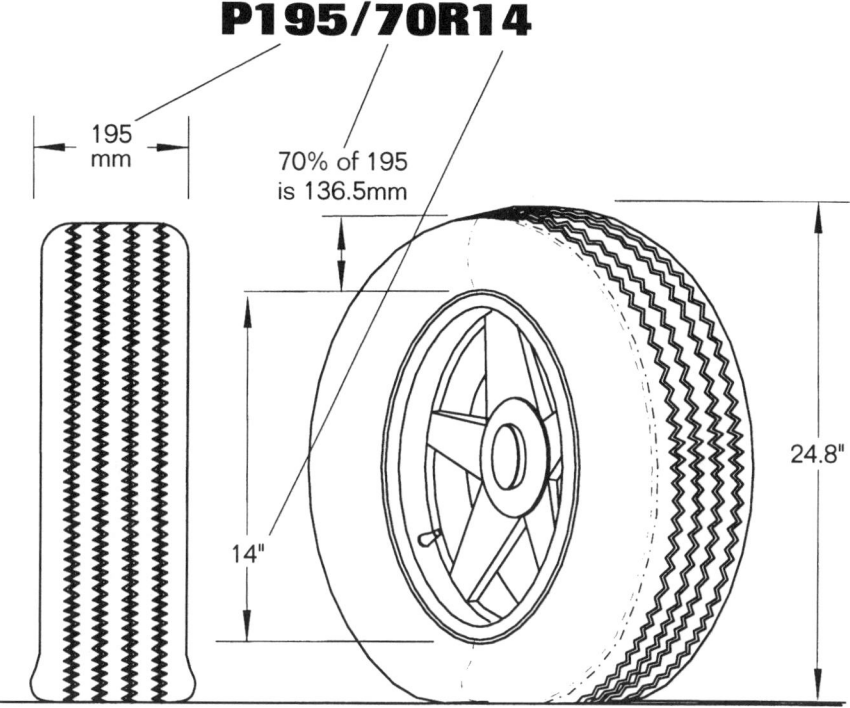

Here is how all passenger tires are sized: The "*P*" stands for passenger tire. The "195" is the width of the tire in millimeters. The "70" is called the aspect ratio, which states the height of the sidewall as a percentage of its width. In this example, the height of the sidewall is 70 percent of 195mm, which is 136.5mm. The "*R*" simply means that the tire is a radial tire. The "14" is the wheel diameter in inches. The total height of the tire can be figured by adding the wheel diameter to two times the sidewall (14" + 136.5mm + 136.5mm = 24.8"). Although these numbers represent what a tire should be, most tires differ slightly from the exact dimensions. In most cases, an expensive tire will be slightly larger than these figures, and an inexpensive tire will be smaller.

emphasis on them. Write the tire size, speed rating, and UTQG ratings down and get ready to shop!

Determining What You Need

Before shopping for new tires, decide what you want. Things like brand name, mileage, speed rating, service, and warranty can have a major effect on how much money you spend. However some features, such as the tire size, should never be changed without the help of an experienced tire specialist. An improper change in tire size can affect the speedometer reading and the anti-lock brakes, because a shorter tire rotates more times than a taller tire to cover the same distance. This gives the speedometer and the anti-lock brake computer a false speed reading, which is not a good thing. **An acceptable change in tire size is one that changes the width of the tire but does not change the height of the tire.** This change in width can be done by changing the first five numbers in the tire size (P<u>195/70</u>R14). The last two numbers, which represent the wheel size, can never be changed unless the metal wheels are also changed. Sometimes, a change in size can save you hundreds of dollars, but you should only do this with the help of a qualified tire professional. It is best to replace tires with the exact same size.

The biggest player in the tire pricing game is mileage. No other factor affects price more than a tire's mileage rating. Tire warranties range from 25,000 to 80,000 miles or more. The question is — in the long run is a 25,000-mile tire really less expensive than an 80,000-mile tire? Usually, when its life expectancy is considered, the answer is no! These low-priced tires often cost the consumer

> An improper change in tire size can affect the speedometer reading and the anti-lock brakes, because a shorter tire rotates more times than a taller tire to cover the same distance.

TIRE LINGO

When calling or visiting a tire store, it helps to speak "tire language." Using the proper terms and language will help establish you as a knowledgeable customer and should eliminate any chance of getting the wrong tires or paying too much. First of all, you should learn how to say the tire size properly. Many customers have ruined their attempt at impressing a tire specialist by calling a P195/70R14 98S tire a, "P, one, nine, five, slash, seven, O, R, one, four,...nine, eight, S." The proper reading is "One-ninety-five, seventy, R, fourteen." Notice the "P" was omitted? Since the "P" stands for passenger tire, the tire specialist already assumes this. The "R" can also be dropped if you feel brave, since all tires are now radials. The "98S" is the speed rating and is not really a part of the size. If you want to ask about the speed rating, tell the tire specialist that you are now running "S"-rated tires. The "98" need not be mentioned.

The UTQG ratings are called "UTQG ratings" or "tire quality ratings." Don't say what the three figures (420, A, B) represent, simply say, "Four twenty, A, and B." The salesman knows what they stand for. Knowing this language will greatly improve your confidence when dealing with a tire salesperson. You may even find that you know more about this stuff than the person selling you the tires!

C A R S M A R T

more *per mile* than a premium tire. Just as you would calculate a car's efficiency in miles per gallon, **you can easily determine how much a tire *really* costs by figuring its cost per mile.**

To do this, simply divide the price of the tire by its mileage (in thousands). This method can be used to accurately compare an 80,000-mile tire to a 25,000-mile tire. For example, if the 80,000-mile tire costs $60, *its cost per one thousand miles is $0.67* (60 ÷ 80). If the 25,000-mile tire is priced at $20, *its cost per one thousand miles is $0.80* (20 ÷ 25). That means the 80,000-mile tire is 16 percent less expensive to own over its lifetime. In addition to its lower long-term cost, the 80,000-mile tire will probably give you a smoother ride and fewer problems than the 25,000-mile tire because premium tires have higher quality standards than so-called "bargain" tires. Of course your budget and how long you plan to keep the car will play a big role in which tire you choose, but the cost-per-mile formula can be used to compare any tires with different prices and mileage ratings. (Tire warranties will be covered in depth a little later.)

Another factor that can have a drastic effect on the price of a tire is the speed rating. Many cars built in the last twenty years are capable of high speeds that could damage an average tire. For this reason, high-performance tires were developed to withstand the heat and stress generated by these speeds. As cars became faster and faster, manufacturers had to continuously improve their tires, and a speed rating system was created to identify a tire's maximum speed capabilities. These speed ratings typically start at "S" (112 MPH) and go up to "Z" (150+ MPH), with several steps in between. The speed rating, if applicable, is printed on the sidewall of every tire, close to the tire size.

Most lower- to middle-priced tires do not have a speed rating at all, while many higher-priced and high-performance tires do. As you may have guessed, as the speed rating gets higher, so does the price. Take for an example the 205/55R16 tire, which is found on several different car models. This tire is available in speed ratings from "S" to "Z," which means there is a wide range of prices for the same size tire. An "S" tire costs around $70, while a "Z" tire may cost over $200. On a set of four, that's a $520 difference! Since the *average* driver never drives over 112 MPH, for most, the "S" tire is always more than adequate.

In some cases, you may want to buy new tires with a different speed rating from the old tires. **A change in the speed rating does not change the tire size, nor will it affect the mechanical or electrical systems of the automobile.** But it can change the price of a set of tires by $500 or more! Today many cars are equipped with tires that have a speed rating that will never be approached by the driver. For example, a Z-28 Camaro may come with 245/50R16 tires that have a "Z" speed rating of over 150 MPH. This car comes equipped with "Z"-rated tires because it is capable of these speeds. To insure safety, the manufacturer must install ultra-performance tires in case they are driven to the limit. The owner of this car may never drive more than 80 MPH, but if he or she buys new tires with a Z rating, they will probably cost over $1,000. However, if the speed rating is dropped to H, which indicates tires capable of sustained 130 MPH speeds, the price drops to around $600. Wow! And if you never exceed the speed the tires are rated for, you will be safe.

Some tire dealers may tell a consumer that they must keep the same speed rating because they want to sell a higher-priced tire. Don't fall for it. **Choose the speed rating that matches *your* needs.** One caution however — if you suspect the car may be driven by you or anyone else to its maximum speed, purchase the tires that will handle that speed. Also, if you sell the car with tires rated for a lower speed than the car will go, be sure to tell the new owner.

TREADWEAR, TRACTION, AND TEMPERATURE RATINGS

Keep in mind that treadwear, traction, and temperature (UTQG) ratings are usually different for every brand and model of tire made. In fact, some tires' ratings have gone up even though the tires did not change. The envelope is constantly pushed higher and higher. Fifteen years ago, a 200 treadwear was considered high; today ratings can be over 600!

The most common Speed Ratings:

S=112 mph
T=118 mph
H=130 mph
V=149 mph
Z=150+ mph

These ratings represent the maximum speed a tire can be driven for extended periods.

Tires have improved over the years, but not as much as their ratings have. Therefore, these figures should be used for comparison only. When you buy new tires, the UTQG ratings don't have to be the same as the old ones. But try to use these ratings to get bargaining power. Point out to a manager that a competitor's tires have a better rating for a lower price. This may prompt the salesman to match the lower price. Many tire professionals don't even know that these ratings don't really amount to much! You can keep it your secret.

Brand Names

What about brand names? Should you buy a name brand tire or a private label? What's the difference? A vast majority of all tires made in the USA are made by the top four or five tire producers. Name brand tires are the ones you see or hear about on the television or radio. A private label tire is usually built by one of these major companies, but is sold by a smaller distributor under its own name. These small distributors seldom advertise on a large scale. But just as you can buy grocery store brand products for less, you can often get a no-name tire built by a brand name company for much less than its brand name cousin. Why is this? The biggest reason is advertising. Have you ever thought about how much a tire company pays for a television ad on Super Bowl Sunday? The top tire makers spend millions on advertising. So to make a profit, they must charge more for their products. Consumers pay for this advertising when they pay extra for a brand name tire.

On the other hand, when a major company sells a tire for a private label, they leave the advertising up to the company buying the tires. If this company chooses not to spend millions to advertise, they can sell tires for much less. Responsibility for tire warranties and liabilities are also handed down to the private label company, and this can also affect the price. So which type is right for you? If you do a lot of traveling or relocate often, a name brand may be a wise choice. This is because the manufacturer's warranty should be honored at any store that sells that brand. Since private brand tires are less common and are often sold only in a local area, it may be hard to find a dealer who carries the same private label in another state or city. If you plan on living in the same location for a while or may sell or trade your car soon, a private label tire can offer considerable savings.

An important exception to the rule is private brand tires sold by a national chain store. These tires may give you a lower price, plus a

T9 - UTQG RATINGS
(UNIFORM TIRE QUALITY GRADE)
FOR USA ONLY / DOT QUALITY GRADES

Treadwear 320   Traction A (B) C   Temperature A (B) C

**All passenger car tires must conform to
federal safety requirements in addition to these grades**

TREADWEAR

The treadwear is a comparative rating based on the wear rate of the tire when tested under controlled conditions on a specified government test course. For example, a tire graded 150 would wear one and a half ($1^1/_2$) times as well on the government coarse as a tire graded 100. The relative performance of tires depends upon the actual conditions of their use, however, and may depart significantly from the norm due to variations in driving habits, service practices, and differences in road characteristics and climate.

TRACTION

The traction grades, from the highest to lowest, are, **A, B,** and **C,** and they represent the tire's ability to stop on wet pavement as measured under controlled conditions on specified government test surfaces of asphalt and concrete. A tire marked C may have poor traction performance. **WARNING:** The traction grade assigned to this tire is based on braking (straight ahead) traction and does not include cornering (turning) traction.

TEMPERATURE

The temperature grades are **A** (the highest), **B,** and **C,** representing the tire's resistance to the generation of heat and its ability to dissipate heat when tested under controlled conditions on a specified indoor laboratory test wheel. Sustained high temperature can cause the material of the tire to degenerate and reduce tire life, and excessive temperature can lead to sudden tire failure. The grade **C** corresponds to a level of performance which all passenger tires must meet under the Federal Motor Vehicle Safety Standard No. 109. Grades **B** and **A** represent higher levels of performance on the laboratory test wheel than the minimum required by law. WARNING: The temperature grade for this tire is established for a tire that is properly inflated and not overloaded. Excessive speed, underinflation, or excessive loading, either separately or in combination, can cause heat buildup and possible tire failure.

All new tires sold in the US are required to have the above information on the new tire sticker. The quality ratings are also printed directly on the sidewall of each tire. As you can see above, tire ratings are not an exact science because of all the variables that take place after the tires are installed. In addition, tire companies are responsible for grading their own tires, and the government does not closely monitor these ratings. Therefore, UTQG ratings should be used as a guide only. (This label was copied directly from an actual tire sticker, and except for the grades, it is exactly the same on all new tires).

national warranty. This is like having your cake and eating it too! There is one thing you must consider about this name versus no-name decision, however. Top tire producers usually keep their best technology just for themselves for several years; also, they sometimes manufacture a private label tire to meet the small company's standards, which may or may not be as high as their own. In many cases though, private label tires are identical to their name brand counterparts, except for the name.

DIAL-A-TIRE

Most everyone knows to shop for tires before they buy. The tire market is so competitive, it is possible to save a considerable amount of money with careful shopping. Shopping however is much more than simply finding the lowest price. There are many other variables to take into consideration, some of which have been covered, and some which will be discussed a little later. The first step is to get out the phone book and warm up your dialing finger. Tire shopping begins on the telephone. Why use the phone instead of visiting a store? Because tire dealers know that a phone shopper is calling many different stores, so they will probably give you their best price on the phone. This is like the "get 'em in the store" routine discussed earlier. You are more likely to get a better price on the phone than if you visit the tire store.

When calling for a tire quote, state that you are shopping around for the lowest price. Don't talk *value* on the phone, talk *price*! You will decide later who has the best value. **Another must is to make sure you are quoted the total drive-out price.** Most tire companies train their salespeople to give you the price for

> **Most tire companies train their salespeople to give you the price for the tire only. This may not include mounting, balancing, valve stems, road hazard warranty, taxes, disposal fees, or service policies.**

the tire only. This may not include mounting, balancing, valve stems, road hazard warranty, taxes, disposal fees, or service policies. The reason for giving you this "tire-only" price is to make the price much lower than what you will pay in the end. This tactic is used in tire advertisements. You will never get the $19.99 tire for $19.99 — you will pay extra for necessities such as mounting, balancing, and new valve stems. At the minimum, all new tires should be balanced and get a new valve stem, and these services are not included in the advertised price. Also, keep in mind that tires are subject to regular sales tax in most states. Some states also require a waste tire disposal charge for your old tires. Many people have been very disappointed or even angry about paying $45 for a $19.99 tire! Be sure you know exactly what you will be getting and what it will cost before giving your permission to have tires installed. Asking for the total drive-out price should get this accomplished.

Another thing to consider when shopping for tires is the service after the sale. At no extra charge, some tire dealers include rotations, balancing, and flat repair for as long as you own the tires. Others sell a separate service agreement for about $10 per tire, or they may offer only free rotations, or nothing at all. This can make a significant difference in the amount of money you spend on the tires over their lifetime. For example, consider a set of 60,000-mile tires that cost $30 every 5,000 miles for rotation and balancing. For eleven visits, this adds up to $330, which could double the cost of some tires! A lifetime service policy, on the other hand, may cost less than $40, which is paid only once, when the tires are purchased. Afterwards, the tires are rotated and balanced for free. Therefore, if you take advantage of the free service, this $40 will be money well spent. A free service policy also encourages people to take better care of their tires because the maintenance will not cost them every time it's needed. As you know, good maintenance adds more life to the tires. When shopping for tires, be sure to ask the tire dealers what services they offer and how much it costs.

TIRE WARRANTIES

You should know what will happen when a tire goes bad before you choose a set of tires or a dealer. The warranty can make a major difference in how much money you ultimately spend on a set of tires. Tire warranties can vary greatly from tire to tire and from dealer to dealer, but this does not mean they have to be confusing.

There are three basic types of tire warranties. The most common is the **limited mileage warranty**. This type of warranty is usually based on a maximum mileage and is a prorated warranty. This means, for example, if you purchase a tire with a 60,000-mile limited warranty, and the tire develops a defect at 30,000 miles, you should get a new tire for 50 percent of the new price. A prorated warranty is a "pay for what you used" kind of thing, based on the percentage of the warranty remaining. The more mileage you get before having a problem, the more you would pay. This may sound unfair at first, but you should consider the 30,000 miles of good service you had before the problem. Think of it as getting a refund for the unused part of your tire, which is applied towards a new tire. This type of warranty actually helps to keep the cost of new tires down. Tire manufacturers and dealers must make a profit, and this type of warranty helps keeps their cost down, which benefits the consumer in the long run.

A mileage warranty usually covers defects only, such as tire separation or out-of-round tires. Most tire warranties do not cover things such as punctures, unexplained blow-outs, damage from a road hazard, and even wear-out. Even wear-out? That's right, most tire warranties are void if the tread wears out before the mileage is achieved. A tire is covered against defects only, and wear-out is not considered a defect. Wear-out is a natural occurrence that happens to all tires. Because of this, warranties are often exaggerated and outlive the tires by several thousand miles! There are exceptions however; some tire warranties *do* cover wear-out. In these cases, if a tire wears out before the warranty expires, it will be treated as defective. This type of warranty is worth more because it guarantees that you will get the mileage you were expecting. Be sure to ask about wear-out when you are calling around, and whether it will be in writing. Many tire salespeople will tell you anything to make a sale, hoping you won't ask for written proof.

Free Tires

Many limited mileage warranties also have a **free replacement period**. This is a grace period that overrides the "pay for what you used" (prorated) part of the warranty for a certain number of miles. This period is usually the first 25 percent of the warranty period. If, for example, a 60,000-mile tire has a 25 percent free replacement period, a defect in the first 15,000 miles would be replaced free of charge. After 15,000 miles, the prorated warranty would start. Most tires have a free replacement period of at least 25 percent; some are longer. Some tires may even come with a 100 percent free replacement period. This means you get a free tire for a defect during the entire covered mileage. The most liberal warranties (50 percent and greater) are usually found in private label tires, in the upper price range. An expensive private label tire may have a very high profit margin, which means a tire company makes enough money from the original sale to allow it to give away a few tires.

When shopping around for tires, be sure to ask about the free replacement period because it can make a significant difference in the price you will pay for a replacement. Store managers or salespeople may "forget" to mention this. Tire dealers can send a defective tire back to the manufacturer and get part or all of their money back — they can make a hefty profit if they can charge you for a tire that should be covered under the warranty *and* get money back from their supplier. Always ask for a written warranty stating both the mileage and the free replacement period.

The other types of tire warranties are **life-of-tread warranties** and **time-based warranties**. Life-of-tread warranties work in much the same manner as mileage warranties except they base the warranty on the amount of the tread remaining on the tire, instead of the mileage. If, for example, you purchased a tire with $^{10}/_{32}$ inch of tread when new, and it was found to have a defect with $^{6}/_{32}$ inch of tread remaining, 60 percent of the purchase price would be refunded towards a new tire (6 ÷ 10 = 60%). This is the same "pay for what you used" routine. Most life-of-tread warranties also come with a free replacement period. Life-of-tread warranties are commonly used on high-performance

Three Types of Tire Warranties:

1) Limited Mileage

2) Life-of-Tread

3) Time-based

A road hazard warranty is an insurance policy for your tires.

and raised-white-letter tires. These tires usually don't last as long, and their mileage can vary greatly depending on how they are used. Don't be afraid to buy a tire with a life-of-tread warranty. Many such tires have a long life if they are treated and maintained properly. If any tire ends up on a car driven by a teenager, however, it will never see 60,000 miles!

Time-based warranties are fairly new and are most commonly used on ultra-premium tires. They base the warranty on time, instead of tread or mileage. It is important to understand clearly how any warranty works, so go over the details when discussing new tires with the salesperson; this will prevent confusion if a problem occurs. Carefully discussing tire warranties also tells the salesperson that you will be expecting your money's worth if you have a tire problem, and that you will not be taken advantage of.

Tire warranties don't always have to be handled by the dealer who originally sold the tires. **Any tire dealer who sells the brand you have *should* honor a warranty for a defective tire.** This can be true for tires that were on a used car when you bought it, the tires on a new car, or tires you bought in another part of the country. The manufacturer's warranty travels with the tire. This nationwide warranty is possible because any tire dealer can send a defective tire (of their brand) back to their supplier and get a refund for that tire, whether they sold it or not. Their warranty policy works on the same prorated basis as the consumer warranty. On a relatively new tire, dealers get 100 percent of their cost back; on a worn tire, they get a percentage based on how much tread is remaining.

The catch is that a dealer who did not make a profit from the original sale may be reluctant to honor a warranty if there's nothing in it for him. However, if you offer to pay an amount that will insure a dealer that his store will not lose money and mention that he will earn your future business, he will probably be glad to take care of your problem. Use the yellow pages to find a dealer in your area who carries the brand of tire you need. Some new *car* dealers take care of tire problems for a short length of time, so check with them first on a relatively new car.

Warranty Exclusions

You may have noticed the term "defective" is being used here. That's the other catch. Tire problems such as a blow-out, damage caused by running a tire flat, or from running over a curb or sharp object are not considered a defect, so they will not be covered by a dealer who did not sell the tire. Most tire makers will not reimburse dealers for these problems, so they are not likely to give you another tire. Also, free service policies and road hazard warranties will be honored only by the dealer who sold these policies. Therefore, you will have to pay for tire maintenance at a dealer other than your own, even if they sell the same brand. The exception to this can be found in chain tire dealers, who warranty *all* aspects of the tire warranty from store to store.

Road Hazard!

A **road hazard warranty** is another purchase you should consider when buying new tires. A road hazard warranty is an insurance policy for your tires. It can be loosely compared to a term life insurance policy in the sense that it is good for only a specified amount of time, in this case the normal life of the tire, and is of no benefit unless you use it. A road hazard policy will pay for part or all of a new tire if the tire is damaged beyond repair while in normal use. The reason this type of warranty is needed is because most tire manufacturers only warranty tires against defects in workmanship, not against damage from outside forces. This is where the road hazard warranty takes over, supplementing the manufacturer's warranty.

Some examples of road hazards are broken glass, sharp metal, and curbs or potholes. When a tire encounters one of these obstacles, it usually soon becomes a swing on a playground. If you have road hazard insurance in such a case, you will get a new tire at no charge, or at a reduced price based on the remaining treadwear. Without a road hazard warranty, you will have to pay the full price for a new tire, even if the tire is only a week old! That is the good side of road hazard warranties. The bad side is, if you purchase a road hazard warranty and never have to use it, the money you paid is wasted and goes right into the tire dealer's pocket. This can be almost as painful!

The price for a road hazard policy is usually around 10 percent of the price of the tire. So an average policy costs about $35 to $40 for most middle- to upper-priced tires. This can add up to a sizeable profit for the dealer based on the law of averages. Tire dealers take in more money than they have to pay out in warranties. Furthermore, a tire dealer pays about 30 to 50 percent less for a tire than you do. Chances are you will not have such a problem and your road hazard money will be wasted. However, like any other type of insurance, if you do use the insurance, it will have been worth it.

So, should you buy road hazard or not? That should be decided by you and you alone. Don't let someone talk you into buying road hazard unless you want it. Many stores pay their salespeople a commission for selling road hazard warranties, so you can expect some pressure to buy them. If you're a gambler, you will probably take your chances, but if you believe in the value of insurance, it will be a safe investment. Please also note: Some companies cover road hazard damage that occurs to the tread area, but not to the sidewalls. This type of coverage is less valuable because tire-destroying damage is more likely to occur in the relatively weak (thin) sidewall area. Be sure to ask about this before purchasing road hazard insurance.

DECISION TIME

Now that you know how to choose the tires that are right for you, it's time to decide where to get them. This will usually be the dealer who has the lowest price on the tires you want. There are of course exceptions. If, for example, the dealer with the lowest price is 20 or 30 miles out of your way, he may not be the best choice. If tires were a "buy and forget about it" product, the 20-mile drive would certainly be worth saving a few dollars. But tires need to be rotated and balanced regularly, not to mention occasional flat repairs or a warranty claim. Long trips can add up to a lot of wasted time and money. In addition to these standard trips, new tires sometimes give problems such as a bounce or vibration that may require several visits to correct. These long drives can get very frustrating if you have to drive past a local dealer who had the same tires for a few dollars more!

If a friend strongly recommends a dealer, there is probably a good reason for this. If this dealer's price and service is reasonably close to the lowest price, he could be the best choice. Also, another thing to consider about the dealer with the lowest price is the service *after* the sale. A dealer who makes only a small profit may not devote a great deal of time to you after the sale is made. He may be reluctant to solve a vibration problem and may be very stingy when it comes to tire warranties. To keep their costs down, these dealers may also hire inexperienced employees and have inferior equipment. On the other hand, dealers with experienced technicians and modern facilities will have to charge more to pay for these assets. And a dealer who makes a reasonable profit on the original sale is more likely to help you with a problem or warranty later. These factors can result in a more pleasant experience both during and after the sale.

Finally, if you like dealing with the same person every time you buy tires or need service, a locally owned store may be a good choice. This is usually where you will find people who are genuinely concerned with making you a satisfied customer, no matter what it takes. These locally owned stores may charge a little more, but it's probably because of buying power, not profit. People are often advised not to choose the building contractor with the lowest bid — this can be good advice for tires and service too. Careful thinking may save you a lot of headaches and money.

BRAKES

THE BASICS

If you keep the same car for more than a year or two, chances are good that it will need some brake repair. Of all repairs other than routine maintenance (oil changes, etc.), brake repair is the most common. The reason for this is that all brake pads and brake shoes eventually wear out. Of course when brakes wear out, they must be repaired. Unfortunately, brake repair is an area where most people are vulnerable to fraud. But it doesn't have to be this way. The following sections discuss some things you need to know to get the most from your brakes and from your repair shop for the least amount of money. This knowledge will make you much less likely to fall victim to a dishonest repair center as well.

CARSMART

To prevent brake repair fraud, it is important to understand the basic principles behind how the automotive brake system works. If you know what happens when you push the brake pedal and understand the terms used in the industry, you will be a confident and knowledgeable customer. A service manager will immediately recognize this and will give you the respect you deserve. This will all but eliminate your chance of being taken advantage of and can save you hundreds of dollars! Don't panic, brakes aren't so difficult. The words in **BOLD SMALL CAPS** are defined in the brake system glossary, and I have included many drawings to help explain the system's functions.

Okay, this is how your brake system works. When you press down on the brake pedal, you are operating a small hydraulic pump. This pump is called the **MASTER CYLINDER** (*see illustration B2*). The master cylinder creates pressure in the brake fluid. This same principle is used in a toy water pistol. The trigger operates a pump, which pressurizes the water to make it spray from the gun. The brake pedal is the trigger, the master cylinder is the pump, but instead of water, liquid brake fluid is pressurized. In fact, the small force you apply to the brake pedal with your foot creates sufficient pressure to stop a 3,500-pound car! However, cars with power brakes (practically every car made today) have a **POWER BOOSTER** (*see illustration B1*). The power booster uses air from the engine to *help* push the brake pedal. This makes a car with power brakes much easier to stop than a car with manual (not power) brakes.

The pressure created by the master cylinder causes the brake fluid to travel through small tubes and hoses down to each wheel (*see illustration B1*). At each wheel, the fluid is forced into small pumps similar to the master cylinder. These pumps are called **BRAKE CALIPERS**. Brake calipers reverse the process that occurred at the brake pedal; that is, the pressure in the brake lines is used to make the calipers move. In other words, ultimately, moving the brake pedal causes movement in the calipers. The outward movement of the calipers is used stop the car. How? Inside each brake caliper are two **BRAKE PADS**. The brake calipers and pads are mounted firmly to the car, but between the brake pads are the **BRAKE ROTORS**, which are mounted to the wheels and spin with the wheels. These rotors are disks, about the size of a Frisbee, and there is one rotor per wheel. When the brake pedal is pushed, the pads are pressed firmly against both sides of the rotors, which slows them down and therefore slows the car. Just like you would pinch a spinning Frisbee between your thumb and forefinger to stop it, the brake pads pinch the

B1 - BRAKE SYSTEM

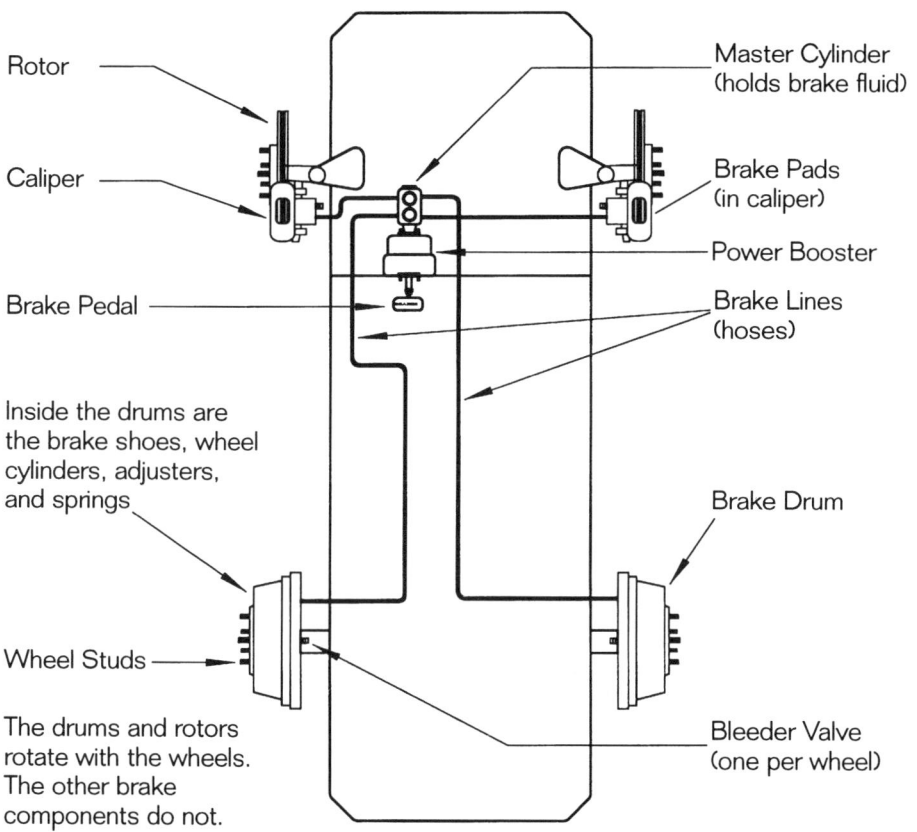

Pictured are the major components of the front disk, rear drum brake system. When the brake pedal is pressed, the master cylinder sends fluid pressure down to each wheel. There, the calipers squeeze the pads against the spinning rotors and the brake shoes rub inside the spinning brake drums to stop the car. Cars with four-wheel disk brakes use rotors and calipers on the rear instead of drums and shoes. Anti-lock brakes have all of these components, with the addition of electronic sensors, control valves, and computers. The master cylinder is divided into two halves, which insures that the car will have brakes on at least two wheels at all times for safety.

C A R S M A R T

B2 - BRAKE MASTER CYLINDER

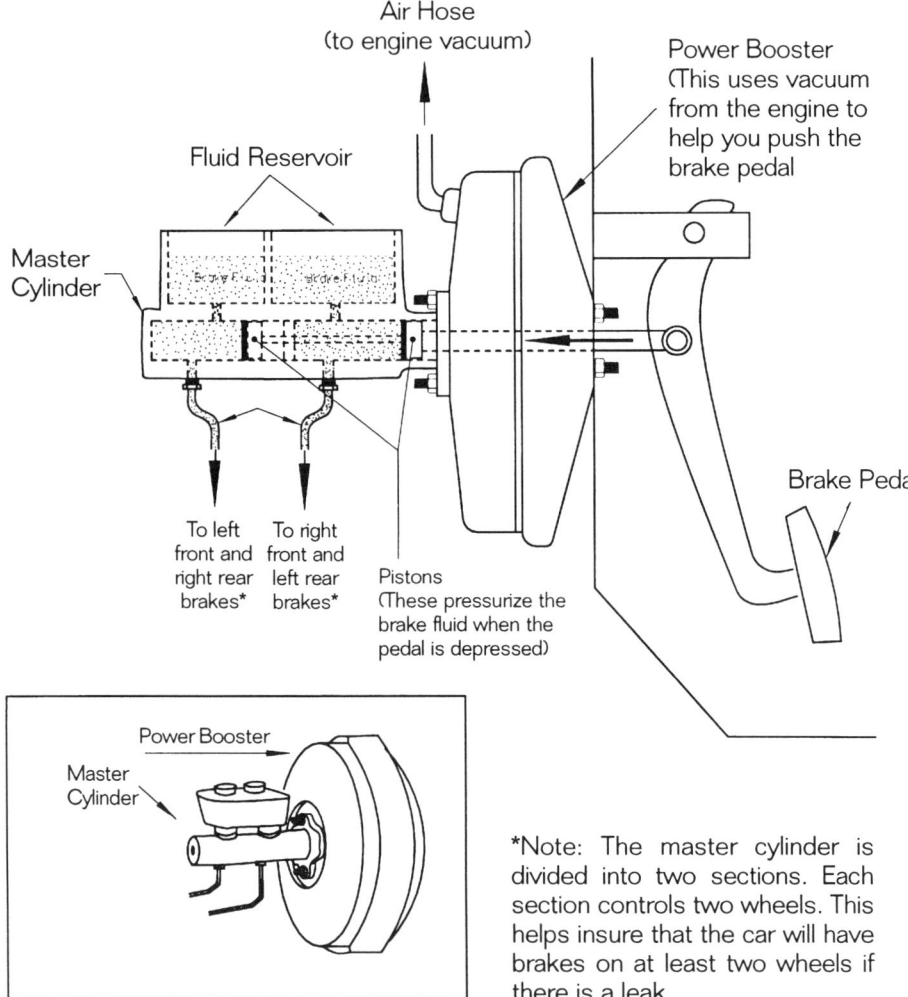

*Note: The master cylinder is divided into two sections. Each section controls two wheels. This helps insure that the car will have brakes on at least two wheels if there is a leak.

As the brake pedal is depressed, the power booster "helps" apply force to the pistons in the master cylinder. This causes fluid pressure to travel down to each wheel where it is used to press the brake pads against the brake rotors, which stops the car.

spinning rotors. (The friction between the pads and rotors not only stops the car, it creates tremendous heat in the brake pads and other brake components.) When you take your foot off of the brake pedal, the pressure disappears, and the pads stop rubbing against the rotors. Although there are minor variations in the size and shape of these brake components, all cars and trucks use some form of this basic design (*see illustration B3*).

DISKS, DRUMS, OR BOTH?

Most cars built between about 1970 and 1985, use DISK BRAKES on the front wheels and DRUM BRAKES on the rear wheels. Before 1970, most cars used drum brakes at all four wheels. But around 1985, a trend to use disk brakes on all four wheels began. This trend started with high-performance and luxury cars, but today just over half of all cars are made with disk brakes on both front and rear wheels. Trucks and lower price cars are some of the last models to still have drum brakes on the rear, but not for long.

What's the difference? Disk brakes use brake pads, brake rotors, and brake calipers to stop the car. Drum brakes use BRAKE SHOES, BRAKE DRUMS, and WHEEL CYLINDERS (*see illustration B4*). Drum brakes use the pressure from the master cylinder to stop the car, but are less efficient than disk brakes, especially under heavy use, because they do not dissipate heat as well. Disk brakes not only work better, they take up less space and can be a little lighter. As a result, more and more cars are built with disk brakes on all four wheels. Eventually, it is likely that all cars will have disk brakes on front and rear. A car with disk brakes on the rear is said to have "four-wheel disk brakes." Although disk

Disk brakes use brake pads, brake rotors, and brake calipers to stop the car.

Drum brakes use brake shoes, brake drums, and wheel cylinders.

C A R S M A R T

B3 - DISK BRAKE SYSTEM

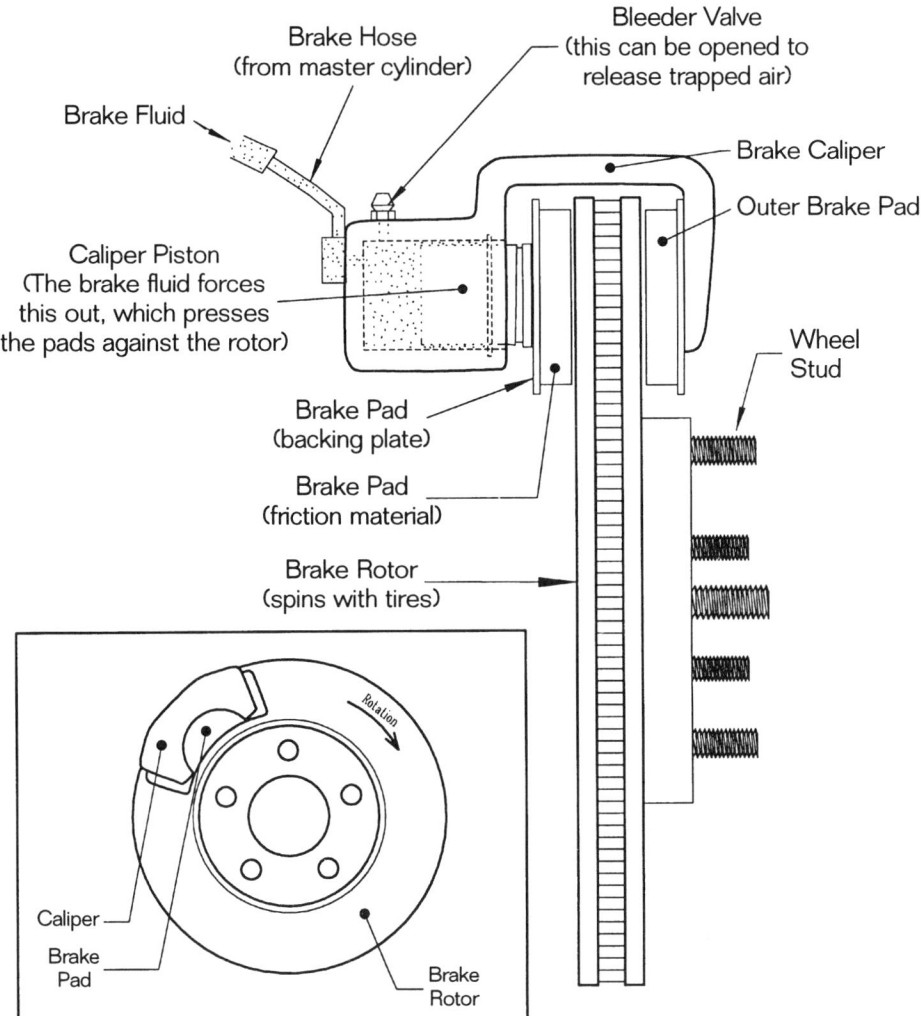

SIDE VIEW

Here are the basic components of the disk brake system. The pressurized fluid from the master cylinder is used to force the caliper piston outward, which squeezes the brake pads against the spinning rotor, which stops the car. Calipers can sometimes leak brake fluid, but more commonly they stick or bind on their mounts and cause rapid pad wear. This disk brake system is used on the front of all cars and trucks and is used on the front and rear of cars with four-wheel disk brakes.

B4 - DRUM BRAKE SYSTEM

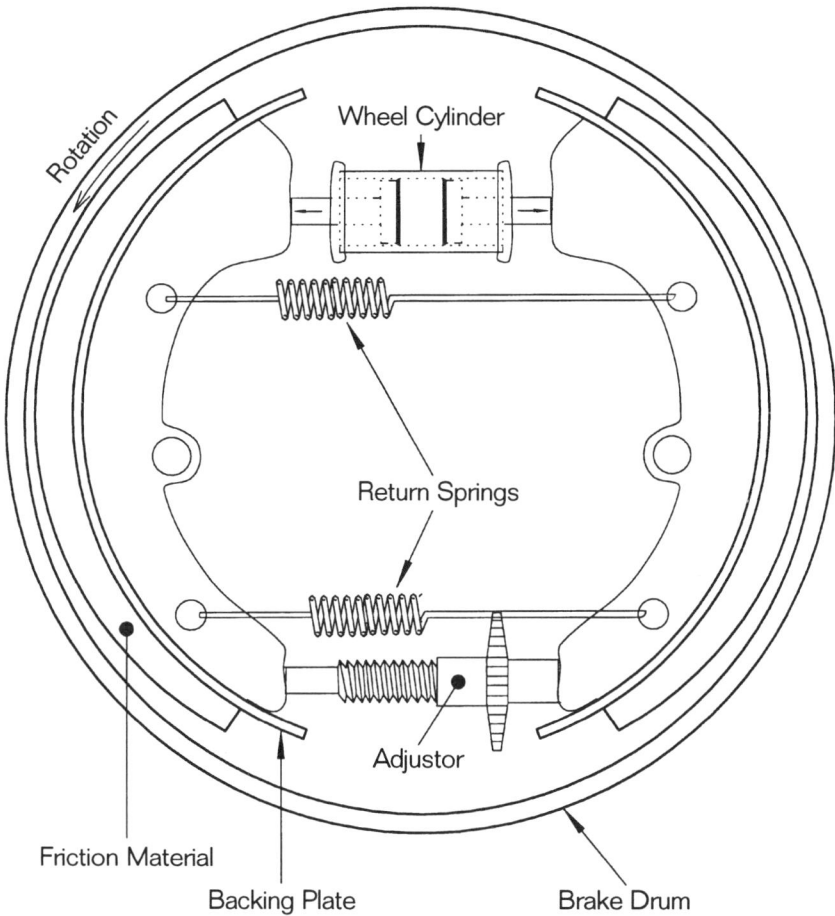

Pictured are the major components of the drum brake system. When the brake pedal is depressed, the master cylinder sends fluid pressure to the wheel cylinder, which forces the brake shoes against the rotating brake drum. This causes the drum to stop turning, which stops the car. When the brake pedal is released, the return springs pull the shoes away from the drum. As the friction material wears off the brake shoes, they get farther away from the drum, which will cause a low brake pedal. The adjuster is used to keep the distance between the shoes and the drum to a minimum so the brakes work as soon as the brake pedal is pushed. Most cars automatically adjust the brakes when the car is backed up, but an occasional manual adjustment may be needed to insure the brake pedal stays high. Drum brakes are found on the rear only, and cars with four-wheel disk brakes have none of these components.

brakes and drum brakes are quite different, brakes shoes serve the same purpose as brake pads, and drums and wheel cylinders are roughly the same as rotors and calipers respectively.

Creating Friction, Destroying Pads

So on disk brakes, brake pads rub against the brake rotors, but what are brake pads? A brake pad consists of an area of FRICTION MATERIAL about one-half inch thick (when new), and a thin metal BACKING PLATE (*see illustration B5*). The friction material and the backing plate are permanently bonded together to form a brake pad. Two brake pads are used per wheel. The friction material is made of a relatively soft material that rubs against the hard metal rotor to create the friction that stops the car. Most brake pads made today contain a small amount of tiny metal particles within the friction material. These metal particles make the friction material harder and therefore last longer. This type of pad is called semi-metallic.

Every time the brakes are used, a small amount of friction material is worn off; therefore, brake pads eventually wear out. This is by design. If the brake pads were made of metal or another extremely hard material, they would damage the rotors, which would create all kinds of problems. In fact, this is precisely what happens when all the friction material is worn off of a pad, leaving only the metal backing plate to rub against the rotor. Most of us have heard the unpleasant grinding or scrubbing sound that occurs when this happens...OUCH! Since brakes pads are designed to wear out, they are also designed to be replaced with relative ease. The next section deals with the ups and downs of brake pad replacement.

Pad & Shoe Replacement

Since all brake pads (and shoes) wear out, there will come a time when your brakes will need to be replaced. The best time to replace the pads is just *before* all the friction material is worn off. If pads are left on the vehicle until there is no friction material left, the metal backing plate will grind into the rotor and quickly destroy it. This will add a significant amount to your repair bill, because in addition to new pads, you will need new rotors. So how do you know when to replace your brake pads to prevent this expensive damage? The only sure way is to check the pads (and shoes) periodically.

B5 - BRAKE PAD

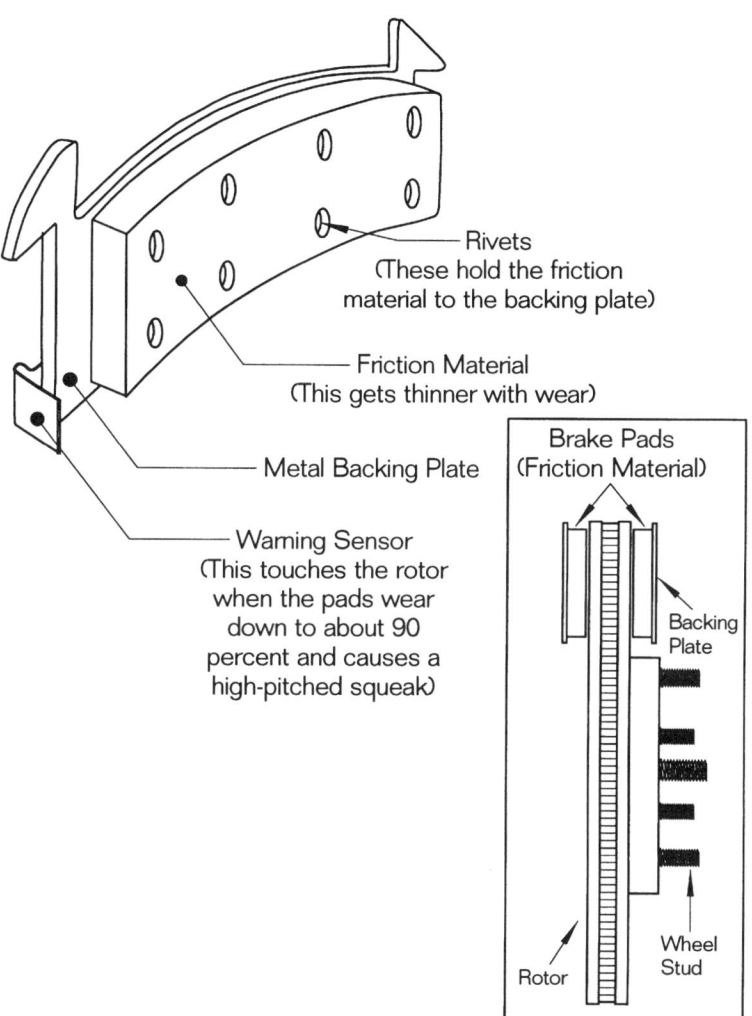

Brake pads are forced against the rotors to stop the car. Brake pads are softer than rotors, so they wear out after about 20,000 or more miles. If the pads are not replaced before all the friction material is gone, the metal backing plate will grind into the brake rotors. There are two pads per wheel, and they come in sets of four, enough for either the front or the rear wheels. All modern cars and trucks have brake pads on front, and about 20 percent of the cars on the road use them an all four wheels.

B6 - BRAKE SHOE

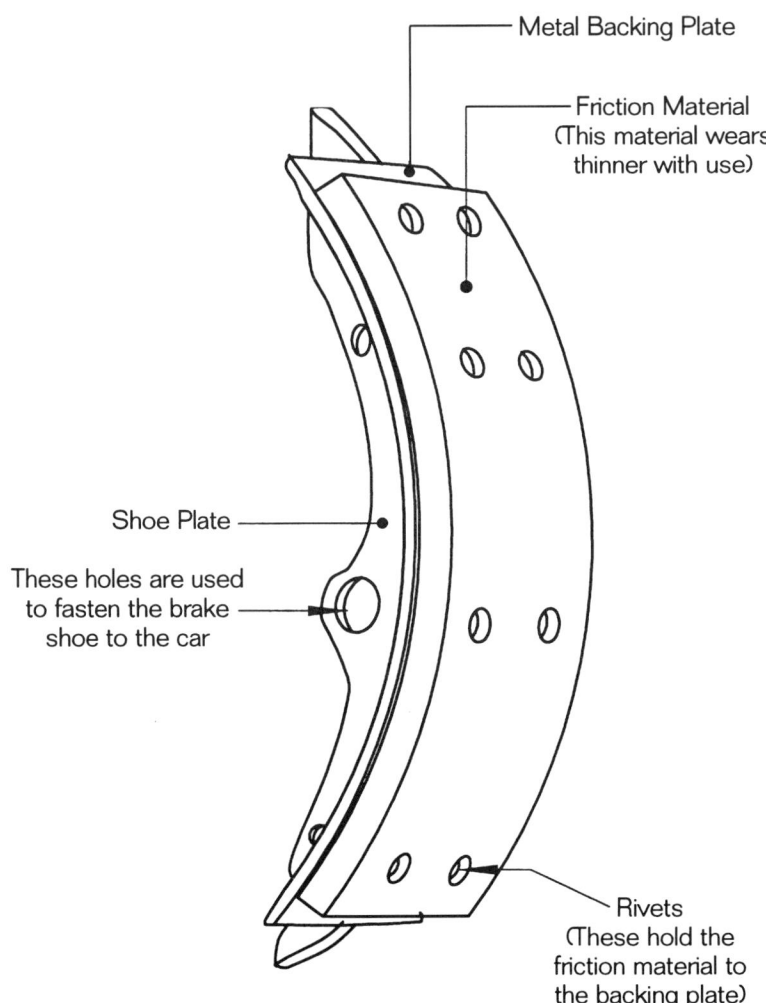

Brake shoes are similar to brake pads and are designed to wear out. They are pressed against the inside of the brake drums to stop the car. Shoes are used only with drum brakes and are found only on the rear of modern cars (1970 and up). Many cars do not use drum brakes at all; these cars have disk brakes on the front and the rear. There are two brake shoes per rear wheel.

Any time the tires are off the car or whenever you hear or feel anything strange from your brakes, your brakes should be inspected. The best time is when you are having the tires rotated, which should be about every 5,000 to 7,000 miles. This relatively short interval almost always allows you to catch the pads before they wear out completely. Even if the shop that does your tire rotation does not repair brakes, someone there can probably tell you approximately how much life is left on them. Simply ask them to look at your brakes while the wheels are off. Most cars can be checked with almost no effort *if* the tires are already off, so many shops will not charge for such a check.

AN EARLY WARNING

Many cars and trucks have a built-in warning system that alerts you about worn brake pads — a device called a WARNING SENSOR. The appropriate slang term is "**squealer**." This squealer makes a high-pitched squeak when the brake pads are about 80 to 90 percent worn. The warning sensor is a small metal finger that gets closer and closer to the rotor as the brake pads wear thinner. When the pads are almost worn out, this finger begins to scrape the rotor as the car rolls (*see illustration B5*). This causes an annoying squeak similar to the sound of fingernails scraping across a chalkboard — ouch! **A warning sensor squeak will usually *stop* when you apply the brakes.** The squealer will not damage the rotor, but it may sound like it is. When this squeak begins, you are probably very close to needing new brake pads!

Nearly all GM vehicles have this warning sensor on the front brakes, as well as many other makes, foreign and domestic. The catch is —

Have the brakes inspected every time the tires are rotated.

There is one sure sign that your car needs brakes. This is the metal-to-metal grinding sound that occurs when all of the friction material is gone and the pad's metal backing plate begins to grind into the brake rotor.

not all cars use warning sensors, so you cannot depend on hearing a squeak from any car. The next time you have your brakes inspected, ask the technician if your car is equipped with warning sensors, then you will know whether or not to listen for the squeak. Also, most cars with warning sensors have only one sensor per wheel. Since there are two pads per wheel, the pad without the sensor could wear out before the pad with it. To add more confusion, some cars will make a high-pitched squeak *during* brake use. This may be a normal sound created by the vibration that occurs between the pads and the rotors and may not indicate a serious brake problem. If you hear a squeak, but are not sure if it's a sensor, have the brakes inspected as soon as possible. This could save you time and money.

Another indication that you may need brake pads is if the brake fluid level is low. The master cylinder, located under the hood, has a reservoir that stores more than enough brake fluid under normal use. When pads wear out however, the fluid level in the master cylinder will go down. This is normal. As brake pads wear thinner, the brake calipers hold more brake fluid, and this can cause the fluid level in the master cylinder to go down by as much as 50 percent. Since many cars are equipped with an electronic sensor to alert you about low brake fluid, worn brake pads may cause the brake light in the dash to glow. Keep in mind though, low fluid level can also be an indication of a fluid leak. If your fluid is low, have the brakes inspected. You may find that you simply need new brake pads, or you may have more serious problems, which will be discussed a little later. If your brake fluid level is low, but still at a safe level, you may want to wait until after the pads are replaced before adding more fluid. When new pads are installed, the fluid level will probably return to normal, but if you add fluid before the pads are replaced, the fluid may overflow when the new pads are installed.

A Little Too Late

There is one sure sign that your car needs brakes. This is the metal-to-metal grinding sound that occurs when all of the friction material is gone and the pad's metal backing plate begins to grind into the brake rotor. This will not only affect your car's braking ability, but can quickly damage other brake components such as rotors and calipers. If you hear the dreaded "scrubbing" noise, have your brakes repaired absolutely as soon as possible. Every mile you drive after this sound begins could be costing you money, sometimes hundreds of dollars!

Shopping for Brakes

When you find that you need new brake pads, first call a few shops to get the price of their basic brake jobs. Make sure you get every detail possible about the brake job you are quoted. Many shops will price you only the very minimum, stripped-down repairs in an attempt to attract you to their shop with a low price, but they may add other repairs later. Be sure to ask about and write down what each shop includes for the price given. Does it include turning the rotors or drums? Are they quoting their best or premium semi-metallic pads? Are there additional charges for inspection? Will there be additional charges for shop supplies? Does the price include tax or other fees for cleaning or waste removal? Charges for items such as these are used by some shops to increase the price you were given on the phone. This sounds a little unfair, but these methods are taught to many service managers or salespeople. **One of oldest tricks in the book is to get the customer in the shop with a low price, get their car on the rack, and then add charges or repairs to the list.**

Don't be afraid to ask questions on the phone. This not only helps eliminate surprises, but it also tells the person at the shop that you are knowledgeable and you will not be a good target for fraudulent repairs or charges. A shop that gives you a higher price for a more complete job that doesn't need add-ons, *could* be more honest, or at least a little less sneaky. Of course, there may be legitimate reasons for additional repairs such as rotor replacement or replacing leaky or damaged calipers or wheel cylinders.

CARSMART

RAPID PAD WEAR

Today's front-wheel-drive cars are harder than ever on brakes — especially the front brakes. Why?

One reason is that modern cars are designed with most of their weight over the front wheels. As a result, cars and trucks must have a proportioning valve that will send most of the fluid pressure to the front brakes. This valve prevents the rear brakes from locking up during a panic stop, which can cause a loss of steering control. To make matters worse, the brake pads and rotors on today's cars are smaller than they were in the past to help cut down on space and weight. These two design factors cause short pad life, but they are only part of the problem.

The worst thing for pads is people who drive fast and then stop quickly. Everyone's in a hurry for one reason or another, and their brake pads suffer. Waiting until the last second to brake while traveling at a fast speed causes excessive heat and makes pads wear quickly. (This heat can also cause the rotors to warp, which will result in a brake-induced vibration in most cars.) With this kind of driving, the front brakes will wear out about every 20,000 to 40,000 miles. There are even some cars that need new pads every 10,000 miles!

If you find that you are replacing your pads about every 10,000 miles, what can you do? Altering you driving style may help more than anything. To prolong the life of your brakes, start braking a few seconds earlier than usual; don't wait until the last second. This could as much as double the mileage between brake repairs. Relax, take it easy — if you have the time.

In contrast to front brakes, rear brakes may last from 50,000 to over 100,000 miles. Why the huge difference? Even when working properly, rear brakes play a small role in stopping a car compared to the front brakes because of the proportioning valve. But when rear brakes are out of adjustment, they do very little at all! Although rear brakes are designed to self-adjust, they often do not adjust fast enough to keep up with normal wear. When this happens, nearly the entire task of stopping a car is given to the front brakes. This can play a role in rapid front brake wear. Therefore to maximize front pad life, the rear brakes should always be adjusted properly. Have the rear brakes adjusted every time you have the front brakes repaired or when the brake pedal feels lower than usual. This simple, inexpensive service will save you money on front pad replacement.

Cars with drum brakes on the rear are usually the ones that need brake adjustment. Most cars with four-wheel disk brakes should self-adjust every time the brakes are used, so you should not pay anyone to adjust brakes on these cars. Check the owner's manual for your car, or ask a technician which type of system you have.

The quality of the brake pads also affects pad life. Just like every other product, there are good brake pads and cheap brake pads. One manufacturer may cut corners and use inferior materials to save money, or may skip important treatments that harden the pads to insure long life. Another may use only the best products and processes, which cost significantly more. Therefore, if you are given a choice between two different pads, and one set costs $20 and the other cost $40, you can bet the $40 set will last longer!

If low quality pads are put on a car that is already hard on brakes, they may last less than 5,000 miles. This is like feeding a hungry lion a can of kitty food! If you own a car with a lion's appetite for brakes, feed it the best quality brake pads you can find. Sure, these premium pads cost more initially, but they will probably cost less in the long run. You will save on labor costs and will waste less of your valuable time in a repair center. When buying brake service, ask the service manager about options and price levels for different qualities of pads. Avoid using inexpensive pads, even if they have a lifetime warranty. These lifetime pads will wear out just as fast or faster than a top quality pad, and you will still have to pay the labor to have them changed.

If you follow these guidelines, you should see a significant increase in brake pad life. However, even if you do all the things mentioned here, and especially if you make frequent or quick stops, you may still get only about 15,000 to 20,000 miles on the front brakes. This may be the normal pad life for your car and your driving habits.

CARSMART

DON'T OVER-REPAIR

How much brake repair is enough? If you have a relatively new car and catch the brake pads before they are completely worn out (they have not begun scrubbing metal to metal), there is a good possibility you may need to replace only the pads. This is simple on most cars: take the wheels off, loosen four bolts, remove the old pads, and install new ones. This should take about 30 to 45 minutes and cost between $50 and $80 for most cars. This price is usually about half parts and half labor. Remember, a brake repair on a very new car, or one that is not as common, will usually cost more because the brake pads will be more expensive. Simple pad replacement is all you need, *unless* you are hearing a scrubbing sound, *or* you are getting a vibration, shake, or pulsation that occurs while braking. These symptoms mean you will need to have the rotors turned or replaced. Because you can detect these symptoms on your own, you can be the judge.

Many service managers may advise you to turn the rotors even if you aren't experiencing any of these symptoms. This may be an attempt to add about $40 in unnecessary labor to your bill. Turning your rotors when they don't need it makes them thinner, which makes them wear faster and more likely to cause problems. In such a case, you may want to tell the manager that you are not having a problem with your rotors and ask him why he wants to turn them. It may be that it is his honest opinion that you will get better service from your brakes if the rotors are turned. In fact, this opinion is held by many in the industry. However, in the past ten years or so, many experts are more inclined to leave the rotors alone unless they are grooved or damaged from excessive pad wear, or if they are causing a brake related vibration. This is known as the "if it ain't broke, don't fix it" philosophy!

ROTORS

Unlike brake pads and shoes, rotors are not specifically *designed* to wear out. But rotors are subjected to a great deal of heat and friction every time the brakes are used and therefore have a limited life. Unfortunately, rotors are a common source of repair fraud, because most people don't understand why and when they should be replaced or how much they cost. Of course, you are about to change this!

The rotors on most modern cars will need to be replaced long before they see 100,000 miles, but this was not the case with cars built in the seventies and early eighties. Then, it was not uncommon for rotors to last for the life of the car. These older cars had oversized brakes, and because they were mostly rear-wheel-drive, the weight of the car was more evenly distributed from front to rear. In addition, most drivers were easier on their brakes back then. These factors put low demands on the brake pads, so they were made of a relatively soft material that did not significantly wear the rotors.

Today's smaller cars and brakes, and the heavy use most brakes are subjected to, brought about the need for SEMI-METALLIC brake pads. These pads have tiny metal particles embedded in the friction material that make the pads harder and greatly increase their life. The bad news is these hard brake pads also wear the rotors much faster. Every time the brakes are used, a small amount of material is worn off the brake pads *and* the brake rotors. Naturally, after thousands of stops rotors can wear out, which means they must be replaced.

THINNING ROTORS

Not only do rotors wear from normal use, they also get thinner when they are MACHINED (turned). Why machine a rotor if this contributes to short rotor life? Turning rotors can not only correct an annoying problem, it can save you money. If a brake pad wears completely out, its metal backing plate will scrub into the rotor, which cuts grooves or valleys into the surface of the rotor. If these grooves are not removed, they will cause the new pads to wear much faster, which costs you money. Also, when a car vibrates during braking, this indicates that the rotor's surfaces are not perfectly flat or even; they are warped. To correct either of these problems, the rotors should be turned.

When a rotor is turned, a thin layer of metal is cut from each side of the rotor to remove any grooves and to make it smooth and flat. Deeper grooves or severely warped rotors require more material to be removed. Naturally when more material is removed, the rotors will be thinner and therefore nearer to the point of being worn out.

Rotors are turned on a machine called a brake lathe. This takes about ten minutes per rotor after the rotor is off the car and will add a little cost to a simple pad replacement. Around $70 to $100 would be average to replace the pads *and* turn the rotors — for both front wheels, or both rear wheels. Be forewarned that semi-metallic pads will wear *tiny* grooves in a rotor, which may not need to be removed. These grooves are slightly larger than the grooves on a record album (if you remember what that is) and will not significantly harm the new pads. The grooves that should be removed are deep, rough grooves that can be easily seen from a distance, or grooves that feel rough, like sandpaper, when you rub across them. (Be careful, rotors can be *very* hot!) Also, the warning sensor or "squealer" found on many cars that warns you of pad wear, will not harm a rotor. Many service managers will suggest that you turn the rotors when it would probably be best to leave them alone. They may want to turn them for profit only. If you can't see any grooves, and if you aren't experiencing a brake vibration, they should not be turned in most cases. Remember, if it ain't broke, don't fix it!

THE PROBLEM WITH THIN

What's wrong with a rotor getting thinner? Heat, is the answer. When rotors get thin, they heat up faster and reach a higher temperature than they do when they are new. Compare a thick cast iron cooking pan to thin steel pan. The cast-iron pan takes longer to warm up; after a while it warms evenly across the entire surface of the pan; it absorbs the heat from the source and distributes it throughout the pan. In contrast, the thin steel pan warms up quickly and can get very hot over the heat source, but stays cool near the edge. The thin pan also cools down quickly compared to the iron pan. The same thing happens to a thin rotor. It heats up quickly around the brake pad and may not carry heat from the pad to the rest of the rotor. Rapid heat build-up and rapid cool-down have several adverse effects. First, higher temperatures cause brake pads to wear much faster. Second, sudden temperature changes can cause rotors to warp, leading to brake vibration. Also, brakes don't work as effectively under

B7 - BRAKE ROTOR

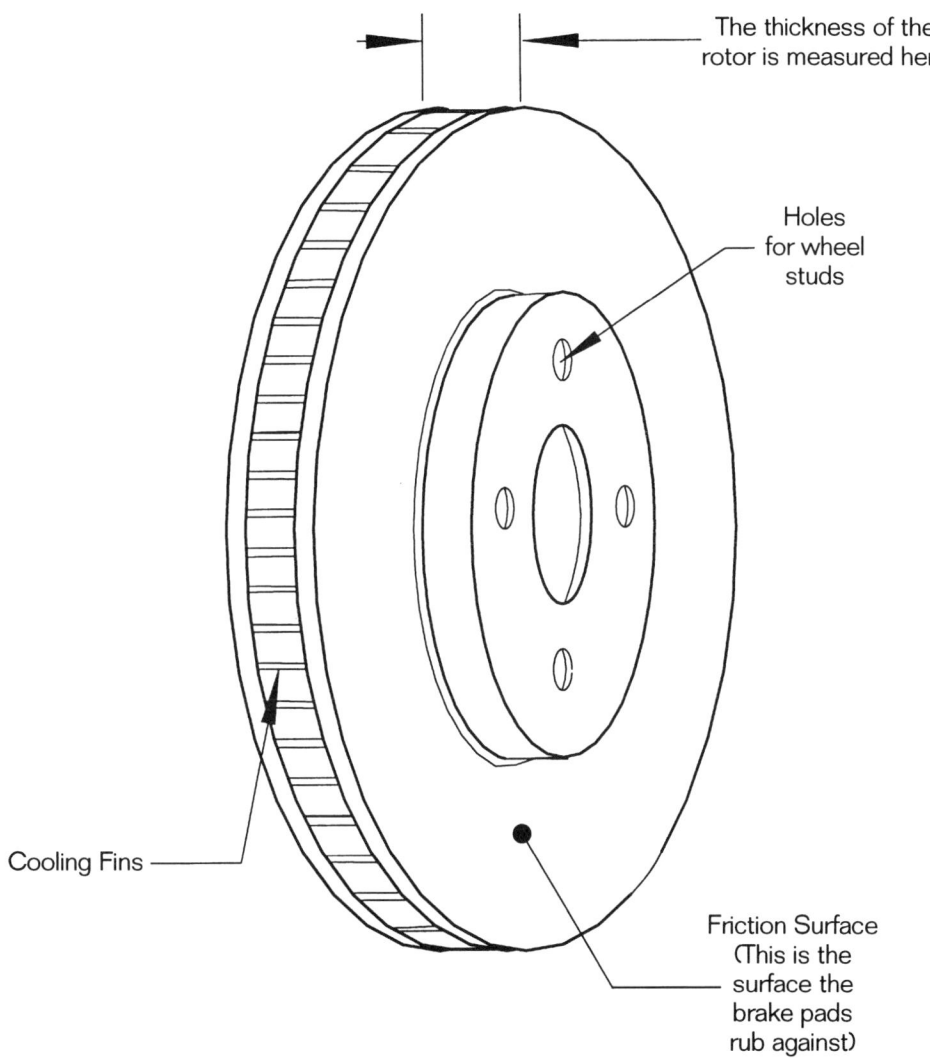

The rotors are mounted to the wheels and rotate with them. When the brakes are applied, the brake pads press against the rotors to stop the car. If a brake pad wears completely out, its metal backing plate will cut grooves into the rotor. If this happens, the rotor should be machined or replaced, depending on its thickness. Once a rotor wears or is machined below a specified minimum thickness, it should be replaced. If the friction surfaces of a rotor become warped or uneven, the car will vibrate when the brakes are applied. This too can be corrected by machining or replacing the rotor.

B8 - BRAKE DRUM

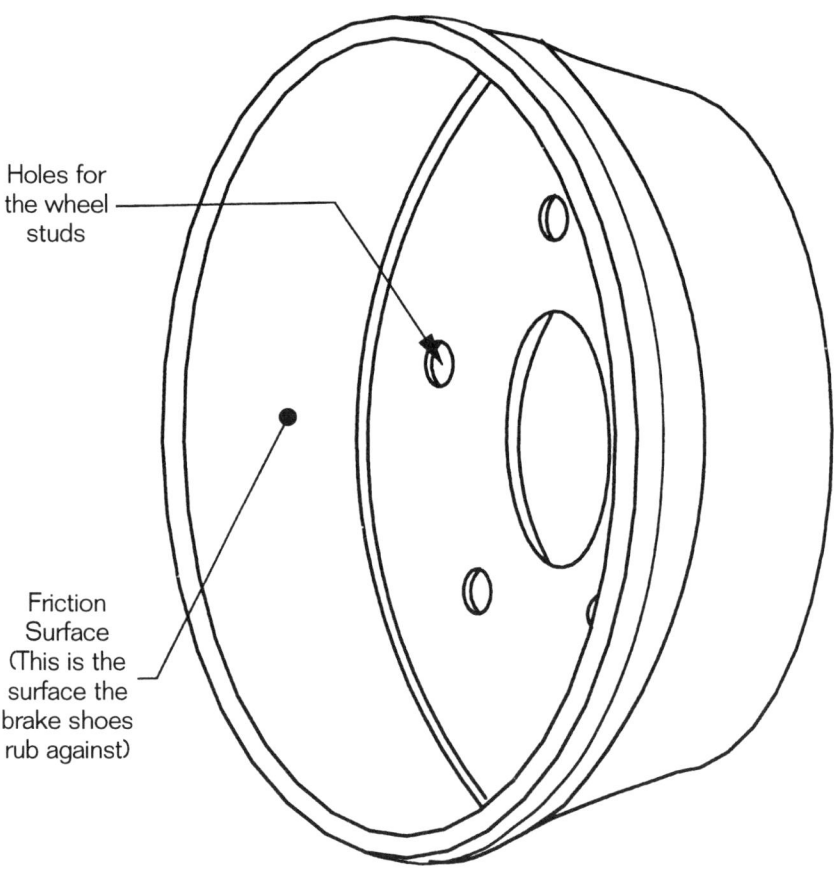

Holes for the wheel studs

Friction Surface (This is the surface the brake shoes rub against)

Brake drums are used only on the rear wheels of cars and trucks with rear drum brakes. Brake drums serve the same purpose as brake rotors: They spin with the wheels, and the brake shoes are pressed against the inside of the brake drum to stop the car. If the rear brakes wear out completely, the metal backing plate of the brake shoe will cut grooves into the drum. These grooves can sometimes be machined out on a brake lathe, or the drum may need to be replaced. Cars with four-wheel disk brakes do not use brake drums.

extremely high temperatures; in other words, your car may not stop as quickly as it should. As you can see, thin rotors must be taken seriously.

How Thin Is Too Thin?

How do you know when a rotor is too thin? Since rotors wear from normal use and from machining, they are made with a "safety zone." New rotors are thicker than a predetermined minimum thickness and are allowed to wear down to this point. All new car manufacturers specify a minimum thickness for the rotors (or drums) on each car model. These specifications are stamped onto the rotors at the factory and are published in technical books. Once a rotor wears past its minimum thickness, it is worn out and should be replaced. A rotor's thickness is measured with a very accurate device called a **caliper** or a **micrometer**. A technician measures the rotor and compares this measurement to the published minimum thickness (*see illustration B7*). Most rotors can only be machined one or two times before they become too thin. In fact, even if rotors are never machined, they can wear out from normal use. Most front rotors will last somewhere between 60,000 and 100,000 miles, depending on use and on how often they are turned. Rear rotors or drums may last much longer. Of course, if the brakes are not repaired quickly after the metal-to-metal grinding sound begins, even relatively new rotors with only 20,000 miles on them will have to be thrown away!

Front rotors may last 60,000 to 100,000 miles — rear rotors, much longer.

Uncommon Knowledge

Before going to a shop for *any* brake repair, even if you don't think you need new rotors, call a parts store to get the minimum thickness for the rotors on your car. Most parts stores have a book with the minimum thickness listed for the rotors on all makes and models. (While you have a parts person on the phone, be sure to ask for the price for a new rotor. If it turns out that you need a rotor, you will know approximately how much it should cost). You may be given two different thickness measurements. Many manufacturers, especially domestic ones, list two measurements for their rotors. One measurement is called the "machine-to" thickness, the other measurement is the "discard" thickness. The machine-to thickness gives the technician the minimum thickness that the rotors can be when he is finished turning the rotor on the brake lathe. This thickness will be slightly more than the actual throwaway thickness. This allows the rotor to wear during the lifetime of the new brake pads. Therefore, a rotor could be below the machine-to thickness, but still be safe, *if* it is not machined thinner.

When going into a shop for brake repairs, you should make the service manager aware that you know the specs for the **machine-to** and the **discard thickness** for the rotors on your car. Replacing rotors before their time is a very easy scam for a service manager to pull, mostly because he assumes the average consumer has no clue about when they should be replaced. Many people are told they need a new rotor because it is below the machine-to thickness; when in fact, if there is no reason to turn the rotor, it should not be replaced. **If a service manager is aware that you know these facts, he will be much less likely to sell you rotors you don't need.** If you purchase new rotors, but suspect foul play, ask for your old rotors and carry them to a parts store. (Rotors are not remanufactured, so you should not have to pay extra to keep them.) Many parts stores turn rotors and can measure them for you. If the rotors were *not* too thin, you know not to go back to that shop again! Give them a call and let them know what you found — this might make them think twice before doing wrong to the next person.

Rotors (or drums) usually cost between $20 and $60 each for most popular cars and can be more than $100 each for some trucks or less common cars. Most rotors are fairly simple to install especially when doing brakes at the same time. Replacing rotors while doing a brake pad replacement should add about a half hour of labor to the job. An exception would be some imports such as the Honda Accord, for example. Some of these cars have the rotors pressed to the front end and can take over an hour to replace. **A word of caution, if you are initially quoted a price for a brake job which *includes* turning the rotors, but** it turns out that you need new rotors instead, there should be *no additional labor charge.* Rotors must be removed to be machined, so it actually takes less time and effort to install new rotors than it would take to turn the old ones! Also, there may be times that only one rotor needs replacing. There is nothing wrong with this procedure, although some service managers may tell you that they must be replaced in pairs. One thing to consider however is that if one rotor is too thin and the other is close to being too thin, it may be cost-effective to replace both while the brakes are already being repaired, preventing an expensive return visit to correct a vibration caused by the thinner rotor becoming warped. It is less expensive to replace two rotors at one visit than to return for one after only a few thousand miles.

BRAKE VIBRATIONS

Although we have discussed rotors along with a brake job, they can also be a problem of their own. A warped rotor causes vibration, pulsation, or shaking that is noticed *only* when applying the brakes. About 99 percent of the time, this means the front rotors are "warped" — meaning there is a variation in thickness from one point on a rotor to another. In other words, both sides of the rotor are not perfectly flat and even. Most experts agree that rotors warp from the extreme changes in temperature they experience each time a car is driven. In extreme cases, a warped rotor can also cause a "clunking" noise. This noise will occur during braking and will slow down as the car slows. It is caused by the excessive movement of the pads and calipers as they come into contact with warped rotors. A warped rotor should be turned or replaced as outlined previously.

About 50 percent of cars will need to have the rotors turned every time the pads are replaced. Some may even need the rotors machined between pad replacement. Many new cars have problems with warped rotors that are covered under warranty. Before paying someone else to turn rotors on a relatively new car, check with your dealer to see if there are any recalls or extended coverage for warped rotors. A common myth in the industry is that brake pads should be replaced every time the rotors are machined. The fact is, if your brake pads are *fairly new, and in good condition* (no heat cracks or grooves), they can be reinstalled with new or newly turned rotors with no problems. Many dishonest service managers tell their customers that pads are damaged or worn to the shape of the warped rotors. This is simply not true. (There are cases where pads will wear unevenly, but a warped rotor is not the cause. More on this later.)

Fluid Leaks

Brake fluid carries the pressure from the master cylinder to the brake components at each wheel. Much like a wire carries electrical energy, brake fluid carries mechanical energy from one brake component to another. Brake fluid is a relatively clear liquid, slightly thicker than water, which is stored in the master cylinder and is held in other brake parts such as calipers, wheel cylinders, and hoses. All of these components must be completely filled with pure brake fluid to function properly, excluding the fluid reservoir, which is a holding tank on top of the master cylinder. This reservoir contains extra fluid in case it is needed and does not have to *completely* full. If a brake system loses enough fluid, air will enter these components and the brakes will not work properly — or at all! Therefore, a fluid leak must be repaired quickly to insure that your brakes are there when you need them.

To catch a fluid leak before it catches you, the fluid level in the master cylinder reservoir should be checked every time the hood is raised. Many reservoirs are made of clear plastic, so you can tell at a glance if the level is okay, others may have small caps that can be removed to inspect the level. Most manufacturers provide minimum and maximum fluid level markings directly on the master cylinder. In fact, on most newer cars, an electronic sensor monitors the fluid level and turns on the brake warning lamp if the fluid level reaches the minimum safe level.

You may wonder why there is a minimum level. Why not keep the master cylinder full at all times? Because there is a natural fluctuation in the fluid level related to brake pad wear. When pads are new, the brake calipers hold a small amount of brake fluid. As the pads wear thin, the calipers hold more and more brake fluid, which means the level in the master cylinder goes down. Then, when new pads are installed, the fluid that has traveled down to the calipers is forced back into the reservoir, filling it again. Therefore, if you add fluid to a system with worn pads, the reservoir will overflow when new pads are installed. Checking the fluid level can be an effective way to *estimate* brake pad wear. If you notice the fluid level is near the minimum level, your brake pads may be worn out. Of course this could also indicate a fluid leak. In either case, the brakes should be inspected as soon as possible. You may also notice that there are two different compartments in a reservoir. This is a safety feature that is designed to insure that a car will have brakes on at least two wheels, even if there is a severe leak. Each half of the reservoir goes to two different wheels. If one wheel develops a fluid leak and all the fluid escapes from that half, the other half will continue supplying fluid pressure to the other two wheels. Naturally, the braking will be inadequate, but it could be enough to prevent a serious accident.

WHERE DOES THE FLUID GO?

If the fluid level goes below the minimum, especially if the brake pads are relatively new, this is a strong indication of a fluid leak. Brake components such as master cylinders, calipers, wheel cylinders, and brake hoses hold brake fluid, and they all have rubber seals that keep the fluid inside. Unfortunately, rubber has a limited life span. After about five years, it begins to dry out and age, although the fact that these seals are soaking in brake fluid helps prolong their life. But just like a rubber washer in a water faucet eventually wears out and leaks, the seals in these components will begin to leak. Keep in mind that brake fluid pressure can be over 100 times stronger than your home's water pressure, so even the tiniest flaw in a seal can allow fluid to escape. In fact, most leaking occurs only during brake application when pressure is high, and there usually will not be any leaking when the brakes are not being used. Every time the brake pedal is pushed, a little fluid is pumped out of the system. If enough fluid escapes, the brake pedal may be lower than normal or the brakes may not work at all. This, of course, is not good.

Most of the time, leaks are from the calipers or wheel cylinders because these components are subjected to extreme heat and a lot of dirt and contamination. This causes the rubber seals to weaken or swell and begin to allow small amounts of fluid to escape every

Keep in mind that brake fluid pressure can be over 100 times stronger than your home's water pressure, so even the tiniest flaw in a seal can allow fluid to escape.

B9 - WHEEL CYLINDER

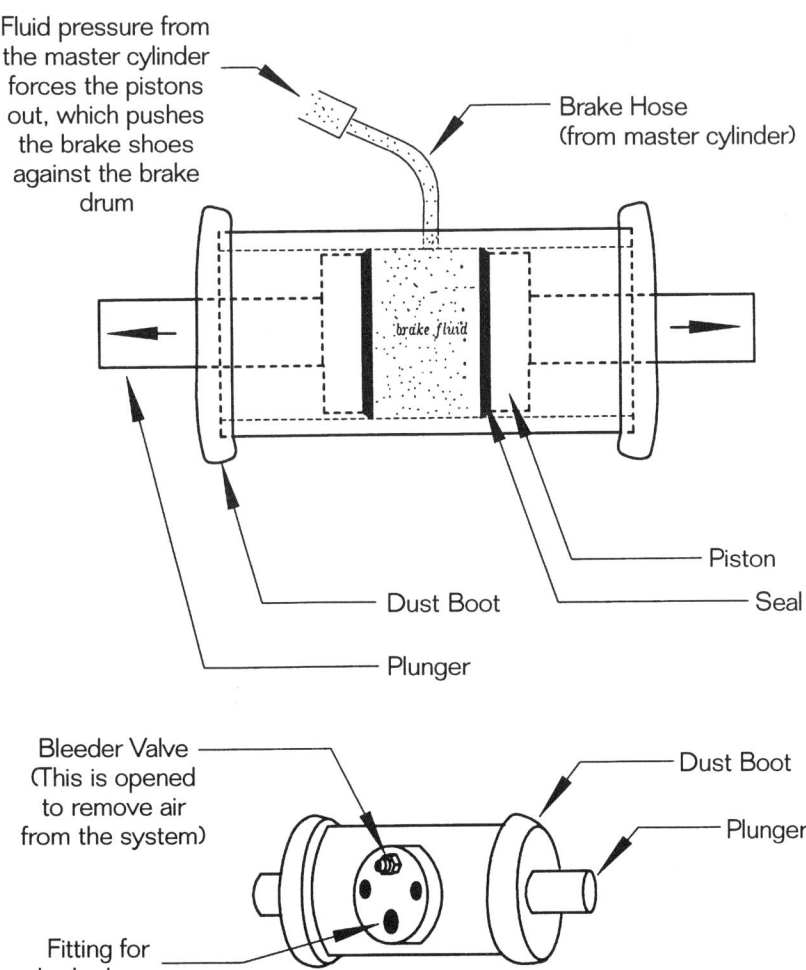

Wheel cylinders are responsible for working the rear brake shoes. When the brake pedal is pressed, the wheel cylinders force the brake shoes against the spinning brake drums, causing the car to stop. Wheel cylinders are also a common source for fluid leaks. The rubber seal inside the wheel cylinder will leak and cause the brake fluid to pour out on the brake shoes, which can cause that wheel to grab or lock up with the slightest touch of the brakes. Cars with four-wheel disk brakes do not use wheel cylinders.

time you apply the brakes. **Calipers and wheel cylinders should be checked whenever the brakes are repaired.** If any fluid leakage or damage to the rubber seals is evident, the calipers or wheel cylinders should be replaced.

A caliper or wheel cylinder usually costs between $20 to $60 each, plus labor of around $15 to $30 each to replace them. Although it is not mandatory, it's not a bad idea to replace both calipers or wheel cylinders on the front or the rear together. There could be slight differences in the new and old parts which could cause a pull or uneven pad wear. This could also prevent a return visit to replace the old part. The system should be BLED to remove the old fluid from the system and to remove any air that is trapped in the brake lines and hoses.

THE FALLING BRAKE PEDAL

Another source of brake fluid leaks is the master cylinder. The master cylinder has several rubber seals or O-rings that can leak. A leaky master cylinder will sometimes be accompanied by a brake pedal that will slowly go to the floor, especially when you are applying gentle pressure on the pedal. The two symptoms do not always happen at the same time. In other words, you may experience the disappearing brake pedal, but notice no fluid leaks, and vice versa. A master cylinder replacement is fairly simple on most cars, requiring about 30 minutes to an hour. The prices for master cylinders vary widely. The best advice here is to call a few parts stores for prices before going to a shop for repairs. Again, the entire brake system should be bled when the master cylinder or any component that holds brake fluid is replaced.

BRAKE PULL

If your car drives straight most of the time, but pulls to one side when the brakes are applied, it has a "brake pull." For a car to stop evenly, both front wheels must apply the exact same stopping power. Usually this is a given, because the brake components on each side are mirror images of one another. But, as you know, cars are not that simple. In fact, a brake pull can be hard to diagnose, even by an experienced technician. Unfortunately, hard to diagnose problems are often treated with the *trial and error* method of repair. A technician takes a guess at the source, and if that doesn't solve the problem, another guess is made, and so on. This can get expensive! Following are a few hints to prevent you from spending too much on a brake pull.

MANY SOLUTIONS...ONLY ONE FIX

A partial list of things that can cause a brake pull includes tires, front alignment, brake pads, rotors, calipers, master cylinders, brake hoses, and caliper mounts. Wow! So where do you start? The tires should be eliminated first, especially if the pull is not severe. First, check the air pressure and have the front tires switched, or rotated to the rear. If this does not change the pull, a visit to a repair shop is next. Explain to the technician what is happening and be sure to go over any recent brake repairs. Be wary if the technician diagnoses the problem without first carefully inspecting your car. Inexperienced technicians often automatically blame the brake calipers. This is definitely a guess!

Calipers are one of the most likely candidates however. Calipers must move back and forth each time the brakes are applied and released. If for any reason one caliper is harder to move than the other, or "sticks," a brake pull may result. A caliper must also be able to slide back and forth freely on its mounts when the brakes are applied. These mounts can become rusty and dry from the lack of lubricant, which may cause the caliper to seize and bind. This will often cause a pull, as well as premature brake wear on one side.

A brake-related pull can also be caused from a restricted brake hose. The brake hoses supply fluid pressure to each wheel. If this rubber hose swells from years of contact with brake fluid and the environment, it may become restricted. A restricted hose will supply less pressure to the caliper on that side. This can cause a severe pull to the side with the *good* hose. A restricted hose will also cause the pads to wear very fast and get very hot. Brake hoses usually cost between $20 and $40 each. It is a good idea to replace hoses or calipers in pairs to insure that you will have even pressure to both wheels. However, if money is an issue, you can try replacing only the defective parts.

TRICKS OF THE TRADE

Brake pulls caused by brake hoses and calipers are the easiest to diagnose, but getting a second opinion is still a good idea. In this situation, do not share the first shop's opinion with the second shop. Let each technician form his own unbiased opinion. Caliper replacement can be expensive on some cars. Therefore, if you are not convinced that this is the problem because you get two or more different opinions from different technicians, you may want to try a simple, inexpensive experiment first: Take the brake pads *and* rotors from the left front, and move them to the right front, and vice versa. This little trick has solved many brake pulls, but usually after hundreds of dollars are wasted on new calipers, hoses, master cylinders, and so on. In fact, if you experience a pull only under heavy brake use, as in a sudden stop, there is a good chance that this will solve the problem. This routine should cost about $30 to $50, but could save big money!

It may also be money well spent to have the brakes bled before authorizing questionable or expensive repairs. Air trapped in a caliper or hose may cause a brake pull, which can be corrected with a $25 brake bleed. A severe pull, however, is usually caused by a brake hose or caliper, so these experiments don't have such good odds in this case.

Low Brake Pedal

Another frequent problem with the brake system is a low brake pedal. On most cars, the brake pedal travels about an inch or two before the brakes begin to work. If the pedal goes much farther than this or feels soft when the brakes are applied, most drivers get a little nervous, and justifiably so. After all, we are talking about brakes here!

Fortunately, a low pedal is normally caused by a simple thing called a **brake adjustment**. Brake adjustment is important on all cars, but can be a problem on cars with rear drum brakes, which is about 80 percent of the cars on the road today. So what is brake adjustment,

Never pay anyone to adjust disk brakes!

> The rear brakes should be adjusted every time the front brakes are repaired or if the brake pedal seems too low.

anyway? As you have learned, brake pads and shoes are pushed against rotors and drums, respectively, to stop a vehicle. You also know that pads and shoes wear thinner with use. Therefore, as the pads and shoes wear thin, more space is created between them and the rotors and drums. This means that they must travel farther to contact the rotors or drums. Since the brake pedal controls the movement of the pads and shoes, it must be pushed farther to make the brakes work. So to keep brake pedal movement to a minimum, the pads and shoes must be constantly adjusted closer to the rotors and drums, to keep the distance between them as small as possible.

Disk brakes adjust themselves every time the brakes are used, so there is no need to worry about brake adjustment on the front of any car. This also means that cars with *four-wheel* disk brakes never need a manual brake adjustment. Never pay anyone to adjust disk brakes! Cars with rear drum brakes are a different story. Drum brakes use an adjusting screw, called an ADJUSTER (*see illustration B4*), that "spins" to move the brake shoes as close as possible to the brake drums. This allows the brake shoes to contact the drum as soon as the brakes are applied, keeping the brake pedal high.

Rear (drum) brakes are *supposed* to self-adjust each time the car is backed up and the brakes are applied, but it doesn't always happen. Many people don't back up often enough to keep the brakes adjusted. Others don't use their brakes when they back up; they simply shift the car from reverse to drive without touching the brake (which is a no-no). Also, these adjusters are subjected to dirt, water, and brake dust, so they often get tight or freeze up. When this happens, as the brake shoes wear, they get farther and farther away from the brake drums, and the brake pedal must be pressed farther down to compensate. To correct this problem, rear brakes can be manually adjusted at a service center. This simple procedure requires removing the rear drums and spinning the adjuster until the shoes are close enough to the drums. This allows the brakes to begin working as soon as the brake pedal starts to move.

Most shops will charge between $10 and $30 to adjust both rear brakes. Some cars even have an adjuster slot behind the wheel that allows brake adjustment without taking the wheels or the brake drums off the car. The rear brakes should be adjusted every time the front brakes are repaired or if the brake pedal seems too low. Proper brake adjustment not only improves brake pedal travel, but it also helps to make the front brakes last longer by getting the maximum stopping power from the rear brakes.

Tiny Bubbles

Air bubbles can also cause a low brake pedal. When air enters a brake system, instead of transferring the brake pedal's energy like brake fluid, it absorbs some of the energy by "giving" or compressing. This can make the pedal too low and make it feel soft or spongy. The more air in a brake system, the more severe these problems will be. In fact, if enough air enters, the brakes will not work at all! So how does air get into a brake system?

Generally, for air to get into a system, fluid must get out. Most of the time, a leaky wheel cylinder or brake caliper will be the source. Other possibilities are brake hoses, lines, and master cylinders. A leaky wheel cylinder, for example, may push out a little fluid when the pedal is pushed and *inhale* some air when the pedal is released. This causes the pedal to get lower and softer each time the brakes are used. Another way for air to enter a brake system is during brake repairs. If any brake component that contains fluid is removed, this will allow fluid to leak out and air to leak in. The components listed above are examples of parts that hold brake fluid. Repairs such as pad, shoe, rotor, and drum replacement should not allow air into a system.

Bleeding Brakes

To remove air from a brake system, the brakes must be bled. This requires small screws at each wheel, called bleeder valves, to be opened, which allows the fluid to flow through all the components and out of the brake system. This flushes out the fluid and any trapped air that may be in the system and replaces it with new, air-free brake fluid. This procedure usually takes less than 30 minutes and should cost about $30 for most cars.

Of course there are other causes for a low brake pedal, such as a bad master cylinder or wheel cylinder, severely worn brake shoes, and others. A rear brake adjustment will correct most low pedals however, and having the brakes bled will correct most of the rest. As a matter of fact, if you are experiencing a low or soft pedal and the cause is not obvious to you or your technician, have him bleed and adjust your brakes before you authorize expensive brake repairs. This simple, inexpensive procedure may correct the problem and save you hundreds in unnecessary repairs. A dishonest service manager may even try to sell you a new master cylinder or new calipers to correct a problem *he knows* could be fixed by a brake adjustment or bleeding.

ANTI-LOCK BRAKES

If the wheels on a car are sliding instead of rolling, your car is controlled only by the laws of physics, not by the steering wheel. Like a raging river, it will take the path of least resistance instead of the direction the wheels are pointing! Therefore, wheel lock-up during brake use can be very dangerous. Anti-lock brake systems were designed to prevent this. They make sure the wheels don't lock up even in dangerous situations such as driving in snow and ice, on a wet road, or during a panic stop. This allows you to steer the car as usual, even if the brake pedal is pushed to the limit.

Since about 1985, more and more cars have been equipped with anti-lock brake systems. Anti-lock brake systems, ABS for short, use all of the basic components that are found on a conventional brake system. They use brake pads, rotors, calipers, master cylinders, and so on. In fact, normal brake repairs on a car with ABS are no different from a standard system, so you do not have to take your car to the dealer or an anti-lock brake specialist for a simple brake job. What makes an ABS system different is the addition of electronic sensors, computers, and valves. These components are used in conjunction with the conventional brake system to prevent wheel lock-up. If your car is equipped with an ABS system, chances are pretty good that you will never have a problem with it. The following paragraphs will help you if you do.

A car with ABS has a **speed sensor** at each wheel. This sensor tells the **anti-lock brake computer** how fast the wheel is turning. The ABS computer monitors each wheel's speed, so it can detect if a wheel abruptly stops turning (locks up). If you depress the brakes hard enough to cause a wheel to lock up, the computer sends a signal to the **control valve,** which in turn decreases the brake fluid pressure to the appropriate wheel for a fraction of a second. This causes the wheel to start rotating again. When the wheels begin to rotate again, if you still have the pedal pushed hard enough to cause wheel lock-up, the cycle will begin again. This cycle will repeat several times a second and will cause a fast pumping sensation or vibration felt in the brake pedal. You may also hear the noise under the hood created by the valves and motors controlling the brake pressure. This is normal, but may seem odd the first time you feel it.

> ...normal brake repairs on a car with ABS are no different from a standard system, so you do not have to take your car to the dealer or an anti-lock brake specialist for a simple brake job.

It is a good idea to read the owner's manual for your car to learn the proper way to use your anti-lock brakes. It may also be helpful to practice using your anti-lock brakes on a wet, secluded parking lot, to familiarize yourself with your ABS system and the noises and sensations it makes during stops. A panic style stop from about 15 miles per hour should do the trick. Make sure there are no other motorists or pedestrians in the area.

Some vehicles are equipped with ABS brakes that control only the rear wheels. Such systems are found on most American light trucks built between 1988 and 1997. These vehicles have sensors and control valves for the rear brakes only. This helps the age-old problem, unique to trucks, caused by the wide range of loads carried over the rear wheels, depending on what is in the back. The rear wheel anti-lock feature keeps the rear wheels from locking up, regardless of the weight on the rear wheels.

The anti-lock brake computer not only controls the valves that limit the brake pressure, it also monitors each electrical component of the anti-lock brake system. If the computer receives a signal from one or more of these components that is not considered normal, the computer will cause the anti-lock, or ABS, brake light to stay on. Usually this will not affect the regular brake system. It will, however, disable the anti-lock feature on most systems. **In other words, the vehicle will still have brakes, but not anti-lock brakes, until the system is repaired.** Some common causes that will turn on an ABS light are a faulty or dirty wheel speed sensor, a blown brake fuse, damaged wiring, or a faulty control valve or computer.

The computer will help a technician find the exact problem by giving a trouble code that pinpoints the circuit that is not normal. This trouble code is retrieved by grounding an ABS test wire and reading the number of coded flashes from the ABS light. The trouble codes can also be read from a testing device, known as a scanner, which plugs into the computer's test connector and monitors the circuits in the computer. These diagnostics require a technician with a good knowledge of anti-lock brakes. After retrieving the trouble codes, the technician should look up the meaning of the code and follow a procedure outlined in a repair manual to determine which part of the ABS system is at fault. It can, and usually will, take some time to perform this type of testing. Also, any time an ABS light is on, the entire brake system should be thoroughly checked. This includes the conventional brake system components at every wheel. In some cases, a faulty conventional part, such as a leaky wheel cylinder, can cause the ABS light to come on.

With this basic understanding of anti-lock brakes, you will be able to ask a technician questions to find out if he or she knows enough to tackle an ABS problem. Some questions to ask are, "Do you have diagnostic equipment for my car?" "Do you have diagnostic repair manuals that cover my car?" and "Are you trained or certified to repair anti-lock brakes by a certification company?" In many cases the only place to find a person with the right answers is at the dealership. Although you will usually pay more for a specific repair at a dealer, they will probably know more about the system and will have the equipment needed for your car. They may be able to diagnose the problem correctly the first time, and therefore save you money. Also, in defense of many knowledgeable and competent technicians out there, let me say that just because a technician does not have certification to repair brakes, or to do any other type of auto repair, it does not mean that he or she is not qualified to do the job. Many competent and experienced technicians simply never take the tests to get these certifications (*for more on problems that are difficult to diagnose, please see the section on driveability*).

CARSMART

BRAKE SYSTEM GLOSSARY

Note: A bold word *within* a definition is defined elsewhere in this glossary.

ADJUSTER: A screw located between the **brake shoes,** which is used to keep the brakes adjusted properly. This screw is turned automatically during braking or can be manually adjusted by a technician. Size: $1/2$" round by 3" long. Price: $20 each (two per car). Location: inside brake drum on both rear wheels.

BACKING PLATE: The thin metal part of a brake pad or shoe. The **friction material** is bonded or riveted to this plate. The backing plate grinds into the **rotor** or **drum** if the brake pads wear completely out. Size: Pad: 2" x 6" x $1/4$" thick; shoe: 2" x 10" x $1/4$" thick. Price: comes with brake pads; see brake pads. Location: see brake pad.

BLEED BRAKES: Small valves are opened at the wheels to allow old brake fluid to escape, as it is replaced with new fluid. This removes all of the air from the lines and components, which is necessary for a firm brake pedal. Price: about $30 for four wheels.

BRAKE CALIPERS: (calipers) These devices use pressure created by the **master cylinder** to press the brake pads against the rotors, which causes the car to stop. Calipers are used with disk brakes only. Size: 4" x 6" x 4". Price: $25–$75+. Location: near wheel, one per wheel.

BRAKE DRUMS: (drums) Brake drums rotate with the wheels. The **brake shoes** rub against the inside of the drums to stop the car. Drums are used only on the rear wheels and only with **drum brakes.** Size: 10" round x 3". Price: $30–$100+. Location: near rear wheels, one per wheel.

BRAKE PADS: (pads) Pads are plates made of a metal **backing plate** and a layer of **friction material**. Pads are pressed against the **rotors** by the **calipers**, to stop the car. Pads are designed to wear out with use. Pads are always used on the front and sometimes on the rear, and are used with **disk brakes** only. Size: 2" x 6" x $3/4$" thick. Price: $20–$50 per set of 4. Location: near wheels, two per wheel.

BRAKE ROTOR: (rotor) Rotors are disk-like plates that rotate with the wheels. **Brake pads** rub against the rotors to stop the car. Rotors are used only with **disk brakes.** Size: 9" round x 1" thick. Price: $20–$100+. Location: near wheel, one per wheel.

Brake shoes: Brake shoes are half-round plates with a metal **backing plate** and a layer of **friction material**. Brake shoes rub against the **brake drums** to stop the car. Brake shoes are designed to wear out with use. Shoes are always used with **drum brakes** and are never used on front. Size: 2" wide x 10" half round. Price: $20–$40 per set of 4. Location: near rear wheels, inside drum, two per wheel.

Disk brakes: Disk brakes are a system, not a specific part. A disk brake system consists of **brake pads, brake rotors,** and **brake calipers.** Disk brakes are used on the front of all modern cars. Many cars have disk brakes on all four wheels.

Drum brakes: Drum brakes are a system, not a specific part. A drum brake system consists of **brake shoes, brake drums,** and **wheel cylinders.** Drum brakes are used only on the rear. Many cars built in the past ten years do not use drum brakes.

Machine the rotors: (turn the rotors) This operation removes a thin layer of metal from a **brake rotor,** to smooth out any grooves in the rotor or to correct a brake-related vibration. This operation can also be performed on **brake drums.**

Friction material: This is a layer of semi-hard material, about one-half inch thick when new, which is bonded to the **backing plates** of **brake pads** and **brake shoes.** This material rubs against the **rotors** and **drums** to stop the car. A semi-metallic pad has small metal particles imbedded into the friction material. Size, Price, and Location: see brake pads.

Master cylinder: The master cylinder is a pump that creates pressure in the brake fluid. The master cylinder is operated by pressing on the brake pedal. This pressure is used to press the **brake pads** or **brake shoes** against the **brake rotors** or **brake drums.** The brake fluid is stored in the master cylinder. Size: 4" x 4" x 8". Price: $30–$130+. Location: under hood, near driver.

Power booster: (brake booster) The power booster uses suction from the engine to help you press the brake pedal. Power boosters are bolted to the **master cylinder** and are found on all cars with power brakes. If a booster fails, the brake pedal will be extremely hard. Size: 10" round x 6" thick. Price: $150+. Location: under hood, near driver.

Proportioning valve: A valve which sends more fluid pressure to the front than to the rear. This keeps the rear brakes from locking up prematurely. These valves rarely fail.

Warning sensor: (brake squealer) A warning sensor is a tiny metal tab, located on the **brake pads,** that begins to rub against the **brake rotor** when the pads are about 80 to 90 percent worn. This creates a high-pitched squeak that usually stops when the brakes are pressed. This noise tells the driver that the pads are ready to be replaced.

Wheel cylinders: Wheel cylinders use pressure created by the **master cylinder** to push the **brake shoes** against the **brake drums,** which stops the car. Wheel cylinders are used with **drum brakes** only. Size: 1" round x 3". Price: $15–$50. Location: inside brake drums, near rear wheels, one per wheel.

ALIGNMENT

This section has some of the most technical terminology used in this book. However, there is a great deal of information in this section that will save you money. If you find yourself getting lost in the first few paragraphs, don't give up. There will be some very useful and easy-to-understand information a little later.

An alignment is not a tangible thing, it is a description of how the wheels and tires are angled on a car or truck. **When you purchase an alignment, you are aren't buying a product, you are paying someone to adjust these angles so they match the angles the manufacturer intended.** When engineers design a car, they determine the wheel alignment that will cause the least amount of wear to the tires and that will make the car drive and handle its best. Before a new car leaves the assembly line, the alignment is set to these specifications. In a perfect world, these angles would stay that way for many years. But this is not, so they don't. When a car is driven, the wheels encounter many bumps, holes, jolts, and occasional accidents — all of which can cause the alignment angles to change. In addition, front-end parts can wear and begin to sag, which also causes the alignment to change. Therefore, manufacturers publish the correct angles, called **alignment specifications,** which are different for every model. These specifications are distributed to alignment shops all over the country who are ready and waiting for someone to come along and ask for, or be sold, an alignment. The sad truth is that unnecessary alignments are done all the time — but you are about to learn how to prevent it from happening to you.

There are basically two types of alignments: **front-wheel** alignments, and **four-wheel** alignments. The obvious difference is that a front alignment checks and adjusts only the front wheels, while a four-wheel alignment deals with both the front and rear. The type you need depends mostly on the type of car you own. On most *cars* built in the last ten or fifteen years, the alignment can be adjusted at all four wheels. On all trucks and most vans, sport utility vehicles, and older rear-wheel-drive cars, only the front wheels can be adjusted. Other cars may be easily adjusted on front, but require special tools and procedures to adjust the rear. Just because a car can be adjusted at all wheels does not mean that it should be. More often that not, the rear wheels don't need to be adjusted as often as the front, so a front alignment may be all that is needed. This little secret is often guarded by a repair center, however, because a four-wheel alignment costs about twice as much. The following paragraphs will help you know when you need an alignment, and which wheels should be aligned. But first you need to know what angles are adjustable and what terms are used to describe these angles. Don't worry, this is easier than it sounds.

CASTER, CAMBER, & TOE

Caster, camber, and **toe** are the three angles that make up an alignment. If these angles are not set to specifications, tires will wear unevenly and the car *may* pull to one side. Bad alignment can even decrease your gas mileage because your car is harder to push down the road. A basic understanding of caster, camber, and toe angles will help you know when you need an alignment, and when you don't, which can save you hundreds of dollars over time. You don't need to become an

ASKING FOR IT!

Could you check my alignment? Translation: "I would like to pay for an alignment, whether I need it or not." This is an exaggeration, but not by much. Since the average car owner wouldn't know if a technician actually adjusted the alignment or not, many times they are charged for an alignment they don't even get. I have seen technicians pretend to align a car that was okay, just so they would get paid for the alignment. In fact, I was recently told by an alignment machine salesperson that he had sold a $20,000 alignment machine to a company that did not do alignments. This sounded crazy at first, but it told me just how easy an individual or company can be ripped off on an alignment. I asked the man, "Why would anyone buy a machine they won't use?" He explained that this company owned a fleet of hundreds of cars that were maintained by independent repair shops. Whenever a repair center was asked to "check" an alignment, it seemed that it was always out and a $30 alignment was in order. The fleet company decided to buy an alignment machine and train someone just to check alignments. Then, the repair centers would only align the cars that actually needed an alignment. This saved the company enough money to pay for the machine in a matter of a few of years! The fact of the matter is, if you ask for an alignment, or a simple check, you will probably pay for an alignment whether you need it or not. The key is to know when you need one and when you don't. The good news is, you don't have to buy a $20,000 machine!

CARSMART

alignment specialist — just learn the basic angles and terms. You may be surprised to discover that many alignment technicians don't fully understand these angles — they know how to adjust alignment with the help of a high-tech machine, but they don't really know what they are doing, or why. Of course, if they make an alignment match the specifications, they are getting the job done.

Like these technicians, you only need to understand the elements that apply to your needs. You need to know how to recognize when you need an alignment and how to communicate effectively with a service manager. If you walk into an alignment center and tell the service manager that you think your toe-in or camber is out of specification, you may get some strange looks, but you better believe you will also get respect as a knowledgeable customer. If you don't catch on to some of this, don't worry, the really important (money-saving) information comes a little later.

> a toe angle that is out of specification by one-half inch can destroy both front tires in a few thousand miles!

TOE-IN...TOE-OUT

The most important alignment angle is the **toe angle,** also known as **toe-in**. This is the most important because it can cause very rapid tire wear. In fact, a toe angle that is out of specification by one-half inch can destroy both front tires in a few thousand miles! The toe is the angle that describes how the wheels are pointing in relation to each other. Imagine that your feet on roller skates are a car's wheels. If both feet are pointing perfectly straight ahead, your toe angle is zero (*see illustration A1*); the distance between your toes is the same as the distance between your heels. When you roll along with zero toe, both feet are pointing in the same direction, and there is

A1 - TOE ANGLES

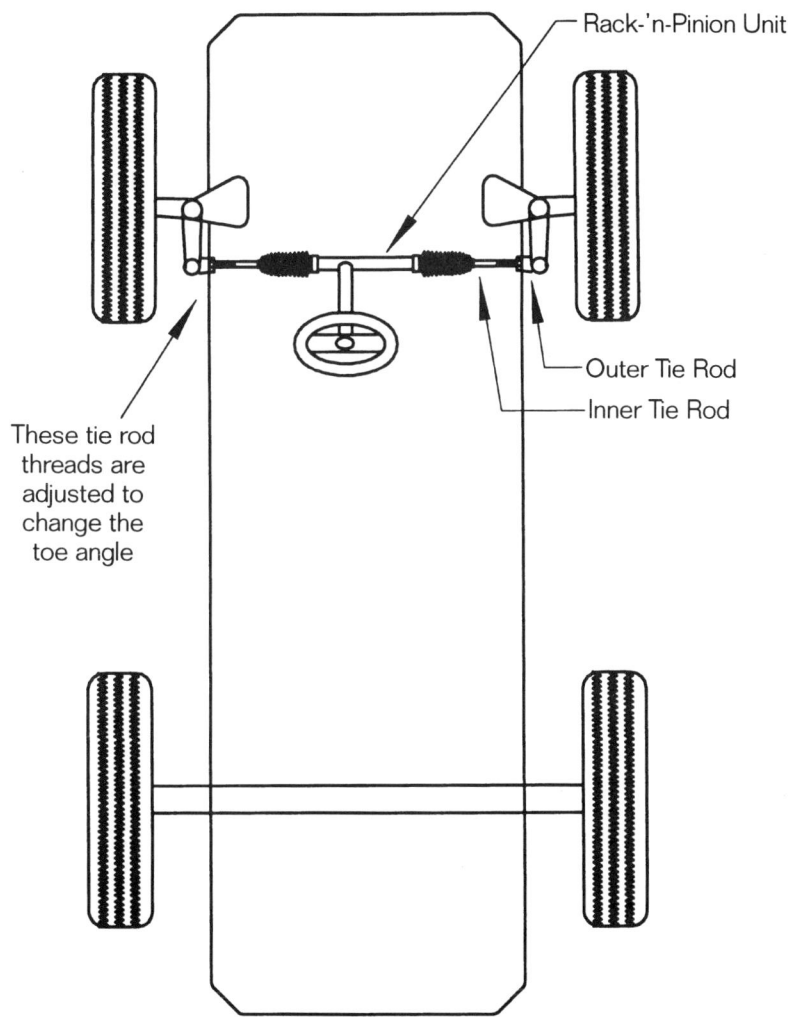

This view from above shows the toe angles of all four wheels. Here, all four wheels are facing straight ahead and are aligned with the direction of the car. This example represents a car with zero toe on the front and rear wheels. This is how most cars are aligned to achieve the least amount of tire wear and drag.

no unnecessary force on your feet or the skates. If you point your toes together, however, they are toed in (*see illustration A2*). If, for instance, your toes are one inch closer together than your heels, your feet are toed in one inch. If you try to skate with your feet pointed together this way, you will have to force one or both skates to slide somewhat against their natural direction. **Toe-out** means the heels are closer together than the toes (*see illustration A3*).

The toe angle on a car works the same way. If the two front wheels are pointed towards each other, they are toed in. The toe angle is the distance between the front of the wheels, compared to the distance between the back of the same wheels. The front wheels and the rear wheels have toe angles, although many cars have toe adjustments for the front only. A car with rear adjustable toe angles may be a candidate for a four-wheel alignment.

An out-of-toe alignment can devour tires in a hurry, because the wheels don't agree which direction your car should go. The left wheel may be pointed to the left, while the right wheel is pointed to the right. Unless your car can go two directions at once, something has got to give. That something is the tires! In this situation, instead of rolling along in a natural, straight direction, the tires are dragged across the pavement at a slight angle. As you know, a rubber tire is much softer than pavement, so the tires lose their tread. A toe angle problem can also cause a vehicle to dart from left to right, especially on a wet road. Since the tires are fighting for two directions, the tire with the most traction will win. On a road with wet and dry spots, a car may wander back and forth as the tires hit these spots and gain or lose their grip.

Excessive tire wear is the most common symptom and the easiest to diagnose. A toe-in problem generally wears *both* front tires on the outside edges, while a toe-out problem wears the inside edges. A severe toe angle problem will cause severe tire wear. The tires may look like new on one side, but are completely worn out on the other. The next time your car is on a rack for an oil change or tire rotation, look at the tires. If you notice uneven wear on the front or rear tires, the alignment is probably out. If the wear is evident on the front only, the rear alignment is probably all right. In such cases, ask for a front alignment only, even if your car is adjustable at the rear. The rear wheels are much less likely to be out of alignment, and you will pay about $20 to $30

A2 - TOE-IN

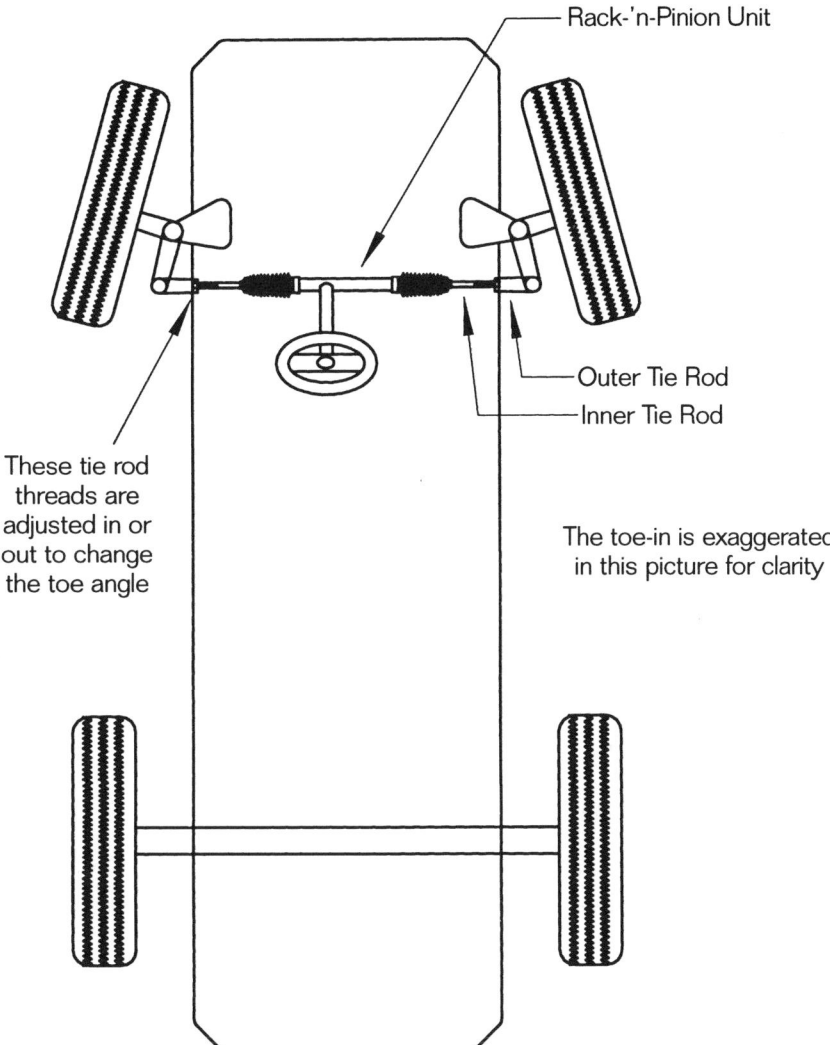

This picture shows the front wheels with excessive toe-in. As you can see, the front edges of the front tires are closer together than the rear edges. This will cause rapid wear to the outside of both front tires, because the tires are fighting to go in different directions. The front toe is most often the angle that gets out of adjustment, but the rear toe can get out in some cases. To adjust the toe, the tie rod ends are adjusted to become shorter or longer.

A3 - TOE-OUT

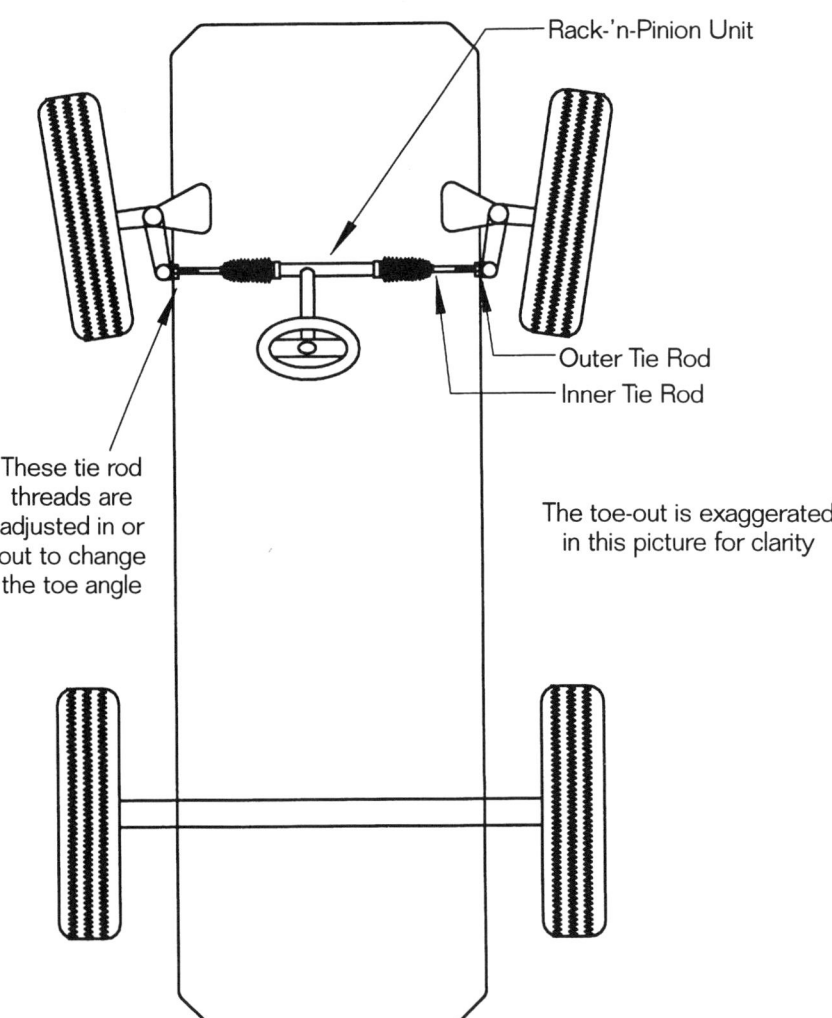

These tie rod threads are adjusted in or out to change the toe angle

The toe-out is exaggerated in this picture for clarity

In this example, the front wheels are severely toed out. This means the tires are angled outward, which causes rapid wear to the inside of both front tires. Since the tires are pointed in opposite directions, they are forced to slide across the road at an angle. This not only wears the tires quickly, but it takes more energy (gas) to push the car. The rear tires on some cars can also have toe angle problems.

more for something you may not need. But if there is any doubt, a four-wheel check can be money well spent.

Standing Tall

The second most important alignment angle is the **camber.** This angle describes how each tire is standing up in relation to the road. If a tire is perfectly straight up and does not lean in or out at the top, its camber angle is zero. If a tire's top tilts *in*, it is said to a have **negative camber** (*see illustration A4*). When the top of a tire leans *out*, this is called **positive camber** (*see illustration A5*). On most cars, the camber angle should be close to zero, which keeps the entire tread in even contact with the road, allowing it to wear evenly. The specified camber angle on many cars may be slightly in or out to compensate for a loaded car, or changes in the alignment during motion. But when a tire leans in or out too much, more pressure is placed on one side of the tire, and the tire will wear faster on that side.

Unlike incorrect toe angle, which wears both front tires, camber wear affects only the tire with the problem. For example, if the left wheel has too much negative camber and the right wheel is okay, the left tire will wear on the inside, while the right tire wears evenly. In fact, a combination of camber and toe problems can cause many wear combinations, such as one tire wearing on the inside, and the other on the outside.

Most vehicles have some type of camber adjustment on the front, but few have camber adjustments on the rear. Many cars without rear camber adjustments can be adjusted by using special shims or bolts however. But here again, this means extra dollars, so if the rear tires show no sign of uneven wear, a front alignment should do the trick.

Straight Ahead

The other angle that is sometimes adjustable on the *front* wheels is the **caster.** This angle is the most difficult to understand because it can not be seen. Therefore, instead of trying to explain the angle, let's just talk about what caster does. The caster angle does two things. It makes the steering wheel automatically return to center after the wheel is turned, and it prevents a car from pulling to one side of the road. How can an alignment angle do all this? The caster angle makes the front of a car raise slightly when the wheels are turned, and lower when they are pointed straight ahead. If you want to feel this, lean against the front of

A4 - NEGATIVE CAMBER

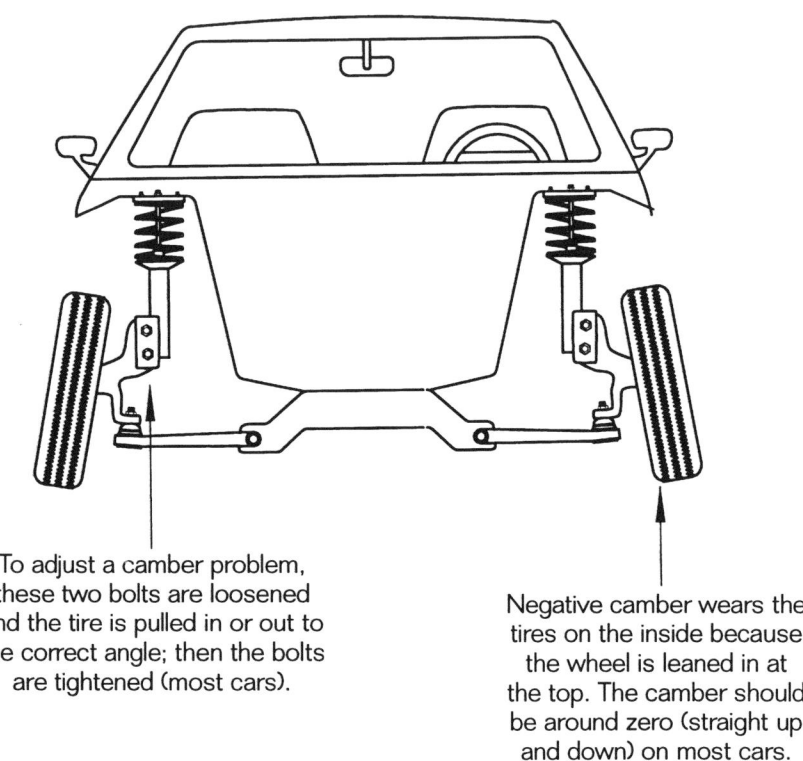

To adjust a camber problem, these two bolts are loosened and the tire is pulled in or out to the correct angle; then the bolts are tightened (most cars).

Negative camber wears the tires on the inside because the wheel is leaned in at the top. The camber should be around zero (straight up and down) on most cars.

The car in this example has severe negative camber. Negative camber will cause a tire to wear on the inside. Both tires, or just one, may be negative. Rear tires can also have camber problems. Negative camber is more common than positive camber, because as a car settles with age, gravity causes the tire to lean in. The above illustration is somewhat exaggerated, but you can sometimes see a camber problem with the naked eye. Many cars have adjustments for camber on the front and rear wheels. If there is no adjustment, a camber problem can be corrected by pulling the frame on a frame-bending machine.

A5 - POSITIVE CAMBER

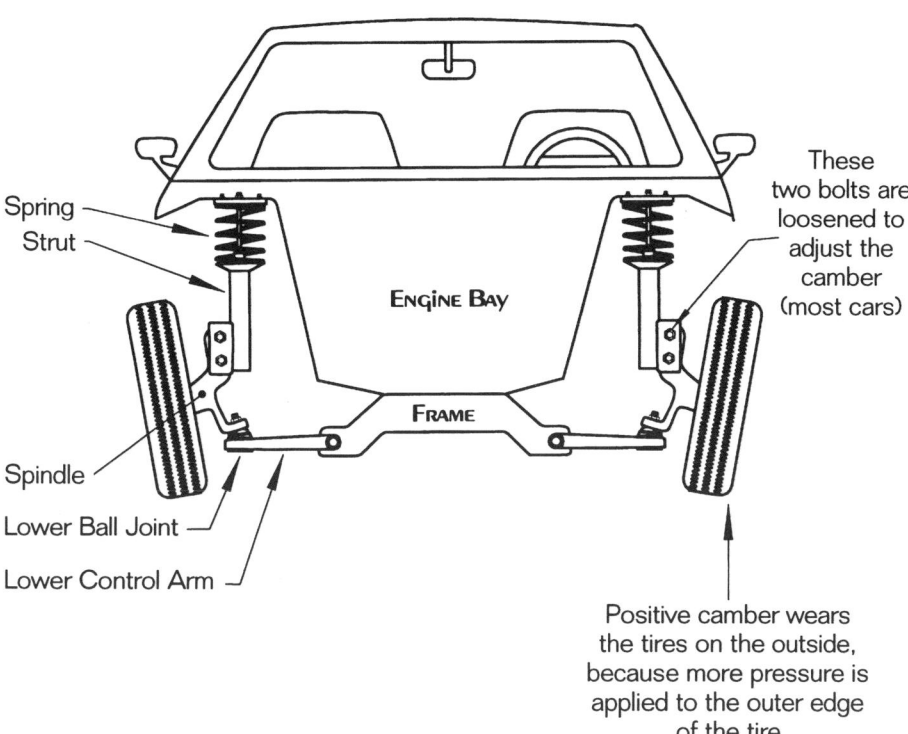

This example shows a positive camber. As you can see, the top of the tire leans out. This causes wear to the outside of the tire. One or both front wheels can have camber problems, as well as the rear tires on some vehicles. Most cars are set at the factory with the camber angle near zero. That is, the tires stand straight up and down.

a car while someone turns the steering wheel. You will feel the car raise and lower. (Some cars move more than others.) The caster angle uses gravity to center the steering wheel. Just as gravity will cause a ball to settle at the bottom of a bowl, it makes a car drive straight when the caster is adjusted properly. The more caster angle a car has, the more it will try to return to center.

For a car to drive straight, the caster angle on the left must be the same as the caster angle on the right. If there is a significant difference, a pull to one side *may* be the result because the natural lowest point no longer occurs with the wheels straight ahead. Instead, the lowest point is shifted slightly to one side and the car will pull in that direction. To correct a caster-related pull, the caster angles are adjusted to specifications.

Unfortunately, the caster angle is adjustable on fewer and fewer cars made today. In fact, most front-wheel-drive cars have no adjustment for caster. Most trucks and rear-wheel-drive cars, however, do. The good news is, most front-wheel-drive cars are very forgiving to slight variations in caster. On these cars, the caster will very seldom cause a pull, unless there is a significant amount of difference from one side to the other. More good news — a caster problem will not normally cause uneven tire wear. Before getting an alignment to correct a pull, be sure to read the next section!

ALIGNMENT PROBLEM?...OR NOT!

Alignments are accused of causing many problems. **The alignment is often blamed for shakes, shimmies, pulls, and uneven tire wear, but many times the alignment is innocent of all charges.** In fact, other than uneven tire wear, alignments normally have no symptoms. Why are alignments so often wrongly accused? Some service centers like to lead customers to believe an alignment will solve unrelated problems as an easy way to make money. But mostly, misdiagnosed alignment symptoms are handed down from generation to generation by *car owners*. Money is thrown away on unnecessary alignments because people assume if a shake or pull can be felt in the steering wheel, the alignment must be the cause. This is not always true. Millions of dollars have been wasted on alignments that should not have been done. The following paragraphs will show how to prevent this from happening to you!

Pulling in Your Favor

Remember, alignment (caster) seldom causes a modern car to pull. But cars pull all the time — therefore something else must be the culprit. The most common reason today's cars pull to one side is...tires! Millions of dollars are wasted because people assume that if a car pulls, it needs a front-end alignment. This myth was once a truth; before front-wheel-drive cars and radial tires came along, the alignment was indeed the cause of most pulls. For over fifty years, people were told they needed an alignment to correct a pull, and this "wisdom" continues to hang around.

Today however, tires cause most pulls. A **tire pull** is caused when one front tire is harder to roll than the other. This can happen because there are slight variations in the internal construction of two tires. If the tire on the left front is harder to roll than the tire on the right, the car will pull to the left, and vice versa. The two tires don't have to be different brands; two identical tires can have different rolling characteristics. Also, if a tire becomes separated (when the steel belts inside the tire begin to unwind), it will usually cause a severe pull. Or a tire with low air pressure can cause a pull to that side because a low tire is harder to roll than a properly inflated one. Trucks, full size vans, and most sport utility vehicles may offer an exception to all this. Many of these vehicles still come with caster adjustments, so on these vehicles a pull can be caused by the alignment. But tires can also be the cause of a pull on these vehicles, so a tire pull should be eliminated first.

Most of the time, a pull can be corrected by simply rotating the tires and inflating them evenly. If you have a car or truck that is pulling,

> **The biggest reason that money is thrown away on unnecessary alignments is because people assume if a shake or pull can be felt in the steering wheel, the alignment must be the cause.**
>
> **This is not always true.**

be sure to check the pressure in all four tires before doing anything. If the pressure is okay, have the tires rotated from front to rear, or if the tires don't need to be rotated at this time, just swap the two front tires. Then, drive the car again to see what happens. If the pull goes away or changes direction, you have a tire pull. If the pull stays the same, or gets worse, you may have an alignment problem, or both. If your car stops pulling after rotating the tires, leave the tires where they are and be happy you saved $40! If the pull switched directions, have the tires thoroughly checked for separation by a tire specialist. If no obvious tire problems are found, try a few different rotations to see if the problem can be corrected. If tires are switched enough, the pull should go away.

A tire pull does not necessarily mean you have a bad tire; many times a tire can cause a pull, but will give perfectly good service otherwise. If rotating the tires doesn't correct a problem, get the front alignment checked, just to be sure. Ask the alignment technician to pay close attention to the caster angles. **Watch out for a shop who charges you for an alignment to correct a pull, and then switches the front tires while the car is on the rack.** They may realize that the problem was not in the alignment, but would rather charge you the $40 for an alignment, than $10 for a tire rotation! This is why you try tire rotation *before* going to an alignment shop. If the alignment checks out okay and you still have a pull, you may have to purchase new tires. Also be aware that a very slight pull to the right may be normal, caused by the slope built into most highways. Many cars will slowly drift towards the low side of a sloping road.

SHAKING THINGS UP

Another symptom that causes many dollars to be wrongfully spent on front-end alignments is a shake or shimmy in the steering wheel. The number one cause of this symptom is, you guessed it, tires! True, years ago, alignments did cause shimmies or shakes, but it is very rare today. If you were to ask your dad, or grandfather what to do to correct a steering wheel vibration, he will probably tell you to get a front-end alignment, but chances are this won't help at all. Modern cars have a very stable front-end structure compared to cars built years ago; therefore, they seldom cause such problems.

On the other hand, a tire that is only a few ounces out of balance can cause vibration in the steering wheel. Tires that are not perfectly round or that are separated can also cause a shimmy or shake. Such a tire may have a "knot" or bulge in the tread, which can cause a very bad bounce or make the entire car wobble from side to side. This is almost never caused by the alignment. Before paying anyone to align the front end to correct a shake or shimmy, have the tires balanced and checked for roundness and separations. This may fix the problem and will probably cost less *and* prevent a trip back to the shop. Many repair shops will try to mislead you into thinking that an alignment will solve a shimmy, knowing full well that the problem is in the tires. This way, they not only charge you for an alignment, but they may also get to balance your tires later!

A defective drive axle can also cause a shimmy or wobble in the steering. A front-wheel-drive car uses two axle shafts, which spin to drive the front wheels. If the inner portion of an axle becomes worn to a point that the axle rotates off center, the entire front of the car may shake violently. You can diagnose the cause of such a problem by paying attention to when the vibration or wobble occurs. If the shake occurs mostly when you are accelerating and stops when you let off the gas pedal, it is probably a worn axle. If speeding up or slowing down has little or no effect, a separated tire may be suspected. If the shake occurs only during braking, more than likely the problem is the brake rotors (*see the sections on front suspension and brakes*). As you can see, the alignment is way down the list for a potential cause of a vibration, and all of these possibilities should be explored before getting the alignment checked.

More Misconceptions

So, now you know you don't get an alignment to correct a pull or a vibration. But uneven tire wear is a sure sign of a bad

C A R S M A R T

alignment, right? Sorry, it's not that simple. **Low tire pressure can cause uneven wear that looks very much like alignment wear, and it is one reason many people get alignments they don't need.** Unlike alignment wear however, which wears a tire on *one* side, low pressure causes a tire to wear on *both* sides (*see Illustration A6*). When a tire is low, more weight is applied to the outer edges, so the tread wears faster there, while the tread in the center of the tire is still good. This type of wear is almost always caused by low pressure, and the alignment may be perfect.

Many shops happily let you spend money on an alignment, knowing that low tire pressure was the cause of uneven wear. To prevent this, you must learn what low pressure wear looks like and check your tire pressure regularly. Radial tires need at least 30 pounds of pressure; anything less will cause rapid wear. If you see a tire with this type of wear, have it checked for a puncture or other causes for a leak. **The only way to know for sure if your tires are properly inflated is to check them with a tire gauge** (*see "Under Pressure" in the tire section*).

Another common mistake made with alignments is assuming that your car needs an alignment when new tires are installed. The truth is, if your alignment was good before the tires were installed, it will be good afterwards. Changing tires does not affect alignment. The best way to determine if you need an alignment with new tires is to look at the old tires. Ask the service manager to show you the old tires after they have been removed from the car. If all four tires are worn evenly across the tread, you probably don't even need to have the alignment checked. Also, if some of the tires are worn equally on both edges, low pressure was probably the cause. When your old tires indicate the alignment is good, you can wait and see how the new tires are doing at the next rotation, which should happen in 5,000 miles. As long as tires wear evenly, the alignment is okay. If there is any doubt, check the alignment just to be sure; after all, you don't want to damage the new tires with a bad alignment. Many tire centers will offer to check your alignment for free when you purchase new tires. Remember to be careful — a free check usually ends up being an alignment.

Finally!

So far, we have covered many reasons *not* to get an alignment, but cars *do* need to be aligned occasionally. Knowing when to get an alignment is as important as knowing when not to. An alignment is needed when a car wears at least one tire on its edge. In fact, this type

A6 - UNEVEN TIRE WEAR

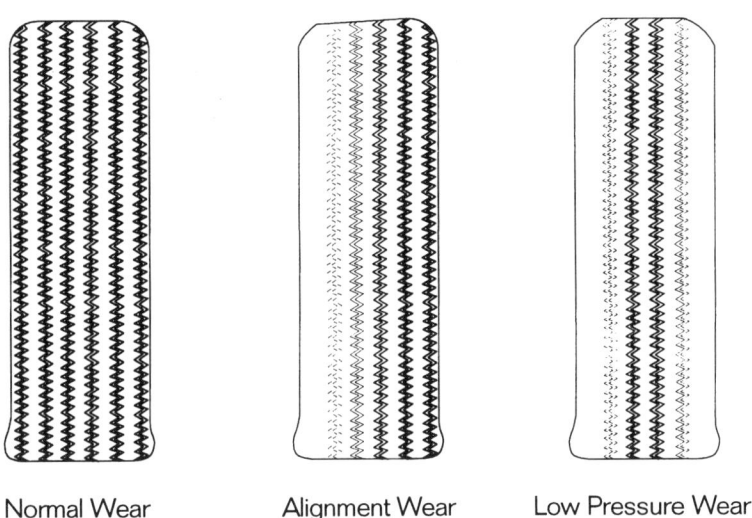

Normal Wear   Alignment Wear   Low Pressure Wear

Here are three examples of tire wear. The tire on the left shows normal tire wear. This tire is worn evenly across the tread, with no noticeable thin areas. A car that wears the tires in this way does not need an alignment. The tire wear on the right is caused by running the tire with low air pressure for an extended period. This wear is equal on both outer edges. If there is no noticeable difference in wear from one edge to the other, the alignment is probably okay. The wear on the tire in the center is caused by an alignment problem such as camber, toe-in, or both. You can see the tread is worn on one edge only. This could be the outer edge or the inner edge depending on the alignment problem. This tire wear can occur on the front or the rear. If the front tires are worn this way, but the rear tires are worn evenly, a front-wheel alignment is all you need.

> ...a regular inspection of the tires should give you plenty of warning about an alignment problem.

of wear is *usually* the only indication of an out-of-specification alignment. Since tire wear is the signal to look for, a regular inspection of the tires should give you plenty of warning about an alignment problem.

It is easy to overlook tire wear when the tires are on the car and the car is on the ground, so the best time to look for uneven wear is when the tires are rotated or when the oil is changed. During these repairs, your car is in the air and you can see the entire surface of the tire with ease. Don't be afraid to ask the service manager to take you to your car and show you the tires. If you notice one or more tires wearing on one side, have the alignment checked. If the front tires are uneven, but the rear tires look okay, just do the front.

Remember, if you have wear on *both* sides of a tire, or an unusual wear pattern, it is probably caused by something else, such as low pressure or a lack of tire rotation. But there is another clue to when you *may* need an alignment — a steering wheel that is tilted to one side when the car is going straight. This indicates that the front or rear toe angles (or both) are out of specification. This does not necessarily mean that the tires will wear unevenly, however. In such cases, the car's "thrust" angle may be off, but the tires may wear evenly (more on this later). One other reminder mentioned earlier: A pull to one side can be caused by an alignment problem, but a tire pull should be eliminated first.

COMMUNICATION IS THE KEY

When going into a service center for an alignment, be sure to state exactly why you want an alignment. If you don't, you diminish your chances for getting the problem corrected the first time, for the least amount of money. Your direction helps the technician know what to look for and places the responsibility for fixing the problem in his hands. It eliminates the "I didn't know you were having *that* problem" excuse. Many people walk into a store and ask for an alignment and never bother to tell the service manager why they think they need one. If the problem was not caused by alignment, their money was wasted.

It's also a good idea to ask about warranties. Most shops will warranty an alignment for a period of time or miles, so ask the service manager what is covered by warranty and for how long. Be sure your receipt reflects the date and mileage when the alignment was done. If the shop has a computerized alignment machine, ask for the computer printout of your alignment. This can be very valuable if a problem arises later.

THRUST ANGLE OR NOT?

A little earlier you read that there are two kinds of alignments: the front wheel, and the four wheel. This was not the whole truth, however. There is a third type called a **thrust angle alignment**. When you go into a shop for an alignment, you may be asked if you would like a thrust alignment, especially if your car or truck is adjustable on the front only. To answer this question well, you must know what a thrust angle alignment is and what is does.

First of all, a thrust alignment is a type of front alignment, because the rear wheels are not adjusted. A thrust alignment insures the steering wheel will be centered, (level) when the alignment is finished, while a regular front alignment may not. How is this? A thrust alignment "checks" the rear wheels and then compensates the steering wheel to allow for any rear alignment problems (*see illustration* A7). It does nothing for the rear alignment problem, but in effect, puts a bandage on it. A front alignment on the other hand *assumes* the rear is okay. Both alignments prevent uneven tire wear, however. So which type do you need? The best advice is to have a regular front-wheel alignment first. The chances are good that the steering wheel will be straight, and you will save about $20. Afterwards, if the steering wheel is not perfectly level, you can either return to the shop and pay the difference for the thrust alignment, or you can wait until the next time you need an alignment and ask for a thrust alignment then. If your car's alignment is good otherwise, an unlevel steering wheel will not cause uneven tire wear, make your car pull, or affect the driving characteristics of you car.

If they are not all that important, why does the service manager try to sell you a thrust angle alignment? Profit! A thrust alignment costs from $10 to $20 more, so you can expect a little pressure to buy one. The service manager may tell you the advantages of a thrust angle alignment, dazzling you with drawings or hand gestures, but the truth is, the only advantage a thrust angle alignment gives you is making the steering wheel straight. Let the service manager know that you know the difference, and he will probably leave you alone! As a matter of fact, before sophisticated four-wheel alignment machines came along, there was no such thing as a thrust angle alignment. Back then, mechanics had to straighten steering wheels by the trial and error method or leave them crooked. Of course, if you own a car that has rear alignment adjustments, an unleveled steering wheel could indicate a rear alignment problem. In these cases, a four-wheel alignment may be a good idea.

A7 - THRUST ANGLE

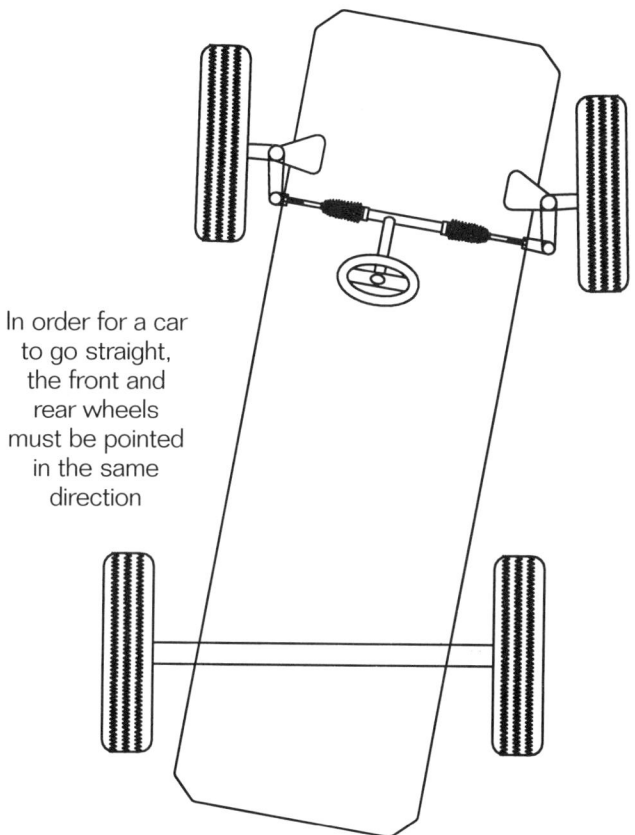

In order for a car to go straight, the front and rear wheels must be pointed in the same direction

If the rear wheels are not straight, the car will go down the road a little sideways! To compensate for this, the front wheels must be steered slightly to one side. This, in turn, will cause the steering wheel to tilt to one side. A regular front-wheel alignment assumes that the rear wheels are straight, so the steering wheel will still be crooked afterwards. However, a thrust angle alignment "checks" the rear wheels, and then adjusts the steering wheel accordingly. Therefore, a thrust angle alignment insures that the steering wheel will be straight even if the rear wheels are out of alignment, but it does nothing about the rear alignment problem. A thrust angle alignment will not improve tire wear compared to a regular alignment; it simply makes the steering wheel straight.

SHOCKS & STRUTS

Any auto repair is a candidate for fraud, but shock and strut replacement is among the most likely. Millions of dollars are thrown away each year by car owners who buy, or more accurately are sold, struts and shocks before they need them. Much like life insurance, many people would never buy struts or shocks unless a salesman first planted the seed. And like life insurance, there is good money in shocks and struts, so sooner or later, some service manager is going try to sell you new struts or shocks for your car. Naturally, struts and shocks *do* wear out and need to be replaced, but this does not occur as often as most people — and service advisors — think. The struts and shocks on many of today's cars can last well over 100,000 miles! As with most other repairs, some basic knowledge will help you avoid spending money you shouldn't, and understanding struts and shocks is probably easier than you think.

What Are Shocks & Struts?

To understand when struts or shocks need to be replaced, you need to know what they are and what they do. Although struts and shocks are very different in appearance, they serve the same purpose: to prevent your car from continuing to bounce up and down after the first time. If you jump up and down on the front bumper of a car with good shocks and struts and then jump off, the car will immediately stop bouncing. If on the other hand the shocks or struts are worn, the car will continue to bounce a few times *after* you jump off. The more it bounces, the more the struts or shocks are worn. In fact, if you took the shocks completely off of a car, it would bounce up and down five to ten times before it stopped.

Shocks and struts are needed because cars have **springs** that support the weight of the car. These springs help the car ride smoothly over dips and bumps, and a spring, as you know, tends to bounce again and again. The shocks and struts help settle the springs down. They also prevent the car from bouncing, swerving, and swaying, and they help keep all the wheels in contact with the pavement so you can maintain control in curves and on rough surfaces.

So how do struts and shocks work? We could get technical here, but there is really no need. Instead, we will say that shocks and struts are filled with oil, which is forced back and forth through small openings inside the shock or strut when the car bounces up and down. Since oil tends to flow through a small opening at a slow, steady rate, this tends to make a car bounce at a slow, steady rate, so it stops bouncing quickly. This can be loosely compared to a nozzle on a spray bottle. If you squeeze the trigger with no liquid in the bottle, it is easy to pull the trigger as fast as you please. If you spray a liquid, however, no matter how hard you pull the trigger, the fluid travels at a steady speed. This simplified explanation gives you the basic idea of how a shock works (*see illustration S1*).

What's the Difference?

Although shocks and struts serve the same purpose, they are very different otherwise. A **shock** is for settling or dampening only, and no other purpose. A **strut** not only serves as a dampening device, but is also a major part of the suspension. Struts are used to connect the front or rear suspension to the body, and they usually hold the springs in place. A strut can be thought of as a part of the suspension with a shock built

S1 - SHOCKS

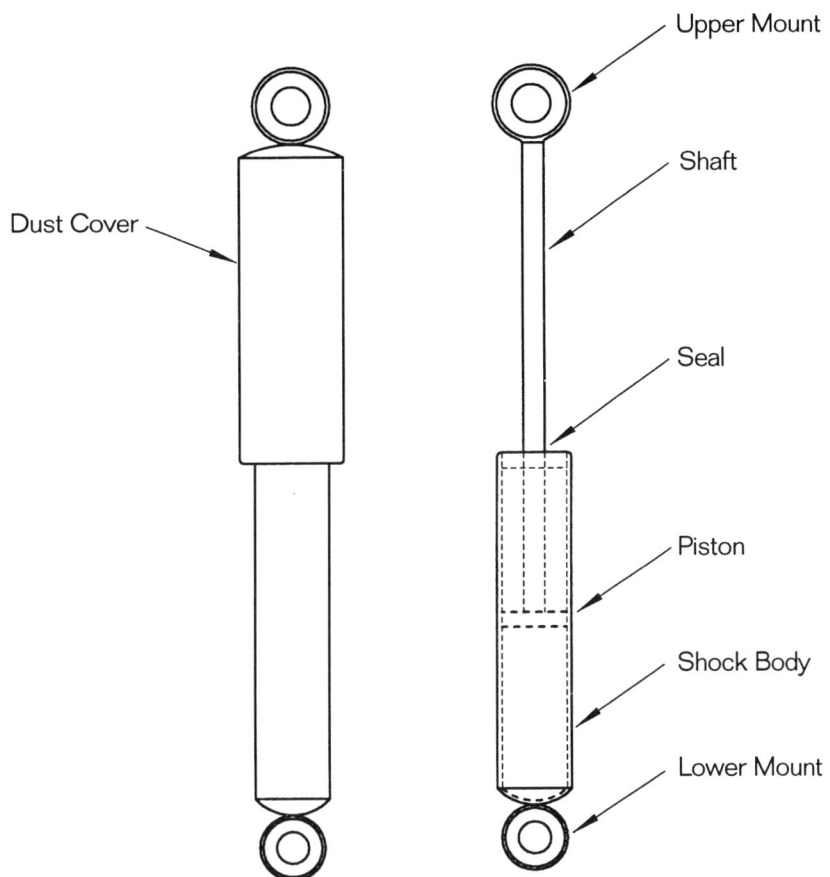

The body of the shock is filled with oil. The shaft moves up and down as the car bounces, forcing the oil back and forth through small holes in the piston and slowing the movement of the shaft to a slow, steady speed. This keeps the car from bouncing more than once or twice. If the seal around the shaft wears out, the oil begins to leak out. If enough of the oil leaks, the shock will not dampen, or steady, the movement of the car. Shocks can also develop internal leaks that will cause them to stop working properly.

Shocks are used mostly on older cars and on trucks and sport utility vehicles. Shocks are designed to settle a car down quickly after it begins to bounce, but unlike struts, they serve no other purpose. They do not hold the car up or change the front or rear alignment. Some shocks do not have the dust cover pictured on the left.

S2 - STRUT

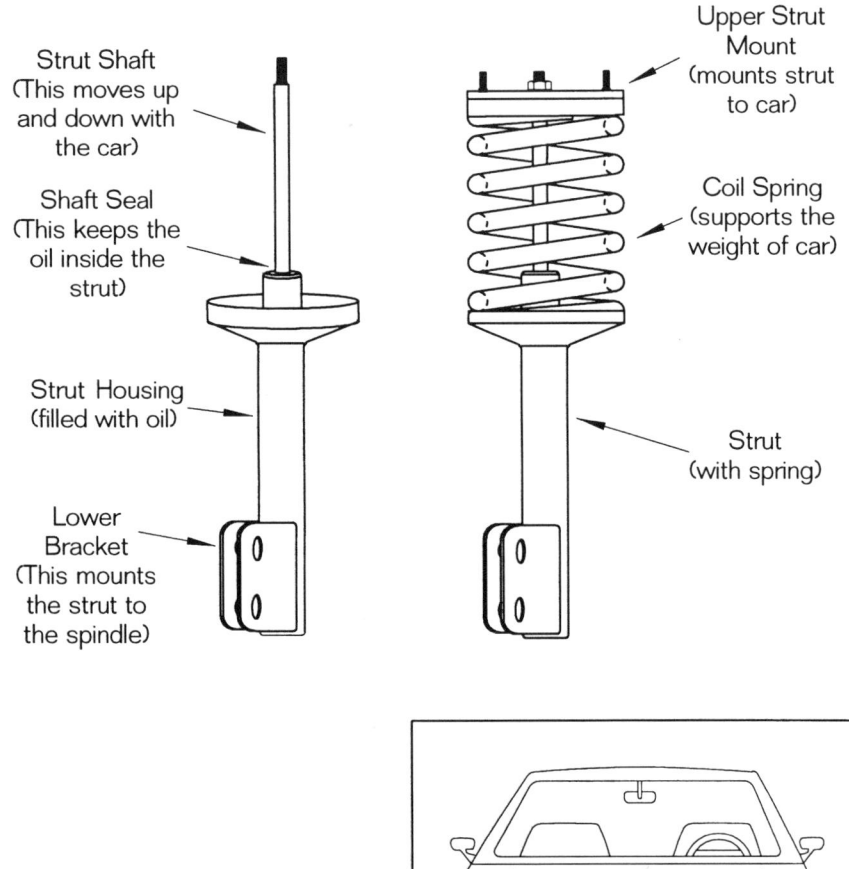

The strut is a major part of the front suspension. It not only dampens any bounces and dips, but it also supports the weight of the car. Struts are used at all four wheels on most cars built in the last few years. Most trucks and sport utility vehicles use shocks instead of struts. As with shocks, if the oil inside the strut leaks out, the strut will need to be replaced soon.

into it. In fact, a car could function with the shocks removed (although it would be a wild ride), but you couldn't even put a car together without the struts (*see illustration S2*).

Usually, the only part of the strut that wears out is its dampening ability. The structural part of the strut has no moving parts and is rarely the cause for replacement. The whole strut must be replaced as a unit however. A handful of cars have rebuildable struts, which allows the dampening part of the strut, called a strut cartridge, to be replaced separately. This can cost significantly less than replacing the entire strut.

Struts and shocks are mounted under the car near the wheels. Whether your car has struts or shocks is determined by its year, make, and model. Most front-wheel-drive cars built in the last fifteen years, have struts on all four corners (one per wheel). Many front-wheel-drive cars built in the eighties have struts on front and shocks on the rear. Older rear-wheel-drive cars and practically all trucks and sport utility vehicles, new or old, have shocks on all four corners. Struts are becoming more prominent because they take up less space and can do the job of several separate components. Therefore, they save space, weight, and money (*see illustration S3*). If you don't know if you have shocks or struts or both, call a parts store and ask them. While on the phone with a parts salesman, get the prices for the struts and shocks for your car. Knowing how your car is made and what the parts cost can prevent a service center from taking advantage of you.

Because a strut is a major part of the suspension, it is usually heavy, usually more than 20 pounds, and is relatively expensive compared to a shock. A good quality shock costs between $20 and $40 dollars, while a quality strut may

Knowing how your car is made and what the parts cost can prevent a service center from taking advantage of you.

cost from about $40 up to $200 or more. The average price for a common strut is around $60. (In case you are wondering, you can't replace a strut with a shock, or vice versa). Probably 95 percent or more of all cars have struts and shocks that can be purchased at any parts store, although some may have to be ordered. A rare few will have to be purchased at a dealer — remember to bring lots of money.

There are different kinds of shocks and struts. Most are **gas charged.** This means they are pressurized with a gas, usually nitrogen. This gas under pressure keeps the oil in the shock from foaming when the car bounces. This foam is made of tiny air bubbles, which can prevent the shock or strut from working properly. Only the least expensive shocks or struts will not be gas charged and should be avoided unless your budget dictates otherwise. Most name brand struts and shocks are offered in two or more price levels (good, better, best) and are warranted for as long as you own them.

OUT OF CONTROL

When a strut or shock goes bad, it loses its ability to dampen the car's movement. Sometimes this ability is lost gradually, sometimes there is sudden failure. Remember, the oil (or fluid) in the shock travels back and forth through small holes, seals, and other valves. If these parts become damaged or wear out for any reason, the fluid will flow too fast, causing the car to bounce or dip more than it should. Furthermore, if the seals that hold the fluid in the shock become worn or damaged, the fluid will leak out, which of course will cause the shock to stop working properly.

You can tell if a shock or strut is leaking by inspecting for an oily substance leaking out from between the two halves of the shock or strut. A leaky shock or strut may work properly for a while, but will eventually need replacing when enough fluid leaks out. Although bad shocks or struts do not present a *major* safety hazard, they should be replaced as soon as possible. A car with bad shocks or struts will not handle as well as it should, which can be dangerous especially in curves, over rough roads, or in panic situations.

YOU BE THE JUDGE

When a shock or strut loses some or all of its ability to dampen a car's movement, it should be replaced. Fortunately, you can figure this out for yourself, so you don't have to place yourself at the mercy

S3 - SHOCKS VS. STRUTS

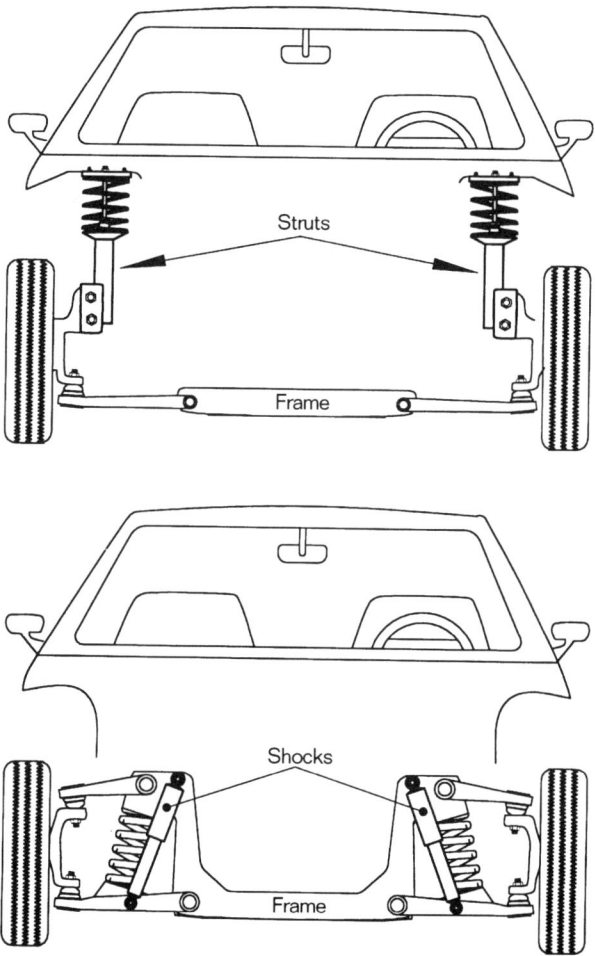

It is easy to see why so many cars come with struts instead of shocks. The top picture shows how much more room struts make in the engine compartment. This allows car makers to build smaller cars, yet stuff more equipment under the hood. Struts also reduce the weight of the car by a few hundred pounds. The struts replace the upper ball joints, upper control arms, and much of the frame. They also move the location of the springs up and out of the engine bay.

> Many people assume, or are told, that if their car sags (rides too low), the struts or shocks are worn out.
>
> This phenomenon is caused by weak or sagging springs, not worn struts or shocks.

of a service advisor who may have much to gain if you buy them from his shop. To check your struts or shocks, push down on the front of the car with all your weight and release. If you can't make the car move more than a couple of inches, ask a friend to help. If the car returns to its original position quickly with no bouncing, your struts on the front are probably okay. If the shocks pass this test, try bouncing the car up and down about three times. If, after you release the car, it settles down after only one bounce, the shocks or struts are fine. On the other hand, if the car bounces several times before stopping, the struts or shocks need to be replaced. Use the same procedure on the rear.

Another way to check the struts or shocks is by driving the car. If the car dips and bounces several times after going over a bump or sways too much in a curve, the struts or shocks are worn. If you find fluid (oil) leaking from a shock or strut, it will need to be replaced soon. To achieve a smoother ride, some large luxury cars are designed with soft suspensions and shocks; these cars may bounce and sway over bumps and dips more than the average car. Many people assume, or are told, that if their car sags (rides too low), the struts or shocks are worn out, but this phenomenon is caused by weak or sagging springs, not worn-out struts.

THE UPS & DOWNS OF REPLACEMENT

It is a good idea to replace struts or shocks in pairs, on the front, or on the rear. A mismatched pair may cause the car to handle poorly. An exception to this would be if the struts are fairly new, and you can replace a defective strut with an identical replacement. In such cases, replacing one strut or shock should work just fine. A myth sometimes supported by people in the service industry is that all four shocks or struts should be replaced together. This is simply not true. In fact, the front struts commonly wear out much more quickly because of the extra weight on the front struts. If you only need front struts, by all means replace only the front, and the same goes for the rear.

Furthermore, never let anyone tell you that your struts need replacing simply because your car has a certain number of miles on it. Mileage is not an accurate way to diagnose bad struts and shocks. Struts may go bad after about 40,000 miles, or they may last 150,000 miles or more. The struts on modern cars ordinarily last about 100,000 miles. Shocks usually last a little less, mostly because they are found on heavier vehicles such as trucks. The only way to know for sure is to check them as described previously.

SHOPPING FOR SHOCKS & STRUTS

When you need struts or shocks, call a few service centers to compare prices and warranties. Most tire dealers, brake repair centers, and independent shops sell and install struts and shocks. When *struts* are replaced, the alignment *will* need to be checked. Therefore, a center that has alignment capabilities is a good choice, although you *could* take your car to another shop to have it aligned. However, don't drive your car more than about 20 miles before it is aligned. If you are replacing shocks only, the alignment need not be checked unless you notice uneven tire wear. Although most better quality shocks or struts are warranted for as long as you own them, this probably does not cover labor. Make sure you ask about this and any other warranty information when you call for an estimate. Since struts make up a major portion of the suspension, the time and labor required to install them will be significantly higher than on a shock. You can expect to pay up to about $60 per strut for labor, compared to about $10 of labor per shock.

When shopping around be sure to ask for brand names. About 90 percent of all shocks are made by just two companies, Gabriel and Monroe, so you will hear these two names again and again. Many people will say their shocks and struts are made by one of these companies, but the brand name won't be on the box, or the shock. These are private label shocks. One of the big shock makers builds them for another company who uses their own name brand. The only disadvantage to a private label is that the warranty will be honored only by the company

> ...the best quality struts or shocks will provide a smoother ride for a longer time.

who sold the shock. A national brand name shock will be warranted at any dealer who carries that brand. Be sure to get all these details in order to make a fair comparison and to help you decide who really has the best price. If your budget can stand it, the best quality struts or shocks will provide a smoother ride for a longer time. Don't be tempted to go with the lowest price just for the sake of saving money, you may be disappointed.

FRONT SUSPENSION

"Front suspension" refers to all the components that allow the front of your car to move up and down, and steer to the left and right. The front suspension of an automobile is very busy. It is responsible for steering the car and helping it ride smoothly over bumps and dips. On front-wheel-drive cars, the front suspension also has the task of rotating the wheels and pulling the car down the road. The front suspension carries a heavy load and takes a lot of abuse from the bumps and potholes in the roads. The components of the front suspension are subjected to a great deal of stress and strain and are prone to wear out and need repairs. Knowing a little about these components and the procedures for repairs can help you save money *and* headaches. This basic knowledge will also greatly *decrease* your chances of being taken advantage of when the time comes to have the front suspension repaired.

A basic understanding of how the front suspension works is essential to understanding what can go wrong. The natural place to start is where it all begins, at the steering wheel. As you know, the steering wheel spins, but the front wheels steer left and right. Somehow, the rotation of the steering wheel must be converted to a side-to-side motion. This is where the **RACK-'N-PINION** comes into play. The steering wheel is linked to the rack-'n-pinion. The rack-'n-pinion's job is to convert the steering wheel's circular motion to a side-to-side motion that can to steer the tires left and right. The rack-'n-pinion is connected to **TIE RODS**, which connect the front wheels to the rack-'n-pinion and to each other. The tie rods push and pull the tires to the left or right, hold the car in alignment, and are actually used to adjust the alignment. The rack-'n-pinion and the tie rods are essentially the only components of a steering system on modern cars, although cars vary slightly from model to model. However, this should give you an idea of what happens when the steering wheel is turned.

RACK-'N-PINION

Although all the components of the steering system are important, the rack-'n-pinion plays the biggest role in the front suspension. It not only converts the rotation of the steering wheel into a side-to-side movement, it also is responsible for power steering, which makes the car easy to steer. The rack-'n-pinion links the other steering components together. As you may have guessed, a part with this much to do can go bad.

When a rack-'n-pinion wears out, the steering can feel very tight and your car may become difficult to steer. One of the first signs of a bad rack-'n-pinion is a noticeable tight spot in the steering or when the steering wheel seems to catch in one place. At first this tends to occur only in the morning when the car is still cold. Cold rack-'n-pinion and power steering fluid do not flow as well as when they are warm. This condition is sometimes called "morning sickness." Eventually, morning sickness develops into steering that is very hard in any direction, hot or cold. This can be dangerous if the steering binds or sticks while driving.

Another sign of a bad rack-'n-pinion, called a "rack" for short, is a power steering fluid leak. The rack-'n-pinion is filled with power steering fluid and has several seals that hold the fluid inside. These seals, or the rack itself, can become worn, and fluid will begin to leak out. This causes the fluid level in the power steering pump reservoir to go down.

Sometimes, the fluid may seem to disappear into thin air because you do not find any on the ground under the car. This is explained by the fact that these seals are inside rubber boots called **BELLOWS** that cover the inner tie rods (*see illustration F1*). These bellows often trap the lost fluid and prevent it from reaching to the ground. If you are having to add power steering fluid, but do not see any fluid under the car, this may be the reason.

If you suspect this type of leak, have a technician remove the clamps from the bellows and check for power steering fluid inside. If there is more than a few drops of fluid in one or both bellows, the rack will need to be replaced soon. A leaky pump or power steering hose can also cause the loss of fluid, but this always creates *external*, visible, leaks. If the only symptom of a bad rack is a loss of a small amount of fluid, you can wait until you can afford the relatively expensive repair, if need be. However, if you are experiencing a dangerous tight or sticky steering problem, you should have the rack-'n-pinion replaced as soon as possible.

Racking Up

Although rack-'n-pinions *do* wear out, fortunately it doesn't happen on a regular basis. In fact, many cars will never need a new rack-'n-pinion. Most will not need replacement until well over 100,000 miles. If you are one of the lucky ones who end up needing a rack-'n-pinion, a remanufactured rack can save you hundreds of dollars compared to buying a new one. Remanufactured rack-'n-pinions are available for 90 percent of the cars on the road today at any parts store.

When a rack-'n-pinion is remanufactured, the skeleton of an old rack is repaired using all new internal parts. They will also have new seals, and many come with new tie rod ends and bellows. Remanufactured racks are often better than new because of improved designs and materials, and most carry a lifetime warranty. Before going to a repair shop to have a new rack-'n-pinion installed, check the price for a remanufactured rack at a few parts stores to get an idea about how much you should pay.

Most good quality rack-'n-pinion's will cost between $100 and $300 dollars. The labor can also be relatively expensive. Most rack-'n-pinion's are mounted under the body of the car, behind the engine. They are connected to the frame, the tie rods, the power steering hoses, and the steering column. They are also hard to maneuver in and out of

C A R S M A R T

F1 - RACK-'N-PINION

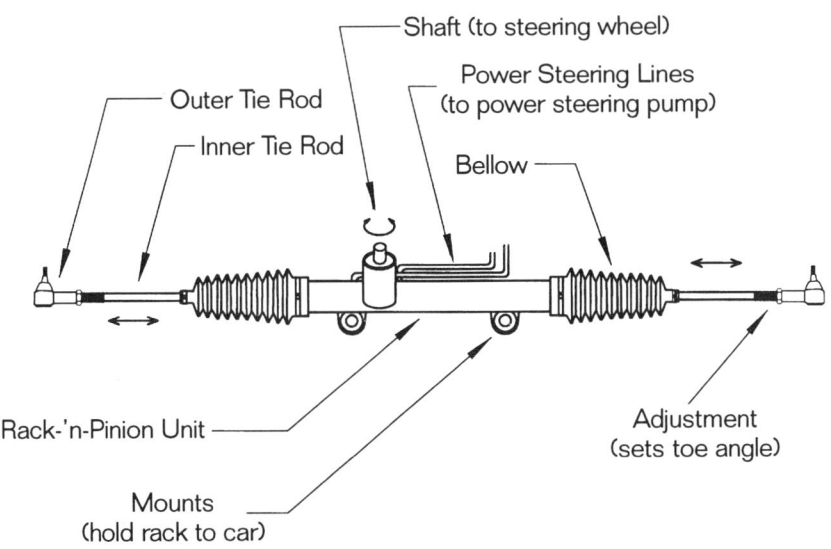

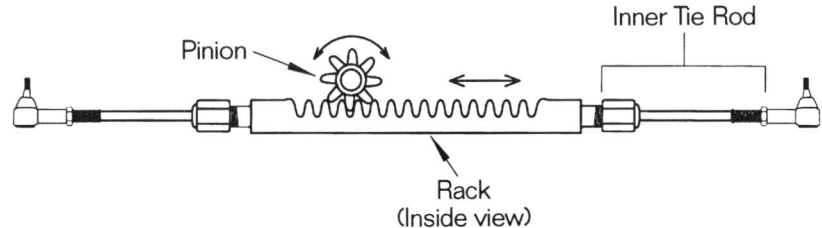

The rack-'n-pinion converts the circular motion of the steering wheel into a side-to-side motion. You can see where the rack-'n-pinion got its name!

the small opening in the underside of the car. Because of this, the time required to replace a rack can be from two to over four hours, which equates to from $100 to over $300!

When a rack-'n-pinion is replaced, the power steering fluid should be changed to remove any dirt and metal shavings trapped in the old fluid. Some shops may install a filter in the fluid line to help insure the fluid stays clean. The alignment will also have to be adjusted immediately after the rack-'n-pinion is replaced.

When calling shops for estimates, be sure to ask for the total price including the parts, labor, fluid, and alignment. Also check the warranty. Many service centers will warranty the parts and labor for a specific time, and the rack-'n-pinion for as long as you own the car. Don't forget to ask for a written warranty stating exactly what is covered. After all, you could be spending $600 or more for a rack-'n-pinion replacement, so consider all these factors when choosing someone to do the job.

TIE RODS

The rack-'n-pinion is the most complex and expensive component of the steering system, but the parts that most frequently go bad are the **TIE ROD ENDS,** also called **TIE RODS** (*see illustration F2*). Tie rods link the front wheels to the rack-'n-pinion, keep them in alignment, and point them in the correct direction. If a tie rod end becomes worn (loose), the front wheels can wobble back and forth and can move independently of each other. In other words, the front wheels can move side to side, in and out of alignment, even though the steering wheel is pointing straight ahead. This will cause the front alignment to change, which will in turn cause the tires to wear prematurely (*also see the section on front alignment*). An extremely loose tie rod can even wear to a point that it breaks, which would cause the loss of steering control. So it goes without saying, a worn tie rod should be replaced as soon as possible.

To check the condition of the tie rods, a technician will jack the car up and try to wobble each front wheel back and forth. If one wheel wobbles without moving the other one, there is probably a loose tie rod. There are other causes for this symptom, such as a loose ball joint or wheel bearing, so a knowledgeable technician is essential for diagnosing the problem correctly.

CARSMART

F2 - TIE RODS

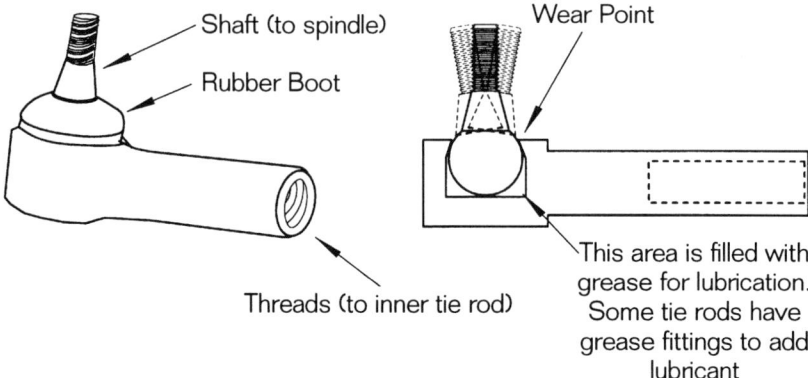

Above is a typical outer tie rod, as found on most modern cars. Below is a typical inner tie rod used on most cars and trucks with rack-'n-pinion steering. Tie rods are used to steer the car by linking the wheels to the steering wheel via the rack-'n-pinion. As shown in the cutaway drawings, tie rods use a ball and socket to allow them to move with the car and the wheels. Over time, these ball and socket joints will wear, which can cause play in the steering. This in turn will cause poor alignment and can cause a thumping noise when the car is driven over dips and bumps. If a tie rod wears to an extreme, the ball can pop out of the socket, causing the loss of steering and possibly an accident. For more details on tie rods, see the drawings for the rack-'n-pinion and front suspension.

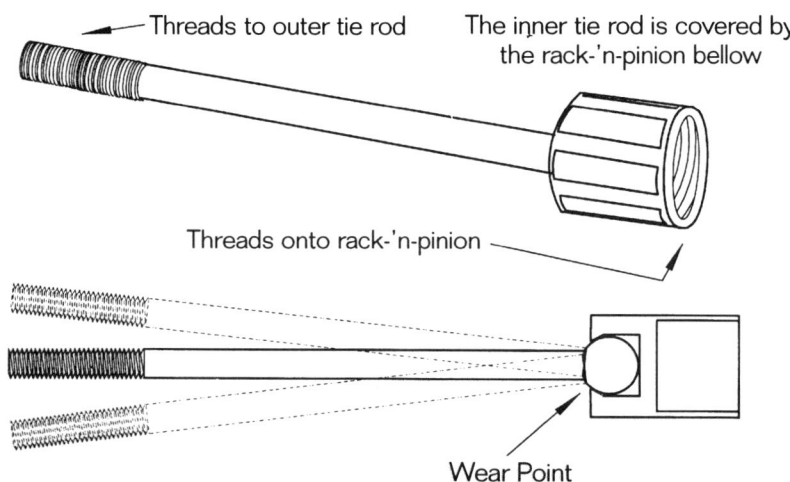

The Ins & Outs

There are four tie rods per car, two inner tie rods and two outer tie rods. Usually the **INNER TIE RODS** wear out on today's front-wheel-drive cars. These are the most difficult to replace because they are mounted under the engine, near the center of the car, on the rack-'n-pinion (*see illustration F1*). They are hard to reach and are covered by rubber boots called **BELLOWS.** To replace an inner tie rod, a technician must remove the outer tie rod, the bellow and clamps, and use a special tool that will reach over the tie rod and into the rack-'n-pinion. The labor will be between about $30 and $60 per inner tie rod. The part itself will usually cost from about $20 for a popular model to over $75 for a less common model.

When having an inner tie rod replaced, have the technician make sure the bellow is in good condition. The bellows protect the tie rods and the rack-'n-pinion from dirt and water. If the bellow is damaged, now is the time to replace it. There should be little or no extra labor to replace a bellow, since it will be off anyway. The front-end alignment will also have to be reset. Changing *any* tie rod *will definitely* change the alignment. All cars and trucks, front- or rear-wheel-drive, have inner tie rods of some form. Some trucks, such as Ford full-size and Rangers, have inner tie rods that are over two feet long and can cost over $100 each.

It is less likely that the **OUTER TIE RODS** will need to be replaced, but they do wear out. Older cars with rear-wheel-drive and trucks are usually the vehicles that need outer tie rod replacement, but front-wheel-drive cars do sometimes wear the outer tie rods. Outer tie rods are relatively easy to replace. They are mounted out near the wheels and are fairly easy to get to. The labor for outer tie rods will usually be around $25 each. The price for outer tie rods is generally about the same as inner tie rods: $20 to more than $75. Again, the alignment must be set after any tie rod is replaced.

Other front suspension components that can wear out are ball joints, sway bar links, wheel bearings, idler arms (on rear-drive cars and trucks), and strut mounts. These don't wear out as often as tie rods, but after a car has about 40,000 miles on it, they should be thoroughly checked every ten thousand miles or so. The service centers most qualified to check these parts are the ones that do front alignments. These shops will have experienced personnel and the right equipment for the job.

Boots, Joints, & Axles

On a front-wheel-drive car, the front suspension not only steers the car, it is also pulls your car down the road. Front drive cars have front suspensions which carry the DRIVETRAIN. The drivetrain consists of the transaxle (or transmission) and two DRIVE AXLES. Drive axles are also called "CV axles," or "half shafts." These axles transfer the rotating motion of the engine and transmission to the wheels. There are two axles per car, which consist of several components. The primary components are the INNER CV JOINTS, OUTER CV JOINTS, INNER CV BOOTS, and OUTER CV BOOTS (CV stands for "constant velocity"). The CV joints allow the axles to spin, to turn left and right, and to move up and down with the car as it steers and bounces over dips and bumps. CV joints are packed with a heavy lubricating grease that keeps the metal parts inside from wearing. Therefore, CV joints are covered by rubber CV boots, which protect the joints by holding *in* the lubricating grease, keeping dirt and water *out*. These boots are held in place by metal bands or clamps (*see illustration F3*).

Since CV joints and boots twist and bend as the car moves and turns, they are subjected to a great deal of stress and strain. CV boots are made of rubber, and like any material made of rubber they tend to dry rot and age as time goes by. This aging process and the constant twisting and stretching will eventually cause most CV boots to break open. **The moment a CV boot breaks, the grease inside the boot and joint begins to sling out and away from the joint.** This takes away the lubrication critical for preventing the joints from wearing out. It also allows dirt and water to enter the CV joint, which speeds up the wearing process even more.

> **When a car is driven after a CV boot breaks, the joint will wear quickly and become permanently damaged.**

F3 - CV AXLE

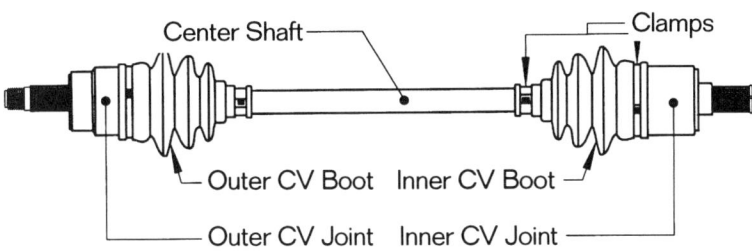

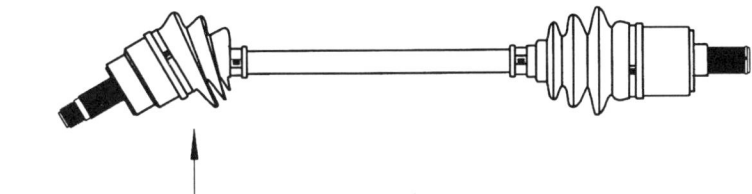

Notice that the outer joint and boot are subject to high stress when the steering is turned sharply

CV axles are also called "half shafts." They transfer the power from the engine to the wheels. The CV joints allow the axles to rotate, bend, and flex as the car steers and bounces. The CV boots protect the moving parts inside the joints from dirt and water, and hold grease inside the joint. If a CV boot breaks open, the CV joint will wear out quickly. A worn-out joint will usually make a popping sound when the car is steered sharply and is repaired by replacing the entire axle on that side. There are two axles per car. (Typically front-wheel-drive cars only.)

> **Since CV boots are prone to break or tear, they should be inspected every time the car is on a lift.**
>
> **This could be when the oil is changed, when the tires are rotated, or during a brake job.**

When a car is driven after a CV boot breaks, the joint will wear quickly and become permanently damaged. In fact, if a busted CV boot is not replaced within a few thousand miles, the CV joint will be ruined. And although rare, a complete failure of a CV joint will cause the car to stop pulling, which means you will be stranded!

Since CV boots are prone to break or tear, they should be inspected every time the car is on a lift. This could be when the oil is changed, when the tires are rotated, or during a brake job. Most repair centers will check the CV boots anyway, not simply out of the goodness of their heart, but because they make money by replacing them. Nevertheless, it is still a good idea to ask the service manager to make sure they are inspected. The reason for the inspection is to try to catch a torn CV boot before the joint is damaged. Since a busted CV boot quickly leads to a damaged joint, it should be replaced as soon as your budget will allow. This is not a repair to put off until next spring, or even until next month.

If you are told you have a bad boot, ask the service person to escort you into the shop to see the boots. Just like a person who has never seen an egg would know a broken egg when he or she sees it, a person who has never seen a CV boot before will know a damaged boot when he or she sees it. When inspecting the boots, you may notice a boot that is dry rotted to a point where you can see cracks or splits where the boot flexes. This is a good indication that the boot will soon split, and it would probably be cost-effective to go ahead and replace it *before* it breaks, especially if your car has over 100,000 miles. A boot replacement will usually cost around $60 to $90 per boot, as opposed to about

$250 or more for the entire axle. As you can see, having the boots inspected regularly can save you some serious dollars.

A **one-piece,** or **solid, boot** is the only type of boot that should be used. This type of boot requires that the joint or axle be removed, which insures that the joint is cleaned and filled with new grease. A one-piece boot will cost a little more than other types, but should last as long as the original. Some shops may try to sell you a **split boot.** This type of boot has a seam that allows the boot to be installed without removing the joint or the axle. These boots do not last, and the joint cannot be properly lubricated. Even if the price is significantly less, a split boot is not worth it!

SOUNDING OFF

If a car is driven with a bad CV boot, the CV joint will soon follow, and the outer CV boot and joint are usually the first to go. When an *outer* CV joint becomes significantly worn, it will begin to make a noise. You have probably heard a car with a bad outer joint, but didn't realize what was causing the noise. This sound is a loud "pop-pop-popping" or "clicking" that occurs when the wheels are steered all the way to the left or right and the car is moving, especially when taking off. The popping noise is caused when the parts inside the joint wear and form grooves. When the wheels are turned to the left or right, the ball bearings inside the CV joint roll back and forth over these grooves, causing the popping sound. This clicking is first heard only when the wheels are steered all the way to one side, but can get worse and can occur when the wheels are only about half way to the left or right.

The severity of the noise increases with the amount of wear, and also if you take off faster. If you hear this noise when the wheels are only slightly turned, you are close to a breakdown! If the noise occurs only when you turn sharply to the *right*, this usually means that the *left outer* joint is bad. If the *right outer* joint is bad, the noise occurs when turning to the left. This is because the wheel on the outside of the turn is subjected to more pressure than the inside wheel. When an outer joint is damaged to the point that it makes a popping noise, it should be replaced. **If you are already hearing a noise from a CV joint, it's too late to replace the boot and grease the joint.** No amount of new grease will replace the metal that has been worn off! Note: There are a few (rare) instances where a joint will go bad even if the boot remains intact.

AXLE REPLACEMENT TIPS

The best way to replace a bad outer joint is to replace the entire axle on that side. This was not always the case, however. When front-wheel-drive cars first came on the market, new axles were very expensive, sometimes over $500 each! At that time, it was cheaper to replace just the damaged CV joint and boot. Now, it is actually less expensive to buy a remanufactured axle assembly than to buy just the CV joint. When an old axle is remanufactured, the worn or damaged parts are remachined or replaced, and the axle will be as good as new, or better. There is another advantage: These axles not only have remanufactured outer joints, but will have a remanufactured inner joint, and *new* boots, grease, and clamps already installed. Replacing the entire axle, as opposed to replacing only the joint and boot, is almost always less expensive *and* less prone to giving you or your mechanic trouble. Furthermore, the labor to replace the entire axle should be a little less than replacing the joint and boot, usually around $50 per axle. Today, remanufactured axles cost from $75 to more than $150 each for most common car models. You will usually need to replace only one axle at a time. It is not uncommon for a car to need an axle on one side, but not the other. When shopping around for a service center to replace an axle for you, don't forget to compare warranties.

A MYSTERIOUS WOBBLE

So far, the outer joint has been the topic of discussion, because they are far more likely to go bad. **Inner CV joints** are not subjected to the same intense twisting and movement as

> Many new tires have been purchased to correct a vibration caused by an axle (inner CV joint).
>
> But remember: a bad tire will cause the car to shake whether the gas pedal is depressed or not.

outer joints, so they don't wear out as often — but they can go bad. The symptoms for a bad inner joint are much different from the popping that an outer joint makes. In fact, a bad inner joint will not typically cause any strange noises. A bad inner joint will instead cause the car to shake and wobble back and forth, mostly when you are speeding up from a stop. This wobble, which makes the whole car to move left and right, can be very severe while pressing the gas pedal, and will then smooth out when the pedal is released. This condition can also come and go. It may happen once in every ten starts, or it may occur every time you take off. This type of wobble or shimmy is almost always caused by a bad inner CV joint and should not be confused with a bad tire. Many new tires have been purchased to correct a vibration caused by an axle (inner CV joint). But remember: a bad tire will cause the car to shake whether the gas pedal is depressed or not.

Like outer joints, a bad inner joint is repaired by replacing the entire axle on that side. Unfortunately, the diagnosis of a bad inner joint is difficult, because you cannot tell which side is bad by turning the wheels and listening for a noise. An experienced technician is needed to correctly diagnose a bad inner joint. The most common method is to jack up one wheel at a time, and determine which axle is causing the vibration by spinning the wheel with the motor. Your technician may not have heard of this method, so if he is having trouble finding the bad axle, mention this trick. If this method does not give a satisfactory result, a trial-and-error method must be used. In other words, the technician makes an educated guess at which side is bad, and if the problem is not solved, the other side is replaced. **This should be done at the risk of the shop if at all possible. Try to place the burden of diagnosing the correct axle in their hands.** You should talk this over with the manager before the job is started. Since the entire axle is being replaced, the price for parts and labor will be the same as described previously.

F4 - FRONT SUSPENSION & DRIVETRAIN (front view)

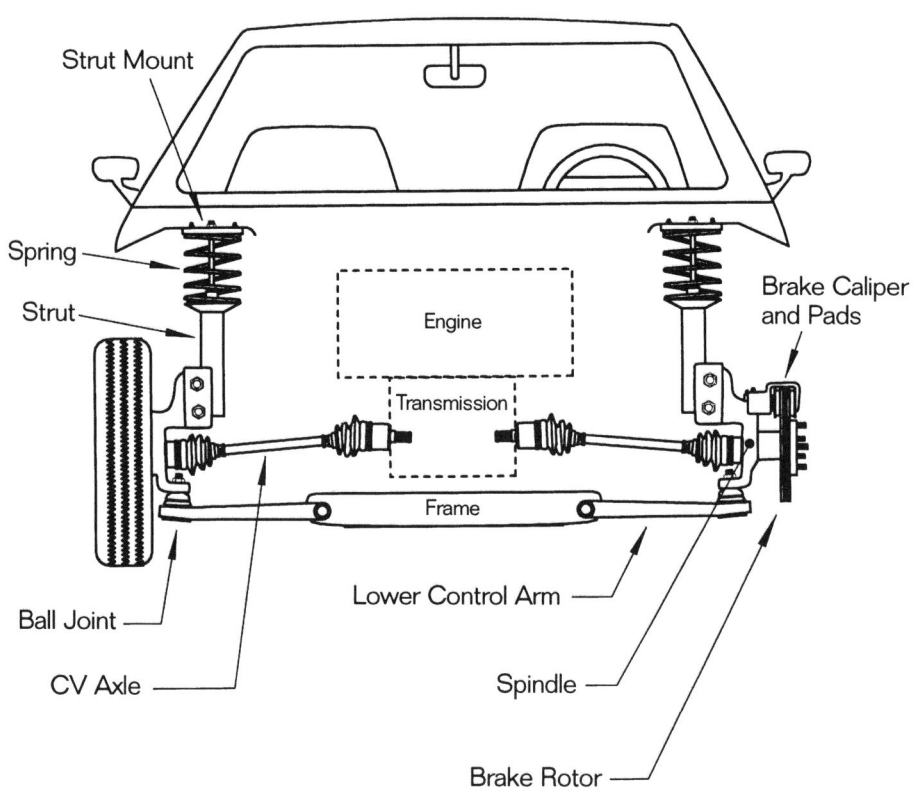

This is a view of some of the front-end components as seen from the front of the car. The struts, ball joints, spindles, lower control arms, and axles all move up and down, allowing the car to bounce smoothly over dips and bumps. (See top view for other components of the front suspension.)

F5 - FRONT SUSPENSION
(top view)

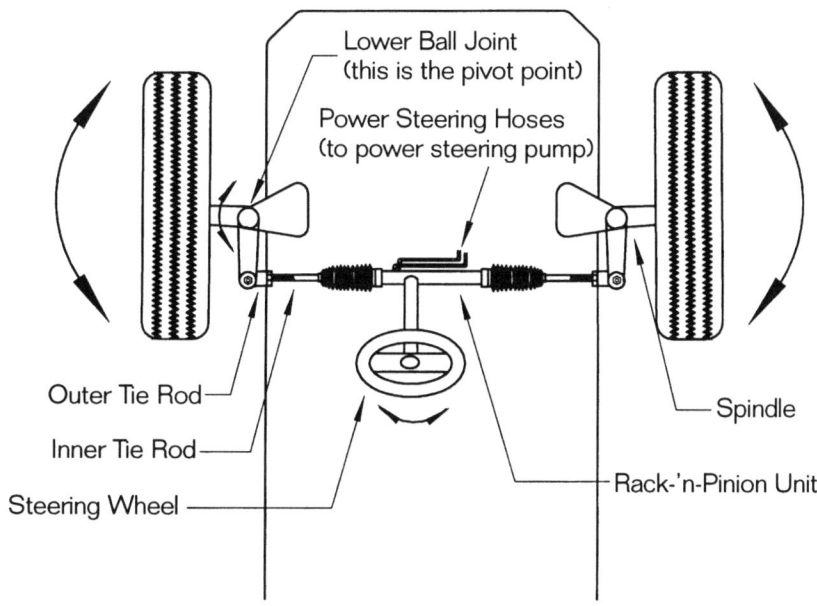

The front suspension components as seen from above show how the rack-'n-pinion converts the rotation of the steering wheel to a side-to-side movement that steers the wheels. Notice that if a tie rod is loose or worn, it will allow the wheels to move independently of one another, causing rapid tire wear.

FRONT SUSPENSION & DRIVETRAIN GLOSSARY

BELLOWS: (tie rod bellows) Bellows are rubber boots that cover the **rack-'n-pinion** and the **inner tie rods.** They protect these parts from dirt and moisture. Size: 3" round x 10" long. Price: $20. Location: under car on rack-'n-pinion.

CV AXLES: (drive axles, half shafts) Axles are assemblies made up of an inner and outer **CV joint** and an inner and outer **CV boot.** The axles link the transmission to the wheels, which pulls the car. A bad CV joint is usually repaired by replacing the entire axle. Size: 6" round x 3'. Price: $100–$200+. Location: under engine, two per car.

CV BOOT: (axle boot) CV boots are rubber boots that cover the **CV joints.** There are two inner and two outer CV boots per car. These boots protect the **CV joints** by holding grease in the joints and keeping dirt and water out. Size: 5" round tapered down to 1" round. Price: $10–$30. Location: outer, near the wheel; inner, under the engine.

CV JOINT: (constant velocity joint) CV joints swivel and allow the **CV axles** to flex and turn as the car moves and steers. There are two inner and two outer CV joints per car. CV joints have metal bearings that can wear and cause a popping noise when the car is steered sharply. Size: 5" round x 8". Price: usually replaced with entire axle (*see CV axle*). Location: on each end of CV axle — outer joints near wheels, inner joints under engine.

DRIVETRAIN: This term describes the parts of the car that transfer the rotation of the engine to the wheels, consisting of a transmission, transaxle, and **CV axles.**

FRONT SUSPENSION: This term describes the parts of the car that allow the car to move up and down and steer left and right. Some components of the front suspension are the **rack-'n-pinion, tie rod ends,** ball joints, shocks and struts.

RACK-N-PINION: (rack) The rack-'n-pinion is the heart of the steering system. It transfers the rotation of the steering wheel to the wheels, which steers the car. The rack-'n-pinion also contains the power steering components. Size: 4" round x 4'. Price: $100–$300++. Location: under car, behind engine.

TIE ROD ENDS: (tie rods) Tie rods are steering components which link the **rack-'n-pinion** to the front wheels. They steer the tires and keep the front wheels in alignment with one another. There are two inner and two outer tie rod ends per car. Size: 2" round x 10". Price: $20–$60+. Location: outer tie rods, near wheels; inner tie rods, under car, mounted to rack-'n-pinion.

DRIVEABILITY

Driveability is a term used in the repair industry to describe the way a car runs or performs. Common driveability problems include cars that jerk, miss, backfire, are hard to start, get poor gas mileage, or simply don't run the way they should, or at all. About twenty years ago, only a handful of parts caused these problems, but today's cars have more and more electronics, and driveability problems are becoming harder and harder to diagnose without proper tools and training. Because of the overwhelming number of cars on the road, there are thousands of possible causes for a driveability problem. A driveability problem could be caused by something as simple as a loose wire, or by something unbelievably complex, or both. To discuss these endless variables and cover every possibility for every car would require a book with a million pages. For your sake, this section on driveability is much shorter than that: It describes how to find the right shop rather than explaining specific repairs.

When you have a driveability problem, the first attempt at repair is done by you. First, if the problem is minor such as a rough idle or a *slight* decrease in gas mileage, you should fill your car up with gas (using a different gas station from the last) and add some fuel treatment. Problems may be caused by water in the fuel or a dirty fuel system, either of which *should* be fixed by the above experiment. Drive the car for that entire tank of gas before seeking professional help, unless the problem is severe or gets worse. Next, have an experienced technician check the basics. Have him make sure there are no disconnected or damaged electrical wires, vacuum hoses, or plug wires. These little villains cause many headaches and many dollars to be wasted on unneeded repairs.

A Safe Bet

A surprising number of driveability problems are caused by the simplest things. Often, something as simple as a dirty air filter or a clogged fuel filter can create big problems. If all of these basics check out okay, try a simple tune-up before paying someone $50 or more to check your car on a diagnostic machine. On most of today's cars, a simple tune-up consists of changing the spark plugs and installing new air and fuel filters. This *could* cure the problem and eliminate the need for expensive and risky diagnostics. If it has been at least 40,000 miles since the last tune-up, your car probably needs it anyway. This small gamble often pays big.

Seeking Professional Help

If the previous suggestions do not cure the problem, the next step is to find the right shop for your situation. The "right shop" is the

> The "right shop" is the one that can diagnose and repair the problem on their first attempt, for a fair price.
>
> This sounds simple on paper, but it's usually not that easy.

ARE TUNE-UPS EXTINCT?

Speaking of tune-ups, they ain't what they used to be! Before on-board computers and fuel injection came along (about 1982), cars actually needed a tune-up about every 30,000 miles. This meant new spark plugs and possibly plug wires plus things like points, condensers, distributor caps, and so on. The engine timing would also need to be adjusted and possibly a carburetor adjustment was needed. These repairs were performed to fine tune or tweak an engine to its best possible condition, which wasn't really all that good by today's standards.

Today, computers and solid state electronics have eliminated all of these parts and procedures except for the spark plugs and plug wires. Now, the computer "tunes" an engine many times per second by constantly adjusting the timing and the fuel delivery, keeping the engine at its best all the time.

So are tune-ups needed today? Not really. A better term would be ignition maintenance. Typically on most modern cars, the spark plugs and plug wires are the only components that wear out; the engine computer takes care of the rest. The trouble is, many people still ask for a tune-up, and a repair center is happy to charge them much more than it would cost to simply replace the spark plugs and plug wires. Therefore, the next time you need a tune-up, don't ask for one. Instead, request a spark plug change and let the thousands of dollars worth of sophisticated electronics under the hood and dash do the rest!

Incidentally, spark plugs are lasting longer and longer as technology improves. Most spark plugs now last over 70,000 miles, and I have seen plugs make it past 100,000 miles, although these were overdue. Plug wires usually last between 75,000 and 100,000 miles. For more ideas on tune-ups, read the owner's manual for your car, and don't forget to change the air filter and fuel filter as needed.

> **Only five out of a hundred technicians really have the talent to solve a tricky driveability problem.**

one that will diagnose and repair the problem on their first attempt, for a fair price. This sounds simple on paper, but it's usually not that easy. This may sound like bad news at first — but the new car dealer may be the best place to repair a driveability dilemma. The dealer has equipment designed especially for your car and technicians who are trained to work on cars like yours. Another factor is experience; dealer technicians work on cars just like yours everyday, which can make a huge difference.

A technician who works on the same brand of car every day will know much more about that car than someone who has to work on every brand. As a matter of fact, he may know what is wrong with your car as soon as you describe the problem, because he has already seen that exact problem on another car. Also, dealers are often linked to each other and receive service bulletins from the factory that give them helpful hints and insights. Sure, a dealer usually charges more for any given repair, but if they can diagnose the problem correctly the first time, they may actually save you money. Millions of dollars are wasted by technicians without the proper know-how and equipment: They guess at a solution, miss it, and you-know-who's money is wasted!

In defense of independent shops, there *are* repair centers out there who have ace mechanics and the right equipment to solve difficult driveability problems. Finding such a shop is the hard part. Only five out of a hundred technicians really have the talent to solve a tricky driveability problem. One of the best ways to find such a technician is to use the phone.

When you call a repair center to describe your problem, notice if they sound interested in solving your problem. If the service manager *reluctantly* agrees to check your car, he may not be confident about his ability to fix it. Ask the manager if his shop has the diagnostic equipment to check *your* car, especially if you have an import. It is also a good idea to ask how experienced their driveability technician is. If the technician has only a few years of experience — look out! Experience can make a huge difference when it comes to diagnosing driveability problems correctly.

The Burden of Repair

Above all, ask if the shop will be responsible for their diagnostics. If they tell you that you will have to pay the full price for any repairs whether they fix your car or not, they may not even care if the problem is fixed the first time. While they continue guessing at the cause of the problem, they make more money and you continue to pay for unsuccessful repairs. **If a shop offers to take at least *some* responsibility for unsuccessful repairs, you can bet they will do everything in their power to get it right the first time.** One way to get commitment from a service manager is to offer to pay enough to cover *their* cost on an unsuccessful attempt. But you must also insist that you are not charged for more diagnostics if the repairs do not fix the problem. If unsuccessful repairs are made and you decide to take your car to another shop, the repair center should, but may not, refund some or all of the diagnostic charges. After all, you paid them to *correctly* diagnose your problem, which they did not do.

There is one thing to consider about a shop that specializes in driveability repairs. A shop that has the right equipment for all types of cars and employs knowledgeable technicians may be as expensive as the dealer, or almost so. They must invest thousands of dollars in equipment and pay top dollar for experienced, intelligent mechanics; therefore they must charge more for their time than a shop who employs the inexperienced. But if they can diagnose and repair a tricky driveability problem the first time, they are worth more than a shop that uses the trail-and-error method.

A Second Opinion

As with any expensive repair, get at least two opinions for driveability problems. This is especially true if the repair is going to cost significantly more than another opinion would. Getting a second opinion may cost you twice as much for diagnostics, but unnecessary repairs can be much worse. You may be told by the first center that you need a new computer that will cost $200, while the next shop finds a loose wire that is fixed for $20! Of course, if you are told by the first service center that your driveability problem can be solved with a $20 or $30 repair, it would be worth the gamble to go ahead and try it.

If you decide to get a second opinion, telling the second shop what the first center found may be a good idea, especially in a case where the repair is relatively inexpensive. If a technician knows what to check first, he may be able to find the problem much faster, which may reduce diagnostic expense. On the other hand, if the first shop recommends a high-dollar repair, or if you have little confidence in their opinion, it may be in your best interest to let the second shop come to its own conclusions. Again, always get the most commitment possible from the shop about their diagnostics. Ask them what happens if the repairs they recommend don't fix your car. **Make it clear you are not in the mood for playing guessing games!**

A TUNE-UP ON A FIGHTER JET

A few years ago, a nationwide auto service center moved right next door to my business. This store oozes high-tech professionalism. This company also has a self-implied good reputation, especially for tune-ups and diagnostics. Not long after the store opened, a parts delivery person told me about the multi-thousand-dollar diagnostic machine my competitor had. The owner of the center had told her, "This machine could fix an F-16, if I could hook it up to one." She was really impressed! Many of my customers asked if I thought this competitor would hurt my business. I will admit, it did enter my mind, but after a few months I realized that I had nothing to worry about.

My business is a relatively small, independent store with a limited budget. We have a diagnostic scanner that costs about $300 and offers only basic diagnostic help. However, with this simple tool, we have shown up the "F-16" machine on several occasions. One time, one of my regular customers, who did not realize we did diagnostic work, brought her car to my shop after an unsuccessful *three-day* visit with my neighbor. They had hooked up their machine to the car's on-board computer and found a sensor which was reading out of range. After replacing this sensor with *three* new ones, the reading was still out of range. They then told her that she needed a $300 computer replacement. This lady had long since lost her confidence in this service center, so she demanded that her old sensor be put back on her car, and she left. She then drove the car across the parking lot to my shop. About five minutes after checking the computer with my scanner, I noticed that the sensor in question was working exactly the opposite of what it should have been. A few minutes later, I found two vacuum hoses that were switched. After the hoses were installed properly, the car ran fine. The original sensor was just fine. She was gone in about twenty minutes!

This goes to show that no matter how good a machine is, there must always be someone with knowledge and experience working on the car. The diagnostic machine is not a miracle fix-it-all, it's just a tool to help the mechanic communicate with the car's computer. Without someone who really understands the automobile, the diagnostic machine is just a high-tech paperweight! A similar example is today's personal computers. These computers are very powerful and have the capability to do thousands of complex operations per second, but many people only use them to play games! Of course I would like to own one of those top-of-the-line diagnostic machines some day, but until then I will depend on knowledge, experience, a service manual, and my $300 scanner.

P.S. The service center next door closed down after about one year in business.

CHECK ENGINE SOON!

These three words, or a form of them, make up what is probably one of the most misunderstood phrases on the planet. When this warning message appears on the dash, people often think their car has a serious problem and is about to break down, or that they will damage their car if they don't stop immediately. This is seldom the case, however. Although systems vary from car to car (read your owner's manual), this little glowing message is usually just a friendly reminder from your car's on-board computer. The computer is telling you that it has found a problem in one of the many components it monitors. Usually this is a minor problem, which is seldom dangerous or detrimental. In fact, in many cases, the car will continue to run fine with no obvious driveability problems. Of course the check engine light *does* indicate that something is wrong, and eventually service will be needed. Therefore, understanding what it means can help you make the right decisions about repairs and help you choose the right repair center, which of course can save you time, money, and headaches.

Artificial Intelligence

Most cars built since the mid-1980s are equipped with an on-board computer. These computers are called different names by different car makers, such as ECM (engine control module), engine programmer, processor, engine controller, and others. Although the names for engine computers vary, they all serve the same purpose — to control the engine's ignition and fuel system. The computer gathers information from various sensors and continually adjusts the timing and fuel for optimum power and economy. For instance, a computer monitors sensors for the engine temperature, how far the gas pedal is depressed, the atmospheric pressure, the amount of oxygen in the exhaust, whether the air conditioner is on, and more. The computer gathers all this information and then determines the exact amount of fuel to "feed" the engine, to give the engine the most power for the smallest possible amount of fuel and to minimize air pollution. The computer reads information from these sensors and adjusts the fuel and ignition hundreds of times per second.

Sensing a Problem

When it is working properly, each computer sensor operates within a given range. If a sensor transmits a value that is not considered normal or sends no signal at all, the computer turns on the check engine light to warn the driver of this situation. If for example, the **engine temperature sensor** normally sends a reading from -40 degrees to +280 degrees Fahrenheit, but if the wire linking this sensor to the computer is broken or damaged, the computer will recognize there is no signal from this sensor, and the check engine light will come on. This is often the only way a driver would know about such a problem because the car may run fine without this information. How can that be? The computer simply stops using the information it was getting from the defective sensor and substitutes a predetermined value. It will continue to use the information it gathers from the remaining sensors to adjust the fuel and ignition to the best of its (now limited) ability. This is sometimes called the "limp home" mode, because the computer does what it can to make the car run properly until repairs can be made.

So, if your car proudly displays the check engine light, don't panic! You should be able to operate the car in a normal fashion until you can get it checked out. Of course, some sensors play a larger role in the system than others, and if a *vital* sensor is defective, the car may not run well, may get poor gas mileage, or may be hard to start.

To get side-tracked for just a moment, let me remind you to read your owner's manual (the little black book in your glove box) from cover to cover, *before* you experience a problem. Different car makers use different phrases for "check engine soon." Most cars also have a warning light that indicates a serious problem, such as low oil pressure or high engine temperature, either of which can quickly destroy your engine. Know which warning lights are which! Besides, you may find lots of other useful information in the owner's manual!

Engine Alert Codes

When a computer finds a problem, it not only turns on the check engine light, but it also stores a code in its memory. This stored trouble code helps a technician diagnose the cause of the problem. In fact, the first step in diagnosing a check engine light problem is to read the trouble codes stored by the computer. The best way to do this is with a **scanner.** A scanner is an electronic device that connects to the on-board computer and scans the computer's memory. The scanner displays these codes to show the technician what to look for. Some scanners even display the actual sensor readings. The technician then looks up the codes in a service manual to find the procedure for testing the listed components.

A technician must use care when diagnosing trouble codes. Often, another problem may produce codes for sensors that are okay. For example, just because a code for the oxygen (O_2) sensor is read does not necessarily mean the oxygen sensor is bad. In these cases, a

> **When a computer finds a problem, it not only turns on the check engine light, but it also stores a code in its memory.**

knowledgeable, experienced mechanic is indispensable; an *inexperienced* technician can easily replace the wrong sensor, or several wrong sensors, before finding the problem. The fact is, trouble codes are often set by loose wires, broken vacuum hoses, or other seemingly unrelated problems. Also keep in mind that there are many things the computer does not monitor, such as spark plugs and plug wires. A bad plug may cause the check engine light to come on, but the computer will not recognize the exact cause; instead, it will set a code reflecting something else. Here again, a veteran mechanic is priceless.

WHERE TO GO

If you have a domestic car, you may be able to find a knowledgeable technician with the right diagnostic equipment at an independent shop, or even at a national chain store. Many such repair centers have diagnostic scanners and trained mechanics for American cars. Imports are a little different, however. There are service centers out there who can *competently* repair computer problems on an import, but because training and diagnostic equipment for imports is more specialized, it can be difficult to find such a shop in some areas. More than likely, the new car dealer will have the most up-to-date equipment and trained technicians for computer diagnostics, especially on imports, along with the highest prices. The good news is, *all* new cars, foreign and domestic, will soon use on-board diagnostics that share a common design. This system is called OBD-II, which stands for second generation, on-board diagnostics. This technology will allow any shop to purchase equipment that will work on *all* cars, instead of buying several different scanners for many different makes and models. This also means that training will be less specialized between car brands. (*For more about finding the right shop for a computer problem, please read the previous section on driveability.*)

WHAT'S THAT SMELL?!

Although I never planned to diagnose any driveability problems in this book, there was one item that kept popping up in my mind. That item is the oxygen sensor. Of the twenty or so computer sensors on a modern car, why the oxygen sensor? One reason is because nearly all cars built in the past fifteen years have one. Another reason is because most oxygen sensors are very much alike, and a bad oxygen sensor in a

Buick acts the same as a bad oxygen sensor in a Ford, Dodge, Toyota, and so on. This is generally not the case with the other computer sensors. These universal symptoms make diagnosing a bad oxygen sensor, called an O_2 sensor for short, easy and *practically* risk-free. I say risk-free because even if the O_2 sensor is not the cause of the problem, it is relatively inexpensive, and a new O_2 sensor is not a bad idea after about 100,000 miles anyway. It's like when your cordless telephone stops working. Even though you know the old battery may be okay, it would certainly be worth the small gamble to install a new battery before taking it to a repair shop. Likewise, if your car has the symptoms of a bad O_2 sensor, this $40 repair (most cars) is a small risk to take when you consider that most shops charge at least $40 for a diagnostic check.

A Lack of Oxygen

So what is an oxygen sensor anyway? Just as its name implies, the O_2 sensor "senses" the amount of oxygen in the car's exhaust and sends this information to the engine computer. When the O_2 sensor detects *too much* oxygen in the exhaust, it *adds* more fuel to the fuel mixture. If the O_2 sensor detects that there is *not enough* oxygen in the exhaust, the computer *decreases* the amount of fuel to the engine. This happens many times per second and maintains a perfect balance of fuel and air in the engine, creating the maximum power and minimum pollution (wasted fuel). In fact, this little O_2 sensor is one of the major reasons that cars make more power with less fuel than they did just 15 years ago. The O_2 sensor is a kind of "thermostat" that tells the computer when to add or take away fuel.

Let's say the thermostat in your home is defective and always detects the temperature to be 50 degrees. The heater will come on and stay on, even after the actual temperature passes 80 degrees, because the thermostat will still be demanding more heat! A faulty O_2 sensor works the same way. If an oxygen sensors *always* sends the computer a reading that indicates that more fuel should be added, the computer will dump more and more fuel into the engine, even if it is way too much. But if the O_2 sensor continues to supply an extremely low reading, the computer will recognize that there is a problem. Then, it will stop using the information from the sensor and will turn on the check engine light. Unfortunately, if the reading is just a little off, the computer will not recognize there is a problem and will continue to add more fuel. The computer will "think" that everything is okay, and the check engine light will not come on.

Smelling Smoke

A defective O_2 sensor is usually accompanied by three symptoms. First and foremost is a drastic decrease in fuel mileage. All the extra fuel dumped into the engine is wasted, and a car that was getting 25 miles per gallon may drop to 15! Another common symptom is black smoke from the tailpipe. When excess fuel is pumped into an engine, much of it does not burn completely and black smoke is the result. A noticeable rotten egg odor is yet another side effect of a bad oxygen sensor. The catalytic converter in the exhaust system is there to help burn any leftover fuel that makes it through the engine; all of this *extra* fuel reacts with chemicals inside the converter to create a powerful sulfur smell. All of these symptoms are caused by a condition known as "running rich." This simply means that more fuel is going into an engine than it can burn. These symptoms may or may not be accompanied by the check engine light. You may not notice all of them, but at least two of these are strong indications of a bad O_2 sensor. Of course there are other situations that can cause any or all of these signals, but as mentioned before, a new oxygen sensor is a good, affordable place to start.

AIR CONDITIONING

THINGS TO KNOW

Automotive air conditioning (a/c) has gone through several changes in the past few years. Most of these changes result from new laws concerning the use of certain chemicals, called fluorocarbons or CFCs, that are found in the **REFRIGERANTS** used in the older systems. It is believed that **FREON** or **R-12,** found in most cars and trucks made before 1993, causes depletion of the ozone layer when it is released into the air. For this reason, the EPA has banned the production of R-12 in the United States. These laws also mandate that *no* R-12 may be released into the air by any person or company. Special recovery machines are required to capture and recycle R-12 so it can be used again, and all businesses that repair air conditioners are required to own and use a recovery machine. Cars made from about 1993 on have a new refrigerant called **R-134A,** which is not believed to cause ozone depletion. To find out what type of refrigerant your car has, check the owner's manual or raise the hood of your car and look near the passenger side, back corner of the engine compartment, or near the front of the engine compartment on a some cars. There you will find a sticker that will say which refrigerant your car uses and how much the a/c system holds.

Because of the ban on producing R-12, the supply of this refrigerant is all but gone. What little there is for sale is very expensive. A 12 oz. can of R-12 now retails for about $30 or more. This same can sold for about $2 in the early 1990s! At last count, about ten or more dollars of this price is federal tax. Every year the price goes a little higher.

So they don't make R-12 anymore, big deal, right? Wrong! There are millions of cars out there with systems that were designed to operate with R-12 and R-12 only. The good news is that the new refrigerant (R134a) *will* work in the old systems, but many cars do not cool as well with R-134a. Also, new R-12 substitutes are hitting the market that may offer better a/c performance in the near future.

A Cool Gas

So what is a refrigerant anyway? In its natural state, a refrigerant is an invisible gas, like air. Unlike air, refrigerants can be used to make other objects become very cold. This happens when a refrigerant changes states from a liquid to a gas. Since a refrigerant is a gas in its natural state, how can it become a liquid? There are two ways to make a refrigerant change into a liquid. One way is to make it very cold (freeze it), the other way is to use mechanical energy to *squeeze* it into a liquid. Since automobiles have lots of mechanical energy to spare, power from the engine is used to make liquid refrigerant in the automotive a/c system.

Once a refrigerant is changed into a liquid under pressure, it is ready to cool. As the *liquid* refrigerant is released from its pressurized state, it turns back into a gas and absorbs heat from surrounding objects. This makes these objects very cold. Air is then blown over these cold objects and into the car to cool the inside. No refrigerant is burned or used up in this process, it simply changes from a liquid to a gas, then back into a liquid, and so on. The only way you lose refrigerant is from a leak in the system.

MORE A/C DETAILS

Now that you know the basics, let's see exactly what happens to the refrigerant as it applies to your car. Cars with air conditioning have a pump called a **COMPRESSOR.** The compressor is located under the hood and is turned by the engine via the a/c belt. The compressor's job is to squeeze (compress) the refrigerant into a liquid. The refrigerant is still a gas when it leaves the compressor however because it is very hot (about $200°F$). So, the refrigerant is sent through hoses to a cooler called a **CONDENSER,** which is mounted near the front of the car. The **ENGINE FAN** pulls outside air through the condenser, which cools the refrigerant enough to change it into a liquid. The pressurized *liquid* refrigerant then travels through more hoses to the **EXPANSION VALVE.** The expansion valve has a small opening that releases the liquid refrigerant at a fixed rate, allowing it to expand back into a gas. This is where things start getting cold, literally! The icy cold refrigerant then goes into the **EVAPORATOR.** The **BLOWER FAN** forces warm air through the evaporator where it becomes cold air. The cold air is then directed through ducts and into the interior, which cools the car. Since the refrigerant is now a gas, it is ready to begin the cycle all over again (*see illustration AC1*).

When the a/c on your car is working properly, turn on the engine and have someone turn the a/c switch on and off a few times while you look under the hood. This will familiarize you with what happens and what changes in sound and movement occur when the a/c is on and working properly. You should be able to see the compressor turn on and off — the belt and the outer part of the clutch, on the front of the compressor, always turn when the engine is running, but the center part of the clutch turns only when the compressor is turning. Take a moment to learn what a normal system sounds like, so you can better detect a strange sound when it happens. You may also want to *very carefully* touch the hoses going into and out of the a/c components to feel where they are hot and where they are cold. This will help you understand what happens during normal a/c operation. If you have trouble finding these components, your auto service manager will probably be glad to show you where they are. This simple investigation may be very helpful in the future if you have problems with your a/c.

CARSMART

AC1 - THE A/C SYSTEM

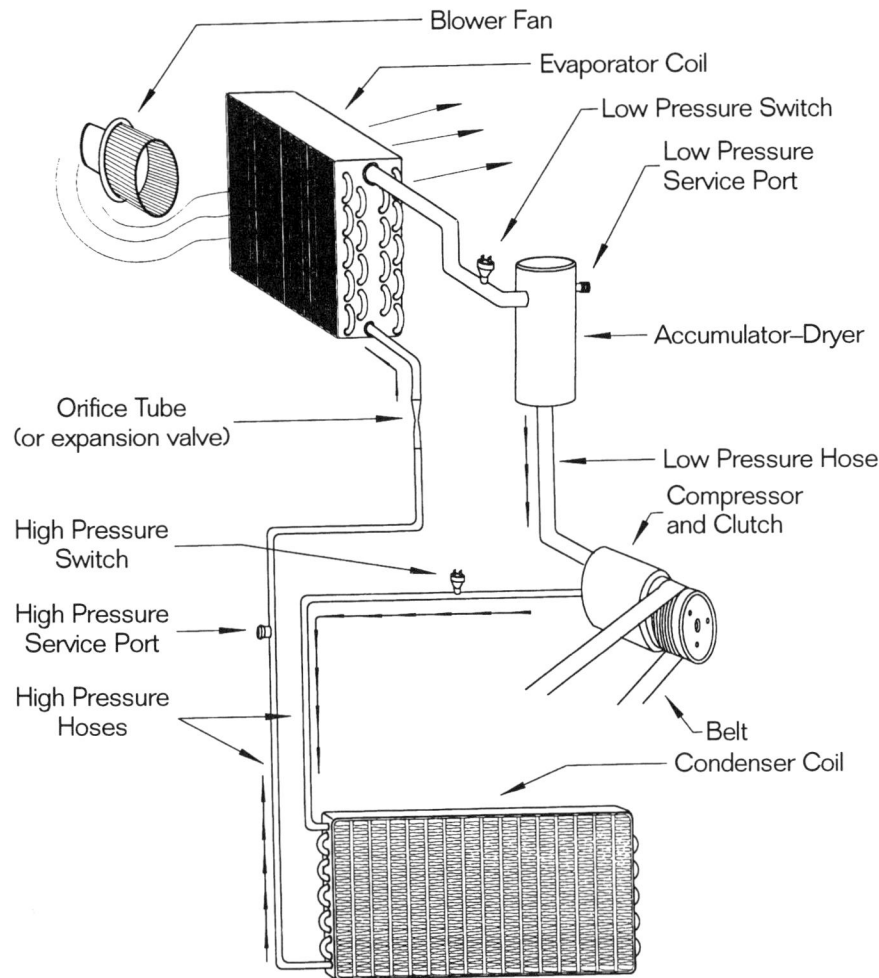

Although a/c systems vary, this drawing shows the basic configuration for most automotive air conditioning systems. All of the components pictured contain refrigerant. If the a/c is not on, the refrigerant just sits there like air in a balloon. When the a/c is turned on, the compressor starts pumping the refrigerant in the direction of the condenser. When the refrigerant is pumped or compressed, it becomes very hot (about 200°F+).

This hot refrigerant must travel through small tubes in the condenser. Air is pulled through the condenser by the engine fan and by the forward motion of the car. This air cools the refrigerant and changes it from a gas to a liquid. The liquid refrigerant then travels on to the orifice tube.

The orifice tube has a small hole in it. This small hole regulates (or restricts) the flow of the refrigerant (similar to a water nozzle on the end of a garden hose). The pressure builds up to about 250 PSI behind this restriction and drops to about 30 PSI at the far side of the orifice tube. This pressure change converts the refrigerant from a liquid back into a gas. Since heat is required to change a liquid into a gas, the refrigerant takes the heat from the evaporator coil and the air around it and causes them to become very cold. The air in the evaporator coil cools down to about 40°F. Warm air from outside is forced through the cold evaporator coil by the blower fan, is cooled, and is blown into the interior of the car. The refrigerant then travels on to the accumulator–dryer where it is filtered and dried, insuring that the refrigerant is a gas and that it has no moisture or contamination in it. Then it's on to the compressor to start the process all over again!

All of the lines, hoses, and components on the high pressure side between the compressor and the orifice tube are under high pressure and are hot (condenser, and so forth). All the lines, hoses, and components on the low pressure side between the orifice tube and the compressor are under low pressure and are cold (evaporator, accumulator, and so on).

The high and low pressure switches monitor the pressure of the refrigerant and will turn off the a/c if the pressure gets too low or dangerously high. The high pressure switch stops the a/c if it sees pressure over about 300 pounds, and the low pressure switch interrupts the a/c if the pressure goes below 23 pounds. This prevents damage to the compressor.

The high and low service ports are used to connect gauges to the system in order to monitor the pressures. These valves are also used to remove or add refrigerant to the system.

Note: Some cars use an expansion valve instead of an orifice tube. An expansion valve will open and close slightly to regulate the flow more accurately than an orifice tube, which has a fixed opening. Cars with expansion valves have the dryer in the line before the expansion valve, instead of after the evaporator.

MORE IS LESS?

Many people feel guilty when they run their air conditioner on maximum. They get the idea that the car will use more gas or that they will overwork the engine or the air conditioner if they use the "max" setting. Most people notice that the a/c makes more noise on max, so they may assume that more energy is being used. The word maximum even sounds wasteful when used in automotive context. But it is not wasteful. The max setting actually uses less energy and cools better than the other selections. Maybe the car makers should find a better term for this position on the a/c selector. Some good choices would be "coolest" or perhaps "high efficiency." Of course these terms would take up too much space on the dash, but they say much more about what you get.

When the a/c is set to max, it is simply using air from inside the car, rather than pulling in air from the outside. This is much easier on the air conditioning system; instead of trying to cool 100+ degree air from the outside, it is cooling 80 degree air from the inside. This not only puts less strain on the a/c, it makes the air from the vents much cooler! (The a/c system in your house is permanently set to maximum.) It takes less energy to cool air that is already somewhat cool. The reason you hear more noise is because you are not only hearing the air coming out of the vents, but also the air going into the ducts under the dash. When it is not so hot outside, you may enjoy the reduced noise from running the a/c in the normal mode, and little or no energy will be wasted. However, when the need arises, don't be afraid to push it to the max!

Note: Some car makers use other terms such as recirculate or a picture of an arrow forming a circle. These are just other (better) ways to say maximum.

REFRIGERANT CONVERSIONS

Since R-12 is no longer readily available, what do you do if your older car uses R-12? If your air conditioning is working okay, don't do a thing. It could work for several more years without any problems. As long as the R-12 stays in your car, it is not harming the environment. Don't think you can do the environment a favor by doing a conversion before you need to. Even if you have the R-12 removed, sooner or later it will find its way into the atmosphere, no matter what. Once it leaves your car, it will probably be recycled and put right back into another car. However, if your a/c suffers from the lack of enough Freon (more on this later), a simple R-12 to R-134a conversion, also called a retrofit, is recommended. A conversion is just what it sounds like — you convert an R-12 system into an R-134a system. Although opinions vary on what should be done to convert old systems to R-134a, we will cover the most sensible, cost-effective, and widely accepted method here.

First, call a few repair shops to get an idea about the range of prices for a conversion. Since there are several methods being used, you will probably get a wide range of prices. Be sure to compare apples to apples. Write down what each price includes. Be sure you compare not only prices, but also exactly what you get for that price. Some shops may do a thorough system flush, for example, and some may only do the minimum amount of work to get the job done. Make sure the shop has a certified air conditioner repair technician. (To become a/c certified, an auto technician must take a test that shows that he or she is knowledgeable about the methods of refrigerant recovery and recycling). Also, a shop doing this type of work must have recovery equipment to capture any old R-12 that may be in your system. Ask if the shop has such equipment and personnel, and remember to ask about warranties that they may offer on the conversion.

The first step in the conversion is to recover any R-12 remaining in your system. Even when a system has leaked enough to stop working, it probably still has some R-12 inside. Because R-12 is so expensive, the shop *may* give you a credit based on how much they recover. Most cars hold between two and three pounds when they are full, so zero to two or more pounds of R-12 may be recovered from an a/c system. Next, the technician should check all the hoses and connections for any signs of leaks. Now is the time to repair any leaks. Some experts recommend a system flush next, and some don't feel that it's necessary. A flush involves removing some of the hoses and forcing a liquid flush solvent through the entire a/c system to remove old oil or contaminants. There is no convincing proof that a flush is a must; it certainly won't hurt, but it will add about $40+ to the conversion.

Next, oil should be added to the empty system. To lubricate the moving parts of the a/c system, all systems require between two to six ounces of a light oil, called **REFRIGERANT OIL,** which is about the same thickness as cooking oil. Next the technician should pull a vacuum on the system, also called evacuating the system, to remove all of the air from the system and then inject the proper amount of R-134a. (The oil is sometimes added at this stage.) The proper amount, or **CHARGE,** will be found on a label under the hood of your car.

When replacing R-12 with R134a, only about 80 percent in weight of the original charge is required to fill the system. If for example a system held 2.25 pounds of R-12, it would only need about 1.8 pounds of R-134a. Special adapters are required to attach the R-134a charging equipment to the old system. These adapters should be left on your car for future repairs. Make sure the technician does a thorough leak check to ensure the refrigerant stays in. A well-equipped shop will have an electronic device called a leak detector, the slang term is "sniffer," that will detect even a tiny leak. You should request an under hood label or notice stating that the system has been converted to R-134a.

Of course, the cost of a conversion varies widely depending on the type of car you have and the type of conversion you choose, but somewhere between $100 and $200 should give you an idea of what to expect to pay. A conversion should be done not only when you have a leak, but when any other repair is done to an R-12 system. The converted system should be as good, or almost as good, as new. Although R-134a works in a system designed for R-12, it is not as efficient as R-12, but you may never notice a difference. R-134a requires more power and some larger components to work as effectively as R-12, but *most* cars have systems that will work satisfactorily with R-134a. As of this writing, most experts do not believe that any components should be replaced when doing a conversion. It was earlier believed that all the major components should be changed, costing close to a $1,000. As time went on however, opinions changed.

It should be noted that new methods and refrigerants are continually being developed. There are now refrigerants available that work much better than R-134a in an old system. However, R-134a is still a good choice as it will always be cheap and readily available, since it is used in all new cars. Some of the less common refrigerants may come and go, which could leave you with the need for another conversion down the road. A knowledgeable a/c service technician should keep you up to date on any new methods or other developments in the industry and help you make the right decision.

Losing Your Cool

Most of us have experienced air from the a/c vents that is just not as cool as it should be. This could be due to the outside temperature. Extremely hot weather can simply overpower an a/c system, especially on a vehicle with a large interior such as a van. But what if the weather is only moderately hot? About 80 percent of the time, the cause of poor a/c performance is the lack of enough refrigerant. An a/c system will begin to lose its cool after only a few ounces of refrigerant have escaped. The most common symptom for low refrigerant is that the air coming from the vents is cool, instead of cold. Another sign is the compressor is switching on and off every few seconds. You can tell when the compressor turns on because you can feel the engine slow down slightly and make a little more noise. The reason the compressor switches on and off is because of a device called a **LOW PRESSURE SWITCH,** which is found on most systems used today.

When a fully charged a/c system is not running (a/c off), the low pressure will be about 100 PSI. When the a/c is on, this pressure will normally drop to around 30 PSI. If this pressure drops below 23 PSI, the low pressure switch will cut off the compressor until the pressure rises again. In fact, if the refrigerant level is extremely low, this switch will prevent the compressor from coming on at all, preventing damage to your a/c system from a lack of refrigerant, and keeping your a/c from getting too cold and freezing over as well. In cool weather switching on and off is normal because lower outside temperature causes low pressure even in a fully charged system. Another note: Most cars are designed so the a/c runs when the defroster is on. This is to keep the moving parts of the system lubricated even when the a/c is not needed.

RECHARGING

Charging, or refilling, an a/c system is one of the easiest auto repairs around. In fact, it only takes about five minutes to charge most a/c systems. Almost any repair center with a certified a/c technician can recharge the a/c without a hitch. Make your phone calls before going to a shop for a/c service, and be sure to ask for the price to check your a/c *and* to install refrigerant. Some service centers may charge a flat rate to check your system, while others will include the check if you go ahead and add the refrigerant. Most shops charge a fixed amount of labor for adding refrigerant and then charge for the refrigerant, based on how much the system holds. Some shops charge you by the pound from a large container, and some use small one-pound cans. The price for refrigerant fluctuates from time to time, so comparison pricing is important.

Before going to a shop, raise the hood and look for a tag taped to the front of the engine compartment or near the windshield on the passenger side. It may be hard to find, but it's there somewhere. This sticker will tell you how much refrigerant your system holds. It will say something about air conditioning and will specify how many pounds of refrigerant are required. You will also find what type of refrigerant your car uses, either R-12 of R-134a. Write this information down, you may need it later.

When you get to the shop, tell the service manager that you have called ahead and let him know that you have already checked on the price. This gives no room for mysterious price adjustments. Also explain why you suspect low refrigerant. When you tell the service manager all the symptoms, you also give him the responsibility to get them fixed. To see if your car

> When you tell the service manager all the symptoms, you also give him the responsibility to get them fixed.

needs refrigerant, the technician will connect gauges to the a/c system that will register the pressures in your system. There are two different pressure readings that should be checked, the "high" and "low" pressures. In a fully charged a/c system, with the a/c on and running, the low pressure is usually around 30 to 40 PSI (pounds per square inch, about the same as your tire pressure). The high pressure reading should be between 150 and 350 PSI, depending on the outside temperature (higher temperature = higher pressure). When the a/c is turned off, the high and low pressure will equalize after a few minutes to about 80 to 100 PSI. If the pressure readings are considerably lower than this, refrigerant should be added until they are normal. Generally, a/c that is cooling will need a pound or so added. Systems with a large capacity (over 3 pounds) may need two or more pounds. Always ask how much refrigerant you are being charged for. If you are charged for more than your entire system holds, you know something is wrong!

BLOWING HOT AIR

If you turn on your a/c switch and all you get is warm air, here are a few of the most common causes, *other* than low refrigerant. First, it helps to understand what happens when the a/c is turned on. As already explained, the compressor uses power from the engine to squeeze the refrigerant. To do this, the compressor's shaft must turn with the engine. So, mounted to the front of every compressor is a CLUTCH. The clutch has the job of transferring the rotation of the engine to the compressor shaft. The clutch uses electricity, supplied by the a/c switch, to "grab" the a/c belt and spin the compressor. If for any reason the clutch does not receive this electricity, it will not spin the compressor shaft, and you get no cool air. So you push the a/c button and it sends electricity straight to the compressor, right? Sorry, it's not that simple.

The a/c switch must first get electricity from the battery through the a/c fuse. This fuse protects the electrical components from an "overdose" of electricity, so it is first in line. If the fuse is good, it sends the electricity on to the a/c switch. When the a/c button is pressed, it sends the electricity, or **"fire"** as we say, to the LOW PRESSURE SWITCH. The low pressure switch will stop the flow of electricity if there is not enough refrigerant in the system or if the temperature gets too cold. This protects the compressor.

From the low pressure switch, the electricity goes to the HIGH PRESSURE SWITCH. This switch stops the flow of electricity if the refrig-

C A R S M A R T

erant pressure climbs to a level that could damage the compressor or blow out the a/c hoses. From there, the fire goes to the A/C RELAY, basically a heavy duty switch that can carry the heavy current required by the clutch. Finally, the relay sends the electricity to the clutch...that is *if* the car's on-board computer says it's okay. The computer monitors the engine temperature to make sure that all systems are "go" before it will activate the a/c relay to turn on the compressor (*see illustration AC2*).

Now that the electricity has finally made it to the clutch, how does it spin the compressor? The clutch is made of two halves. One half always spins with the engine, the other half is mounted to the compressor shaft. When the clutch is energized by the fire from the relay, the halves are "slapped" together as a magnet to metal, and the compressor turns (*see illustration AC3*). Believe it or not, almost all cars use a system very similar to this, and if any one of these electrical parts fails, you will not engage the clutch, or get cool air. Most failures are due to relays, usually found under the hood, and low pressure switches, also under the hood on an a/c hose. The price for relays and pressure switches is usually around $20, and they are easy to install on most cars. The hardest part for the technician is figuring out which of these many components is the culprit. Of course the logical place to start is to check the fuses!

A/C LEAKS

Almost all systems lose small amounts of refrigerant over several years. Refrigerant under high pressure can escape through tiny holes in the rubber seals or through the pores in the rubber hoses. These very small losses may not affect the a/c for a few years and can

> ...if you add only a pound or so of refrigerant once every year or two, there is probably no reason for alarm.
>
> In such cases, be cautious of claims by a repair center that you need expensive leak repairs.

AC2 - A/C ELECTRICAL

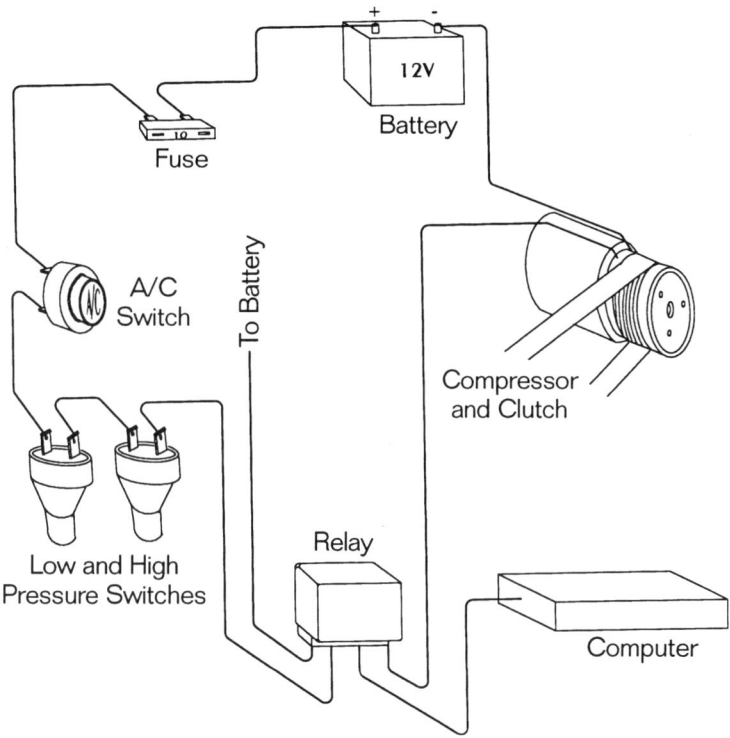

For the a/c to work, the clutch must get a 12-volt supply from the battery to engage the compressor. The voltage first goes through a fuse (labeled a/c). The fuse protects the components from an overload. From the fuse, the voltage goes to the a/c switch. When the a/c switch is pressed, the power goes to the low and high pressure switches. The low pressure switch, or clutch cycling switch, will cause the compressor to stop if the refrigerant is low or if the temperature is too cool. The high pressure switch will cut off the compressor if the pressure reaches a dangerously high level. If the pressures are acceptable, these switches pass the power onto the a/c relay. The relay is a heavy duty switch that can carry the current needed by the clutch. Before the relay will engage the clutch, the engine computer (ECM) must "okay" your request for cool air. The computer monitors the engine to make sure that all systems are "go," and then activates the relay, which engages the clutch and causes the compressor to turn. Systems vary slightly, but most cars use some form of this layout. If one of these components fails, the clutch will not get the power it needs and the a/c won't work.

AC3 - COMPRESSOR & CLUTCH

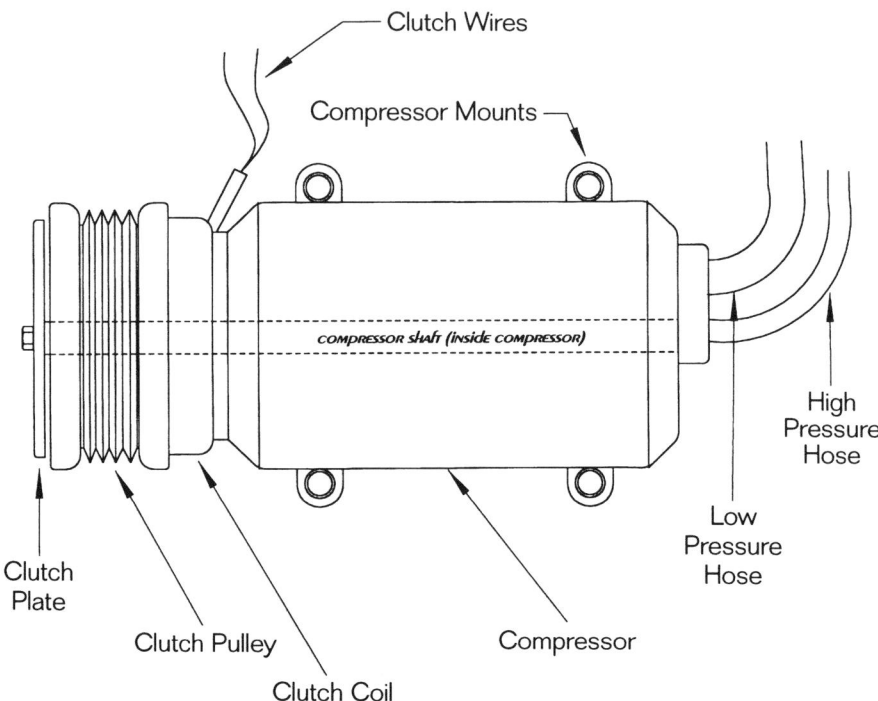

The compressor is the heart of the air conditioning system. As its name suggests, it compresses the refrigerant to convert it into a liquid, which cools the car. The clutch assembly is mounted to the front of the compressor. The clutch is made up of three components: the plate, the pulley, and the coil. The pulley always spins when the engine is running. The plate however is connected to the compressor shaft and does not turn unless the a/c is on. When the a/c switch is pressed, it sends electricity to the clutch wires and the coil becomes a magnet, which pulls the plate tightly against the rotating pulley. This causes the compressor shaft to turn, compressing the refrigerant. When a/c is turned off, the plate moves back to its original position, and the compressor shaft stops turning. The compressed refrigerant exits the compressor through the high pressure (discharge) hose and returns through the low pressure (suction) hose. The mounts hold the compressor to the engine.

be considered normal. Therefore, if you add only a pound or so once every year or two, there is probably no reason for alarm. In such cases, be cautious of claims by a repair center that you need expensive leak repairs. Check with other shops before authorizing any major leak repairs. If your system is *more* than a pound or so low on refrigerant, you may have a significant leak, and you should have the system thoroughly checked for leaks. Many leaks are relatively inexpensive and easy to repair. Adding refrigerant two or three times a year, on the other hand, can get expensive, and a leaky a/c can quit at the most inopportune times.

A Bad Connection

Since leaks are common on many cars, it's probably a good idea to become familiar with some of the most common a/c leaks. On most Ford cars and trucks, there are connections in the a/c hoses that leak *often*. These connections consist of two O-rings and a spring that locks and seals two hoses or lines to each other. Most Ford cars and trucks have about four of these. These connections are designed to fit loosely to allow free movement of the rubber hoses during normal engine vibration and movement. But this constant movement causes the rubber O-rings to wear out and leak. Usually you can see an area of a dirty, oily substance around a leaky connection. The proper fix is to install new O-rings and new springs at each connection. Unfortunately, this is only a temporary fix that will last about two years. There is hope however as some manufacturers have designed a special, add-on clamp that will hold the connection together tightly and may help prolong the repair. If you own a car with these leaks, ask your shop if they use these clamps and if they have had success with them. These clamps should cost around $10 to $15 each, and are easy to install.

In the last few years, these leak-prone connections have shown up on a few other car makes. These connections are probably used just to save money. On an assembly line, they can be snapped together in a split second, as opposed to the several seconds it takes to screw a leakproof, threaded connection together. More bad news is that these connections usually last just long enough for the warranty to expire!

Leaky Hoses

On many American cars and some imports, the rubber a/c hoses are a common source for leaks. These hoses route the refrigerant from one a/c component to another. A hose assembly is made up of two or more reinforced rubber hoses with metal ends crimped onto them. Most cars have two of these hose assemblies. Refrigerant sometimes escapes through the pores of the rubber, or leaks near the crimped hose ends. Most refrigerant leaks can be pinpointed by finding dirty, oily residue around the source of the leak. This dirty residue forms when the refrigerant oil leaks out of the system and collects dust. This is one of the best methods of identifying a leaky hose. This inspection is often better than an electronic sniffer because leaks can be very small and spread over a large area.

A new hose assembly should be installed to repair a leaky one. Hose assemblies usually cost around $100 each, and in many cases, they will have to be purchased from the new car dealer. Before buying from a dealer, however, check with a few parts stores. A few aftermarket companies manufacture a/c hose assemblies for the more popular models, and they should cost significantly less than a dealer hose. Remember as well, now is the time to do a conversion if you have a car with R-12. After repairs have been performed, the technician should pull a vacuum and recharge your system with the proper amounts of refrigerant and oil. Ask them to check again for leaks and give you a written guaranty on the repairs.

More Serious Problems

If you have a leak, and it's not a hose or O-ring, you may have more serious problems. In this case, *at least* two shops should thoroughly check your system for leaks. Ask each shop to give you an exact description of the leak and the parts that need replacing on a written estimate. A shop will spend a significant amount of time and will possibly use a little refrigerant to check for a leak, so you can expect to pay for these checks. A reasonable price would be between $20 and $40. Ask each shop if the price you pay for the check will be refunded if you allow them to do the repair later. Some may offer this, especially if the repair is relatively expensive.

The reason for getting two different opinions is because these leaks are often very hard to pinpoint exactly. Unlike the telltale dirty, oily signs of a leaky hose, these leaks often leave no evidence behind. Because refrigerant is invisible, special detectors are needed, and it requires some skill to find the location of some leaks with certainty. Do not share the shops' opinions between them, instead let each shop come up with their own unbiased opinion. If two or more technicians agree on the source of the leak, you can feel pretty sure that you're on the right track.

One common refrigerant leak, though much less common than an O-ring or hose leak, is from the seal in the a/c compressor. The compressor seal is a small rubber ring inside the compressor, which surrounds the compressor shaft. This seal can become worn or damaged, either by natural aging and wear to the rubber, or by a defective compressor. Once the seal is damaged, refrigerant will leak out around the front of the compressor. The most effective way to repair a compressor seal leak is to replace the compressor. This can be expensive. On most cars, it will cost about $600 to $1,000 for a complete compressor replacement.

There is one possible option, however. If you can find a *very* competent a/c repair technician, he may be able replace only the defective seal. This requires removing the compressor and taking it apart, so it's not a job for the novice. A seal replacement is not inexpensive either, unless you compare it to the complete compressor job. There is catch to this repair, however. Many times a compressor seal leak is caused by a defective compressor, so the new seal may not last. Be sure the shop will guaranty the work for at least 90 days or more. A seal replacement is a gamble, but it could save you hundreds of dollars if it is successful. More on compressor replacement later.

Another somewhat rare source for an a/c leak is the **EVAPORATOR COIL,** also called an evaporator core. This is a rectangular shaped coil of small aluminum pipes through which the cold refrigerant flows. The **BLOWER FAN** blows air over these icy coils to cool the inside of the car. These thin aluminum tubes can corrode over time and begin to leak. This is one of the most difficult a/c leaks to find because the evaporator coil is usually in a remote location under the dash and behind a maze of ducts and wires. For this reason, the evaporator coil can also be difficult (read expensive) to replace. It takes about four hours to change in most cars, so the labor charge can be $200 or more. The cost of the part can be significant also. Evaporator coils can cost around $200 for some cars and are as high as $400+ on others. This is often a dealer item, but some common car models have aftermarket coils available at a parts store for much less. Check into this by calling a few parts stores before going to a shop for repairs.

A coil similar to the evaporator coil is the **CONDENSER,** found in front of the engine, ahead of the radiator. In fact, the condenser looks very much like a radiator. It cools the compressed, hot refrigerant to help convert it to a liquid. It can also be the source of an a/c leak. It is made of thin aluminum tubes and can be easily punctured by an auto collision or by small rocks kicked up from the road. These condensers are also available in the aftermarket, and the price for parts and labor is usually slightly lower than for the evaporator coil.

AFTER REPAIRS

After any leak has been repaired, the system must be evacuated, which is also called "pulling a vacuum." This procedure removes any air from the system before it is recharged. A special vacuum pump sucks all the air out of the a/c hoses and components to insure that your system will contain 100 percent refrigerant. If a system contains a mixture of air and refrigerant, the a/c will not cool as effectively as with pure refrigerant, so evacuating the system is very important.

In a case where there was a severe leak, as in all the refrigerant was lost in a matter of days, the ACCUMULATOR or DRYER may also need to be replaced. When this type of leak occurs, all the pressure is released from the system and atmospheric air and moisture can enter the system. Moisture also decreases the effectiveness of the a/c, and the dryer's job is to remove moisture and trash from the system. If enough moisture enters the dryer, it may lose its ability to filter the system effectively. If a leak is discovered *before* all of the refrigerant has escaped, however, the dryer should be okay. A new dryer usually costs around $60, so if there's any doubt, it's probably a good idea to replace it.

> When a compressor wears out from normal wear and tear, there may be no cut-and-dry symptoms.

Compressor Failure

Now, down to the heart of the a/c system, the compressor. The compressor is really the only moving part in the a/c system. Since its job is to compress refrigerant when it turns, what does it mean if the compressor turns when the a/c switch is pushed, and still no cool air? One thing we know is that all the electrical parts and devices are working properly, so it's not a relay or a switch. The next step is to check the pressure to make sure the system has the proper amount of refrigerant. If the pressure is okay, this could indicate a bad compressor.

When a compressor goes bad, it will usually turn, but will not sufficiently pump or compress the refrigerant. This is usually caused by normal wear to the metal, plastic, and rubber parts that move together inside the compressor. Another cause of compressor failure is a lack of lubrication (oil) to its moving parts, which can cause the moving parts to overheat and seize (lock up). When a compressor locks up, you will probably get a broken a/c belt. You may also smell a burning odor and see smoke coming from under the hood, as the belt tries to turn an object that refuses to move. This is a sure sign that you need a new compressor!

When a compressor wears out from normal wear and tear, however, there may be no cut-and-dry symptoms. An experienced, knowledgeable technician is required for a diagnosis; other problems can trick a less than competent a/c repairman into incorrectly faulting the compressor. A few of these demons are an overcharged system (too much refrigerant), an undercharged system, a restriction that stops the flow of refrigerant through the hoses, or a bad valve that fails to control the refrigerant flow. You may have already guessed that you should get two or three opinions before authorizing a compressor replacement. Again, don't tell the next shop what the first shop has found until after hearing what they have to say. Note: There is one symptom that may give you a clue that a compressor has worn out — an increased (more than usual) amount of noise when the compressor is running. However, a low charge of refrigerant can sometimes cause slightly increased compressor noise.

Compressor Replacement

When you're sure you need a new compressor, there are a few thing to know about the repair. First of all it will be relatively expensive. Most *complete* compressor jobs cost from $600 to $1,000 or more. Other

> **The most cost-effective method of buying a compressor is to purchase a remanufactured compressor.**

components must be replaced along with the compressor. One of these is the accumulator, or filter–dryer, a metal can about the size of a 20 oz. Coke bottle that removes contaminants and moisture from the a/c system. This filter can become saturated (full) and cause problems if not replaced.

Another component that should be replaced is the ORIFICE TUBE, found on most Ford and GM cars, or the EXPANSION VALVE, found on most Chryslers and imports. These valves have very small holes in them that cause refrigerant to flow at a fixed rate. If these valves get dirt or other material lodged in them, they will restrict the flow of refrigerant and oil to the compressor, possibly causing it to fail. You must replace these items because compressor failure dispenses small bits and pieces of metal and rubber into the system, which generally lodge in their tiny holes. If a new compressor is installed with the old valves and filters, it can be damaged. In fact, most compressor manufacturers will warranty a compressor *only* if these components are replaced with the compressor. These parts will add about $100 to $200 to the total repair, but will pay off in the long run.

Many experts agree that the system should be flushed at this time also. Flushing the system with a liquid solvent insures that all of the metal particles are removed before the new parts are installed.

CUTTING COMPRESSOR COSTS

When getting repair estimates, be sure that everyone is pricing the same components and will give an itemized list of these parts on the invoice. Also, be sure you know exactly what the warranty does and does not cover and for how long. The repair should carry at least a

90-day warranty on all parts and labor, and compressor warranties can go from at least a year to as long as you own your car. Don't be afraid to take your car back before the warranty is out to have them make sure everything looks and sounds okay and to make sure the system is still fully charged (no leaks).

The most cost-effective method of buying a compressor is to purchase a remanufactured one. Many companies are in the business of rebuilding old parts that are very expensive to purchase new. They use the "skeleton" of an old part and replace the damaged internal parts with new ones. These remanufactured parts are often as good, or better, than the original. A rebuilt compressor is one of the best examples. It costs hundreds less than a new compressor and will probably last just as long. A plus in purchasing a remanufactured compressor is that it will usually have a rebuilt clutch already installed. In many cases, the clutch is damaged when a compressor fails, so it's a good idea to replace both. Clutches aren't cheap ($100+), and most *brand new* compressors *do not* come with a new one. Of course, if the old compressor did not lock up, and you can't find a compressor with a clutch, the old clutch on the new compressor should be fine. Finding a rebuilt compressor can be difficult and some technicians may not mention this option, but it can be done. You may have to put your foot down!

A New Clutch

In some cases, only the a/c clutch will fail. Clutches have both mechanical and electrical components that can wear out or break. When a clutch goes bad, it will not be able to turn the compressor, so the a/c will not work at all. Clutch failure can also cause the same broken belt and burning odor as a bad compressor, but competent technician should be able to tell you whether you have a bad clutch or compressor, or both. He should also advise you on whether to replace the entire compressor–clutch assembly or just the clutch. Although the clutch is attached to the front of the compressor, it is not really a part of it, therefore it can be replaced separately. The key here is that if you replace *only* the clutch, not only will this eliminate the need for a compressor, but also for all the components that go along with a compressor replacement such as the dryer, accumulator, expansion valves, and so on. Sometimes this can be done without removing the compressor or releasing the refrigerant. As you can see, this can save you a lot of money. This procedure does carry some risk however, because a bad compressor can cause clutch failure. Be sure you are dealing with a competent technician before attempting a clutch replacement. Ask the repair shop what they will do if a new clutch does not correct the problem. They may be willing to refund some of the money, if you allow them to repair the rest of the system.

A Compressor Bypass

The a/c belt has been mentioned several times in this section, and it should not be overlooked. Since, the a/c belt links the engine to the compressor, it must be there and in good shape for the a/c to work properly. If the belt is broken or missing, the a/c will not work at all. If the belt is badly worn or loose, the a/c may lose some, or all, of its cool.

There are two types of belt systems used on cars now on the road. One system in the V-belt system, which uses up to five different belts to drive one or two components each. In other words, a car with V-belts may have one belt for the engine fan, one for the a/c, one for the alternator, and so on. On such a system, if the compressor locks up, the belt can be removed, if it hasn't already removed itself, and the car driven until you are ready to do the repair. The V-belt system is fast becoming obsolete, however.

Since the mid-eighties, nearly all cars and trucks were built with a "serpentine" belt system. This system uses only one belt to drive all of the engine accessories, including the air conditioner. The advantage to this system is that one belt uses less energy than four or five, therefore it uses less gas and makes more power. The *disadvantage* to this system is if the belt breaks, all of the accessories stop, including the water pump, the alternator, and the power steering. Big problems! If the compressor locks up on one of these cars, it will have to be replaced, even in the middle of winter. It can be very unpleasant to spend a thousand dollars on your a/c when the temperature is 20 degrees! There is, however, a trick that will work on some cars with the serpentine system — installing a shorter belt that bypasses the compressor while still turning everything else. If money is tight, this gives you some time to scrape up the grand. The bad news is that this trick will not work on all cars; on some cars the placement of the other accessories simply will not allow skipping the compressor (*see illustration A4*).

AC4 - BUYING TIME

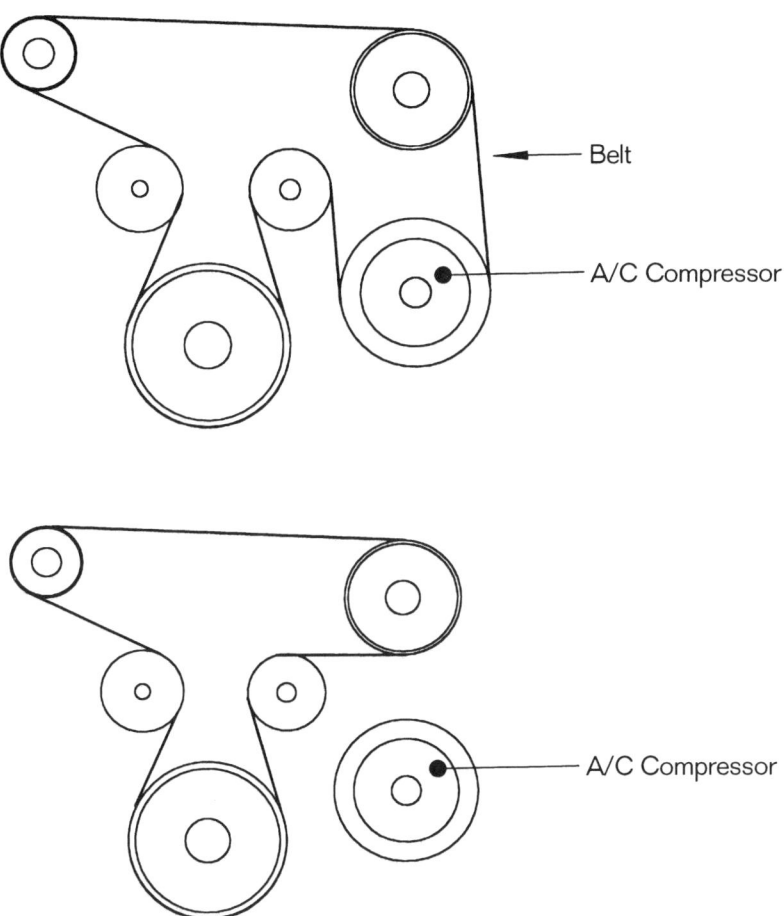

The belt and pulley system above is similar to those found on most of today's cars and trucks. This system is called serpentine, because the belt curves back and forth in two directions like a snake. This system is very efficient because it uses only one belt to drive all the accessories, instead of three or four different belts. The only drawback to this system is that if one component fails, the entire system stops turning. Therefore if the a/c clutch locks up, it must be repaired before the car can be driven. A trick that can be used on some cars is to bypass the a/c pulley and use a shorter belt. Of course the a/c will not work, but the car will be driveable. This may give you some time to get the money together for the expensive compressor and clutch replacement. This trick will not work on all cars because the new belt routing may not clear all of the other engine components.

AIR CONDITIONING GLOSSARY

A/C RELAY: A small electrical switch that carries electricity from the battery to the **compressor clutch.** This relay is controlled by the a/c switch and the computer. Size: 2" x 2" x 2". Cost: $15–$25+. Location: under hood.

ACCUMULATOR: A metal can with two hoses attached that contains a substance that filters the moisture from a/c system. Size: 4" round x 10" tall. Price: $30–$75+. Location: under hood.

BLOWER FAN: An electric motor that forces air through the **evaporator coil** to cool the inside of the car. This motor is controlled by the fan speed switch on the dash. Size: 6" round. Price: $40–$100+. Location: under hood near dash or under dash.

CHARGE: This is the amount of **refrigerant** required in an a/c system. The units for the charge is usually pounds. The average charge is around 2.5 pounds.

CLUTCH: A clutch uses electricity supplied by the **a/c rela**y to turn the **compressor.** The clutch becomes a magnet and pulls itself tightly against the compressor, which causes it to rotate with the engine. Size: 6" round x 3". Price: $100+. Location: under hood, mounted to the compressor.

COMPRESSOR: The main component of the a/c system. The compressor pumps the **refrigerant** to "squeeze" it into a liquid. The compressor is pulled by the a/c belt. Size: 6" round x 12" long. Price: $150–$400+. Location: under hood, mounted to engine.

CONDENSER: An aluminum, radiator-like coil that cools the hot **refrigerant** after it has been pressurized by the compressor. Outside air is pulled through the **condenser** by the engine fan. Size: 24" x 30" x 1" thick. Price: $150–$300+. Location: under hood, at the very front of car.

EVAPORATOR COIL: An aluminum, radiator-like coil made up of small tubes. In this coil, the **refrigerant** changes from a liquid back into a gas, causing the evaporator coil to become very cold. Air from the **blower fan** is passed through the coil to cool the inside of the car. Size: 12" x 12" x 4" thick. Price: $200+. Location: under dash, passenger side.

Expansion valve: A metal block with one or more small holes in it that controls the flow of **refrigerant** through the system and maintains the **refrigerant** temperature around 40°F. Most cars except GM and Ford use an **expansion valve.** Size: 1" x 2" x 4". Price: $30–$50. Location: under hood, near dash or under dash.

High pressure switch: A switch designed to cut off the a/c if the **refrigerant** pressure rises to an unsafe level, which can prevent damage to the **compressor** or hoses. Size: 1" round x 2" tall. Price: $20–$30+. Location: in an a/c hose or in the compressor.

Low pressure switch: A device which causes the a/c to cut off if the **refrigerant** pressure gets too low. This prevents damage to the **compressor** and maintains the temperature around 40°F. Size: 1" round x 2". Price: $20–$30. Location: under hood, in an a/c hose.

Orifice tube: A tube with a small hole through it, about the size of a pencil lead. This tube regulates the flow of the **refrigerant** through the system. It also has a small filter that traps small particles from the system. An orifice tube is used on most GM and Ford products to control the temperature of the a/c. Size: $1/2$" round x 3". Price: $6–$10. Location: in an a/c hose.

R-12: The old **refrigerant,** also known as Freon, used in most cars made before 1993. This refrigerant is believed to deplete the ozone layer when released into the air.

R-134a: The new **refrigerant** used since about 1993, which does not harm the ozone layer. This **refrigerant** is not as efficient as **R-12**, but is safer for the environment.

Radiator fan: An electric motor turns a fan that pulls air through the **condenser** and the radiator. This fan should always run when the a/c is on. Price: $50–$100+. Location: under hood near front.

Refrigerant: A gas used in air conditioning systems. When this gas is compressed into a liquid, and then decompressed, it becomes very cold. This cold refrigerant is used to cool the inside of the car.

Refrigerant oil: A relatively thin oil used to lubricate the a/c **compressor.**

INDEX

(Bold items also appear in glossary)

	Page No.	Illustration
ABS (anti lock brakes)	144-147	
air conditioning	215-239	
accumulator	232, 234, 235	218
belts	217, 233, 236	218, 237
blower fan	217	218
charge	222, 224	
clutch	225, 226, 234-236	227, 228
compressor	217, 225, 230-231, 218, 227, 228	233-236
condenser	217, 231-232	218
conversions	221-223, 230	
dryer	232, 234, 235	218
evacuating	232	
evaporator	217, 231	218
expansion valve	217, 234, 235	218
fans	217	218
fuses	225, 226	227
hoses	229-230	218
leaks	226-232	
o-rings	229	
oil (refrigerant)	222, 223	
orifice tube	234	218
pulling a vacuum	232	
R-12	215-216	
R-134a	215-216	
refrigerant	215-216	
relay	226	227
seals	229, 231	
switches	225-226	227
alignment	151-171	
camber, caster	159-162	160, 161
pull	159, 163-164	
shake, shimmy, vibration	162, 164-165	

	Page No.	Illustration
steering wheel	159, 162, 164, 169-170	
thrust angle	169-170	171
tire wear, uneven	154-159, 162, 165-168	167, 83
toe in, toe out	152-159	155, 157, 158
axles	(*see suspension/drivetrain*)	
boots	(*see suspension/drivetrain*)	
bounce	(*see shocks/struts: also see vibration*)	
brakes	113-150	
adjuster	126-127, 141-143	119
adjustment	126-127, 141-143	119
air	143	
backing plate	120, 125	121, 122
bleeding (bleeder valve)	143-144	115, 118
calipers	114, 117, 137, 140	118
disk brakes	117	118
drum brakes	117, 120	119
fluid	114, 124, 136-139, 143-144	
friction material	120, 129	121, 122
hoses, lines	114, 137, 140	115
leaks	136-139	
low pedal	139, 141-144	
machining	125, 128, 129, 133-135	
master cylinder	114, 124, 139	116
pads	114-128	121
power booster	114	116
proportioning valve	126-127	
pull	139-141, (*also see alignment*)	
pulsating, vibrating	128-135	
rapid wear	126-127	
rotors	128-135	131, 118
scrubbing	120, 125, 127, 133	
semi-metallic	120, 126	

	Page No.	Illustration
shoes	117, 120-123	122, 119
springs	119	119
turning, machining	125, 128, 129, 133-134	
warning light	124, 146	
warning sensor	123-124, 130	121
wheel cylinder	117, 137-139	138, 119
check engine soon light	209-214	
computer		
brakes	144-147	
engine	203, 209-214	
cv joints	*(see suspension/drivetrain)*	
engine diagnostics	201-214	
inner tie rods	*(see suspension/drivetrain)*	
machining rotors	*(see brakes)*	
oil change	67-71	
oxygen sensor	212-214	
popping	135, 188, 193, 195	
power steering leaks	184-185	
pull (to the left or right)		
while driving	90, 159-163	
under braking	139-141	
rack-n-pinion	*(see suspension/drivetrain)*	
rotors	*(see brakes)*	
shake, shimmy	*(see alignment)*	
shocks/struts	173-182	175, 176, 179
bounce	174, 178, 180	
leaks	178	175
testing	178-180	
speed sensor	*(see brakes)*	
steering wheel	*(see alignment)*	
suspension/drivetrain	183-199	
axles	190-195	191, 196
bellow	185, 189	186
boots, cv boots	190-193	191
cv joints	190-195	191
popping	193, 195	

	Page No.	Illustration
power steering leaks	184-185	
rack-n-pinion	184-187	186, 197
tie rods, inner, outer	184, 185 187-189	186, 188, 197
tires	73-111	77
balance	84-92	
bounce, vibration	84-92	
brand names	102-104	
cupping	81-84	83
flats	79-80	
inflation	75-79	74
out of round	89, 92	
patch	79-80	
plugs	80	
pressure	75-79	74
pull	90, 183-184	
quality ratings, UTQG ratings	101-102	103
road hazard warranty	96, 99, 101-102	
rotation	80-84	85, 86, 87
separation	89-90	91
size	96, 98, 99	97
speed rating	100-101	
temperature, traction, treadwear	101-102	103
warranty	105-110	
wear, uneven	75, 80-81, *(also see alignment)*	
toe in, toe out	*(see alignment)*	
tune ups	202, 203	
vibration		
brakes	128-135	
alignment	162, 164-165	
tires	84-92	
suspension/drivetrain	194-195	
wheel cylinder	*(see brakes)*	